WOULD YOU CONVICT?

PAUL H. ROBINSON

WOULD YOU CONVICT?

Seventeen Cases That Challenged the Law

New York University Press • *New York and London*

B/T   345.73   28.95

8/2000

NEW YORK UNIVERSITY PRESS
New York and London

© 1999 by New York University

Library of Congress Cataloging-in-Publication Data
Robinson, Paul H., 1948–
Would you convict? : 17 cases that challenged the law / Paul H.
Robinson.
    p.   cm.
Includes bibliographical references and index.
ISBN 0-8147-7531-4 (pbk. : acid-free paper)
ISBN 0-8147-7530-6 (cloth : acid-free paper)
1. Criminal law—United States. 2. Trials—United States.
I. Title.
KF9218 .R634 1999
345.73—dc21   99-6451
                    CIP

New York University Press books are printed on acid-free paper,
and their binding materials are chosen for strength and durability.

Manufactured in the United States of America

10 9 8 7 6 5 4 3 2 1

Contents

Acknowledgments

This work is the product of many people. Mark Plichta and Kevin Metz, both of Northwestern University Law School, class of 1999, and Alex Paul and Hallie Mitchell, class of 2000, worked on the project as research assistants and contributed enormously to it. Mike Przyuski of Northwestern and Rozona Kelemen and Trudy Feldkamp of University of Michigan Law School provided typing and administrative help. Dean David Van Zandt of Northwestern provided financial and moral support. The Stanford Clinton, Sr. Research Professorship at Northwestern allowed me the time to undertake the work. Marcia Lehr and many other librarians at Northwestern University Law Library unstintingly helped with our often challenging and sometimes bizarre research problems. Sally Schwartz, Sarah Robinson, Katie Siegenthaler, and John McAlpine commented on an early draft.

Finally, many people helped with research into the facts of the individual cases. Regarding the case of Larry Eugene Phillips, we thank Sergeant Ian Grimes, of the Glendale (California) Police Department, for his interview; Tom Reisinger, editor of *Soldier of Fortune* magazine, for facts and photographs; Gene Blevins, freelance photographer, for photographs.

Regarding the case of Joseph B. Wood, we thank Professor Randy Roth, of Ohio State University in Columbus, Ohio, for facts and newspaper citations; Paul Carnahan, reference librarian at the Vermont State Historical Society in Montpelier, Vermont, for photographs and research leads; Paul Donovan, reference librarian at the Vermont State Historical Society, for photographs and facts; Jeffrey D. Marshall, archivist and curator of manuscripts at the University of Vermont, for photographs and facts.

Regarding the case of Canna Baker, we thank Mary Ann Messick, local historian in Baxter County, Arkansas, for photographs and facts.

Regarding the case of Julio Marrero, we thank Andrew Fine, Marrero's attorney with the Legal Aid Society, for court documents and insights; Mary Price, senior court clerk, Supreme Court of New York County, for court records; Anna Lucena for photographs; Beth Sauer Robinson for field research.

Regarding the case of Ray Edwin Billingslea, we thank Virginia Billingslea, granddaughter of Hazel Billingslea, for an interview; John Hagler, Billingslea's appellate attorney, for facts and help with court records; Deke Austin, Billingslea's trial attorney, for insights on the case; Ray Edwin Billingslea for an interview; Joel Sauer for field research.

Regarding the case of Linda Ruschioni, we thank Linda Ruschioni, Ricci Ruschioni, and Dudley P. Haney for interviews; John Ronan, Haney's attorney in the civil suit, for information and insights.

Regarding the case of John Charles Green, we thank Beverly Holder, reference librarian at Little Dixie Regional Library in Moberly, Missouri, for facts and newspaper photographs; Joan Krauskopf, Green's defense counsel, for facts and insights; C. M. Hulen, another Green defense attorney (retired), for research leads; Tim Kneist, director of public relations, Missouri Department of Corrections, for photographs.

Regarding the case of Johann Schlicht, we thank Judge Michael Bohlander for help finding German court documents; Delf Buchwald for court documents, other information, and field research in Germany; Sarah Schaeffer for translations.

Regarding the case of Motti Ashkenazi, we thank Jonathan von Samek for interviews of Israelis; Dr. Ron Shapira, of Tel Aviv University Law Faculty, for Israeli statutes and newspaper articles; Ronen Avraham for translations and field research in Tel Aviv.

Regarding the case of Bernice and Walter Williams, we thank Anthony Savage, Jr., the Williamses' defense attorney, for facts and insights; Gil Zimmerman, of the Sawyer Company, for field research; Chris Lane, Washington Department of Corrections, for research help.

Regarding the case of Janice Leidholm, we thank Irvin B. Nodland, Leidholm's defense attorney, for documents and insights; Professor Tom Lockney, of the University of North Dakota School of Law, for research leads.

Regarding the case of Barry Kingston, we thank Charles Taylor, Kingston's barrister, for documents, an interview, and assistance in arranging an interview; Colin Wibley, Kingston's solicitor, for documents; Professor Keith Topping, at University of Dundee, for help in locating Mr. Kingston; Barry Kingston for an interview and photographs.

Regarding the case of David Kenny Hawkins, we thank Mike Spechio, Washoe County (Nevada) public defender, for facts; John Petty, also of the public defender's office, for an interview and court documents; Tim Randolph, the Reno prosecutor of Hawkins, for an interview; Edwin Basil, also of the prosecutor's office, for an interview; Officer Roger Linscott, Reno Police Department, for an interview and field research in Reno; Carol McHenry, of Gladding and Michel, Inc., for field research; Karen Fraley, deputy city attorney (Reno), for help in obtaining documents and photographs.

Regarding the case of Richard R. Tenneson, we thank Frederick Hess, director, Office of Enforcement Operations, Criminal Division, U.S. Department of Justice, for help obtaining department records; John Andrews, intelligence specialist, U.S. Army Materiel Command, for research help.

Regarding the case of Alex Carbarga, we thank Lieutenant Richard Gordy, of the Concord (California) Police Department, for an interview.

Regarding the case of Robert Sandifer, we thank Professor Tom Geraghty, of the Northwestern University School of Law, for documents and research leads.

Also to be thanked are the several hundred people whose "sentences" for these seventeen cases are reported in this book, including students from the entering class of Northwestern University School of Law in 1997 and students from the entering class of University of Michigan Law School in 1998.

As always, my greatest thanks go to my family for their patience and support.

N.B. The facts recounted in these stories are true, as best as we can determine from our research of court documents, newspaper articles, and personal interviews. In places, I have added what I think is reasonable speculation about a person's motivation or state of mind as it appears from the person's conduct and circumstances.

Prologue

Criminal law is different. In other bodies of law, be it contract law, torts, employment discrimination, tax law, or something else, the legal rules might be called "man-made"; they could be formulated in any number of ways, depending on the specific objectives, objectives that may change with time and circumstances. Criminal law, in contrast, is generally understood as having the goal of *doing justice*, and "justice" is understood by civilized people as having an independent meaning. Thus the criminal law is not free to fashion any rule it chooses. It is bound by the shared intuitions of justice of the community it governs. The ultimate criminal law experts are not the judges and legislators who create it, but rather average people, the community. This book taps into that intuitive expertise of every reader and uses it to help evaluate the success or failure of modern criminal law.

Every mentally competent person, whether educated or not, has such intuitions of justice because the inclination to blame an offender as he or she deserves is a universal and distinctly human trait. Popular culture's endless books, movies, and television shows about crime, criminals, police, criminal courts, judges, lawyers, and trials give evidence of the basic human impulse to blame where it is due and to punish where it is deserved. It is an impulse as human as love for one's children or the desire to be part of a social group. But, unlike other desires, blaming and punishment require a previously existing social structure with shared norms. There can be no violators without rules.

It is no surprise, then, that every society creates a distinct body of criminal law, separated and labeled as distinct from all other bodies of law. This recognition of a distinct criminal law transcends political, cultural, religious, economic, and geographic differences. The communist Chinese have distinct criminal and civil systems, as do the democratic Swiss and the monarchist Saudis. The criminal-civil distinction is a basic organizing device for Islamic Pakistan, Catholic Ireland, Hindu

India, and the atheistic former Soviet Union, industrialized Germany, rural Papua New Guinea, the tribal Bedouins, wealthy Singapore, impoverished Somalia, developing Thailand, newly organized Ukraine, and the ancient Romans. Apparently every society sufficiently developed to have a formal legal system uses the criminal-civil distinction as a basic organizing principle.

What are the shared intuitive principles for doing justice that a criminal law should embody? How well do the formal legal rules express these principles? These are the questions that this book examines.

The average person has a sophisticated sense of justice, and so the analysis here is full and robust, not watered down. The seventeen real cases examined raise all of the most important issues in constructing a criminal law. For each case, you are given the full story of the people involved and the events leading up to the offense, then you are asked what liability and punishment, if any, ought to be imposed. Once you have sorted out your own view, there follows a discussion of the case that may cause you to rethink your view or may reaffirm your commitment to it. With that, you will hear how other people sentenced the same case after reading the same facts you read, and then will learn how traditional legal rules would deal with the case. Finally, the story of the case is finished; you will learn what actually happened in the case and what has since happened to the people involved. Thus, for each case, you will test your intuitions of justice against those of others, test our collective intuitions against the formal legal rules, and see how the formal legal rules actually operate in practice.

This book has three goals. First, it aims to help readers refine their own thinking about what justice means. More thoughtful and sophisticated potential jurors mean greater justice in the courts. The book's second purpose is to give a sound education in criminal law. The seventeen cases discussed here cover the same matters that law students cover in their basic criminal law course. (Indeed, these seventeen cases are used as the vehicle for teaching criminal law in some law schools.) Third, the book is intended to encourage people to think about the gap between law and justice. The rules of criminal law do not always match our intuitions of what justice requires. Citizen and legislative awareness of the law-justice gap can help close it.

I

Punishing Intent, Harm, or Dangerousness?

WHAT SHOULD THE criminal law focus on when it assigns punishment? A person's mental state? (What was the person's purpose? Were the conduct and its consequences intentional or accidental?) Whether there was actual harm? (Did the harm or evil defined by the offense actually occur, or did the person just intend or risk it?) Whether the person is dangerous? (Was this offense an aberration of character, or, if released, will the person commit another offense?) Are all these factors—intent, harm, and dangerousness—relevant? If so, how and when? What effect should they have? And how do they relate to one another?

The three cases that follow ask you for your answer to these questions, and sketch the law's answers. They also reveal some serious inconsistencies in the law's response, serious enough to suggest that what is needed is a rethinking of the nature and goals of modern criminal law.

ARE EVIL INTENTIONS A CRIME?

On a night in late October 1993, Sergeant Ian Grimes is patrolling in an unmarked car in Glendale, a suburb northwest of Los Angeles. A Thunderbird squeals its tires as it pulls out of a gas station and speeds north on Pacific Avenue toward the Ventura Freeway. Grimes gives chase and pulls the car over, for speeding, before it reaches the freeway on-ramp. He approaches the passenger side and talks to the driver through the passenger window. The driver gives the name "Dennis Franks," but has no license, claiming he left it at home. In response to Grimes's questioning, the driver seems confused about his home address. The passenger explains that the car belongs to the driver's mother, but Grimes has already learned over his radio that it is a rental car from the airport.

Left: Larry Eugene Phillips. (Archive Photos); *Right:* Emil Matasareanu. (Archive Photos)

He directs the driver to step out and stand at the right rear of the car, where he can see both men as he talks further to them. Both are big. The driver is six feet, 210 pounds; the passenger, six feet, 340 pounds.

The driver stands in an odd way as he talks, holding his body at an angle. He claims not to be armed, but Grimes realizes the man's odd stance is to make his shirt hang over and hide a nine-millimeter Glock 17 in his waistband. Grimes takes the weapon and backs up, taking cover behind a nearby planter on the sidewalk. The driver won't respond to Grimes's commands, nor for a moment will the passenger. Finally, Grimes hears a "clonk," which turns out to be the passenger dropping a Glock that he was holding. The passenger puts his hands out the window and Grimes holds the two in that position until backup arrives.

A search of the car reveals the following:

- one Norinco folding stock, semiautomatic rifle
- one MAK 90 wood-stock, semiautomatic rifle
- one Springfield Armory .45 pistol
- one Colt .45 pistol
- 1,649 rounds of 7.62 x 39 mm ammo, most loaded into 40-round magazines, taped three-together

- three seventy-five-round drum magazines loaded with 7.62 x 39 mm ammo
- 967 rounds of 9 x 19 mm JHP ammo
- 357 rounds of .45 JHP ammo
- six smoke bombs
- two improvised explosive devices
- one gas mask
- two sets of National Body Armor Level III-A vests
- two 200-channel, portable, programmable scanners with earpieces
- sunglasses, gloves, wigs, ski masks, stopwatch
- two spray cans of gray Studio Hair Color
- three different California automobile license plates
- $1,620 cash

The driver initially refuses to answer questions, but is subsequently identified as twenty-three-year-old Larry Eugene Phillips. The passenger is twenty-seven-year-old Emil Dechebal Matasareanu.

At the station, the men explain their load of weapons by telling police they are on their way to a shooting range in the Angeles National

The Glendale Police Department and bomb squad investigate the red Ford Thunderbird. (Gene Blevins, *Los Angeles Daily News*)

Top: Two semiautomatic assault rifles found in the trunk of the red Ford Thunderbird that Larry Phillips was driving. (Gene Blevins, *Los Angeles Daily News*); *Bottom:* 200-channel programmable police scanners and gloves found by Sergeant Ian Grimes and the Glendale Police Department. (Gene Blevins, *Los Angeles Daily News*)

Evidence room at the Glendale Police Department where the contents of the red Ford Thunderbird were laid out. (Gene Blevins, *Los Angeles Daily News*)

Forest known as "Kentucky." It is just before Halloween, "Devil's Night." The disguises and other material may be needed for a Halloween party after the shooting range.

The police, and later the prosecutors, have little doubt the police have stumbled onto two robbers on their way to a job. The arsenal and supplies are a classic "bank robbery kit."

The two men are probably liable for at least some weapons offenses. (Their assault rifles are not at the time illegal in California.) Should the two also be held criminally liable for attempted robbery? If so, what amount of punishment would you impose for attempted robbery?

no liability	☐	1 year	☐
liability but no punishment	☐	3 years	☐
		7 years	☐
1 day	☐	15 years	☐
2 weeks	☐	30 years	☐
2 months	☐	life imprisonment	☐
6 months	☐	death	☐

(In answering this and similar liability questions throughout the book, if you would impose a punishment other than imprisonment—a fine or community service—translate that sentence into a term of imprisonment of equivalent punitive bite, in order to allow easier comparison of assigned punishments.)

People's Intuitions of Justice

Few people are likely to believe Phillips's story that the two are on their way to a shooting range and then a Halloween party. Homemade explosives? Police scanners? Stopwatch and gloves? It doesn't fit. And unless they are going to be shooting at each other at the party, why bulletproof vests? Clearly these folks are up to something bad. That the items together make what the experts call a "bank robbery kit" only confirms the suspicion.

At the same time, most people faced with these facts seem hesitant to hold Phillips liable for attempted robbery or conspiracy to rob. Rob what? Where? When? We know nothing about what the two specifically intend. Another concern is how real the intention is. Even if the two had a plan, would they really have done it, or is this a Walter Mitty pair who has watched too many television shows? Was their intention sufficiently formed and resolute that they really would have gone ahead with a robbery if they had gotten to a bank or whatever their target was?

Even if the *intent* to rob was clear, people typically have a sense that a person must do enough toward committing the offense for it to count as a crime. Bad intention may be enough for sin, in a religious sense, but criminal liability requires sufficient *conduct* toward the offense.

In one Mississippi case, a burglar was caught with a list in his pocket of items needed for the burglary, in an envelope conveniently labeled "Preparations for a Burglary." Assume Phillips had such a "Preparations for a Robbery" envelope, so his intention was clear. Would it make this case clear, or would we still have some concern that these two would-be robbers still have not done enough to make a crime? They have raised strong suspicion, but has it matured into proof of a crime?

Several hundred people have been given the facts of this case (and all the cases in this book) and been asked to sentence the defendant using the same scale that you were given above. Here is how the people in the survey sentenced Phillips:

no liability	59%	1 year	7%
liability but		3 years	19%
no punishment	3%	7 years	4%
1 day	—	15 years	4%
2 weeks	—	30 years	—
2 months	1%	life imprisonment	—
6 months	2%	death	—

Mean = 2.4 weeks.

Even on such suspicious facts, 59 percent of the people would not impose liability for attempted robbery.

The Law's Rules

The intuitions of this majority match the law's high requirements. The law requires proof of both an intention to commit the offense beyond a reasonable doubt and sufficient conduct toward commission of the offense. The facts of this case—carrying a robbery kit and giving a doubtful explanation—do not present a strong case for attempt liability.

Jurisdictions disagree as to how much conduct is enough. Some require that the person be in "dangerous proximity" of committing the offense—that he present an imminent threat. Others require only that the person has taken a "substantial step" toward its commission. Most of the legal requirements for minimum conduct are vague, like these two. Thus, when juries are given legal instructions, they probably just express their own intuitive sense of how much is enough.

Why such intention and minimum conduct requirements for criminal liability? Our intuitive notions of justice typically don't see thinking bad thoughts, or even acting on them in a preliminary way, as sufficient to be criminal. Most people seem to feel that punishment is deserved only when, first, the intention is sufficiently developed and firm and, second, the person has come sufficiently close to committing the offense.

Background

Larry Eugene Phillips, born on September 9, 1970, gets his first exposure to the life of crime on his sixth birthday, when the FBI knocks on the door of the family home in Denver. Before Larry's eyes, they arrest his father, Larry, Sr., who has been a fugitive from a Colorado prison since his son's birth. A few years later Larry's mother, Dorothy Clay, finalizes a divorce and moves with her son to a suburb of Los Angeles. His mother is no stranger to crime, once serving ten years for drug possession and stabbing a prison guard. At the age of nineteen, Phillips gets arrested for the first time after stealing four hundred dollars from a Sears store in Alhambra, California.

Phillips and Emil Dechebal Matasareanu meet in 1989 and quickly become friends. They both enjoy weapons and like to go shooting together. Although four years the younger, Phillips, controlling and manipulative, becomes the duo's leader. "You can't imagine how manipulative my brother was," explains Phillips's half-brother later. "He tried to break your mind down and then build it up again so that you would become one of his crew."

Phillips, a clean-shaven bodybuilder, dreams incessantly of wealth, fantasizing about spending one hundred-dollar bills by the handful. He idolizes the 1980s robber baron Michael Milken and the movie-screen legend the "Godfather." To pass the time, he sometimes drives around the chic neighborhoods of Los Angeles, watching the celebrities come and go, and pictures himself living their lives.

Matasareanu, born in Romania on July 19, 1966, moves to California as a child and grows up in Altadena, a suburb fifteen miles northeast of downtown Los Angeles, and other areas. Matasareanu's mother, a former singer who defected from the Romanian state opera, describes her son as a very intelligent boy. She struggles to raise him on her own. As a chubby boy, he is the butt of teasing from other children and classmates. The isolation of his youth turns him early to computers as an outlet. He gets formal computer training at the DeVry Institute.

In his twenties, Matasareanu returns to Romania, marries, moves back to the United States, has a son, and starts a computer business. Not long after his marriage, a blocked artery in his brain causes him to begin suffering epileptic seizures that require surgery. Soon after, his computer business fails.

In 1990 the twenty-year-old Phillips takes the California real estate examination and passes. However, officials in the Department of Real Estate discover his 1989 theft conviction through a routine fingerprint check, and the state turns him down for a license because his application failed to disclose the conviction. About that time, Phillips, with no license, tells his probation officer that he is making a lot of money, about two thousand to four thousand dollars per transaction, as a real estate agent.

In 1991 Phillips, now twenty-one, is arrested again, this time in Orange, California, on weapons charges, when a police officer spots a semiautomatic nine-millimeter pistol in his waistband and an extra clip of ammunition and a knife hidden inside a compartment in his BMW. He insists he needs the gun for protection because he is going to pick up a large amount of cash from a real estate transaction. Detectives in the Orange Police Department, while investigating the weapons charges, link him to a real estate scam involving forged title documents.

Phillips also goes by the names Larry Franks, Dennis Franks, and Denis Rene. He regularly changes his address within the same city and gives false addresses.

In 1992 Denver police link Phillips to a residential burglary and arrest him. He pleads guilty but skips the sentencing hearing and returns to California. Denver police also link Phillips and Matasareanu to the robbery of an armored car, but by the time they have gathered enough evidence to arrest the pair, they have gone back to California.

Throughout the early 1990s, police and repossession agents search diligently but unsuccessfully for Phillips, repeatedly checking for him at a house he once rented in Altadena. In 1993 Phillips, going by the name Larry Martinez, marries a woman he met while in Denver, Janette Teresa Federico, who is the mother of a young girl by another man. After the two move back to Los Angeles, they split up.

Then comes the bad luck traffic stop in Glendale.

The Aftermath

That Phillips has a criminal history at the time of the traffic stop in Glendale only confirms our suspicions about his intentions. But that history does not alter the fact that, when stopped, he had not yet done much toward commission of a specific robbery.

Deputy District Attorney James Grodin initially charges Phillips and Matasareanu with conspiracy to commit robbery and holds them on bond as prosecutors figure out what to do. Grodin sees real problems with the prosecution because they have no evidence of a criminal agreement between the two to rob, which conspiracy to rob requires, and little evidence of a specific robbery planned, thus no grounds for attempted robbery. Says Grodin, "We didn't have a lot. I didn't know what the men were doing. . . . I wanted to charge him with whatever I could. We actually sat around thinking what we could do. . . . We didn't have a lot of proof. . . . These assault weapons were not the AK-47s. . . . They were copycats that you could have legally at the time."

Phillips pleads no contest to one felony and one misdemeanor weapons charge and serves ninety-nine days in jail. Matasareanu serves seventy-one days. Both are placed on probation for three years, but rarely see their probation officer.

Defense attorneys request the return of the seized weapons and property, and a judge grants most of the request. After their release, the two reclaim their bulletproof vests, hollow-point bullets, the two .45-caliber pistols, the MAK-90 rifle, police scanners, gas mask, wigs, fake mustaches, stopwatch, gloves, clothes, and sunglasses. Some material is returned with a specific requirement that it be sold.

Free again, Phillips reenters the real estate scam business, but with little apparent success. In 1995 he and two other men are ordered to pay $140,000 in principal and interest to reimburse a mortgage title company for forged deeds. During part of this time, he moves back in with his mother and a girlfriend, April Coleman, along with the couple's illegitimate son. Less than a year later, Coleman moves out and obtains a court order for $152 monthly child support.

Unfazed by their 1993 arrest, Phillips and Matasareanu return to high-stakes robberies. In 1995 they rob an armored car and kill the guard, then attempt to rob another armored car. In May 1996 Phillips and Matasareanu rob two Bank of America branches in San Fernando Valley near Los Angeles. They enter the bank dressed in combat fatigues, fire shots into the ceiling and vault to scare the customers, and order everyone to the floor. The robberies seem amazingly well timed and come just after the banks have received large shipments of cash. Police and the FBI begin investigating whether the unknown robbers have ties to organized crime groups or paramilitary organizations. "It's obvious these guys did their homework," one investigator says. The robbers net about $1.5 million. The two begin living the high life, wearing $500 suits, $200 shoes, and Rolex watches, and driving BMWs, Jaguars, and Lincolns.

In August 1996 Matasareanu's wife, Christina, leaves him, taking their two- and five-year-old sons with her. At the same time, state investigators begin closing in on him and his mother for the abuse and neglect of patients at her day care center for elderly and disabled people.

On February 28, 1997, Phillips and Matasareanu start to assemble gear for what they hope will be their biggest heist yet: another Bank of America branch, this one in North Hollywood on Laurel Canyon Road. They hide a getaway car—a gray, late-model sedan—in a Mission Hills neighborhood, and plant two mayonnaise jars filled with gasoline in the trunk for use in later blowing up the car to cover their tracks. They also stock the car with a hundred-round drum of high-powered ammunition. They steady their nerves with doses of phenobarbital.

At 9:17 A.M., a few minutes after the bank opens, the two men burst in carrying fully automatic AK-47 assault rifles, spraying bullets indiscriminately. Screaming customers dive for the floor. Some are herded into the safe deposit box area.

When they find only $304,000 in the vault, the men fly into a rage. (Since Phillips's May 1996 robberies and similar ones at Bank of America branches around Los Angeles, the bank has begun keeping less cash at each of its locations.) Phillips and Matasareanu viciously beat one branch official because he cannot produce more money. The brief indulgence throws off their military timing as they ignore the stopwatches sewn to their gloves. Witnesses call police, who are already responding to a silent alarm.

The police soon close in on the bank and call for reinforcements, aware that recent Southern California bank robbers have been heavily armed. News helicopters hover above, broadcasting the scene live across the country.

When the two men emerge from the bank, they are met by a police blockade. But Phillips and Matasareanu are ready. The pair are wearing Kevlar body armor, which is almost impenetrable to ordinary bullets. In the fusillade that follows, bullets bounce off the two as if they are supermen. They spray the crowd of bystanders and police with hundreds of rounds, tearing up trees, signs, mailboxes, and windows. The SWAT team arrives but realizes that it too is outgunned. They visit a local gun shop to get additional armaments. The shoot-out goes on for twenty minutes.

The two men try to escape east on Archwood Street. Phillips, on foot, has his escape route cut off, but continues to shoot at anything that moves. At 9:52 A.M. on Archwood, less than a block from the bank, he shoots himself in the head with his nine-milimeter semiautomatic

Surveillance photos from Bank of America of robbery in progress. (the FBI)

14

One of the gunmen as he shoots at Los Angeles police officers in front of Bank of America. (Gene Blevins, *Los Angeles Daily News*)

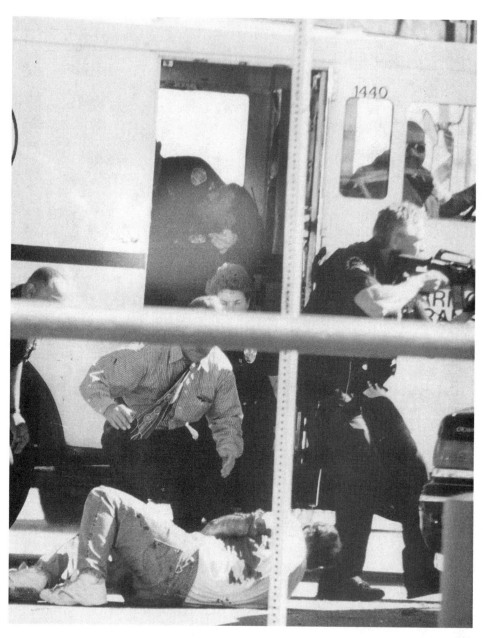

LAPD officers and SWAT team, as they use an armored car to rescue a man who was shot six times during the shoot-out. (Gene Blevins, *Los Angeles Daily News*)

pistol. Simultaneously, a police sharpshooter's bullet slams into his neck, severing his spinal cord.

Matasareanu drives east in the getaway car, a white Chevrolet sedan. Police shoot out two of the car's tires. Four blocks down Archwood, Matasareanu tries to commandeer a Jeep pickup truck. He lets go a burst of gunfire with his AK-47 through his own windshield into the Jeep. Its driver, fifty-two-year-old William Marr of Burbank, is struck by flying glass and shrapnel. He jumps from his truck and flees.

As Matasareanu tries to start Marr's Jeep, a black and white squad car, loaded with SWAT officers, approaches at high speed and pulls in front of the two stopped cars. Matasareanu gets out of the Jeep and crouches behind his Chevy as the officers open fire, now at close range.

For two minutes, the police and Matasareanu blast away at each other, just a car length apart. Matasareanu is shot twenty-nine times, and surrenders. Officers handcuff him at 9:59 A.M. and call ambulances for the gunman and his last victim, Marr.

Afraid that the two robbers have rigged bombs to themselves or might have nearby accomplices, police refuse to let paramedics touch either body for several minutes. In that time, Matasareanu bleeds to

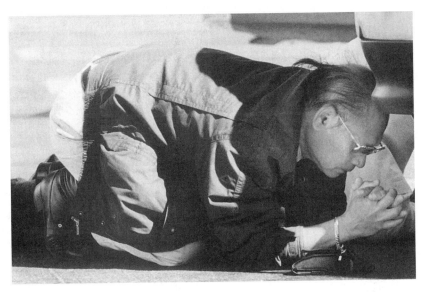

An LAPD officer prays while taking cover behind a squad car as gunmen fire. (Gene Blevins, *Los Angeles Daily News*)

LAPD officers survey the dead robber. (Gene Blevins, *Los Angeles Daily News*)

death. "His actions were more like a suicide," says Matasareanu's mother, Valerie Nicolescue. (But she later sues the police department for wrongful death for letting her son bleed to death.)

Eleven police officers and five civilians are wounded in the shoot-out. In the trunk of the men's bullet-ridden car, police find two mayonnaise jars filled with gasoline, each rigged with triggers to ignite the bombs and destroy the car after the planned getaway.

Police clad in flak jackets search Phillips's Altadena house after the shoot-out. A search of Matasareanu's rented sprawling, multilevel Rowland Heights home turns up two high-powered rifles, a pistol-grip shotgun, two bulletproof vests, police T-shirts, patches with police insignia, and paramilitary and survivalist literature. In the trunk of Matasareanu's Buick Century, parked in the garage, they find a Tupperware bowl containing plastic explosive with wires attached.

In the days following the shoot-out—the largest in California history—news reports show the gun battle over and over.

When the earlier arrest of the two men comes to light, there is much hand wringing. Clearly, if the requirements for attempt liability were less demanding—if a highly suspicious intention were sufficient, for example—Phillips and Matasareanu would have been convicted of attempted robbery and would still be in prison. The North Hollywood shoot-out never would have occurred. Despite this obvious cost of the more demanding requirements for attempt and despite the televised spectacle of a morning of automatic weapons fire in North Hollywood, there is no suggestion that the minimum requirements for criminal attempt be weakened. The excesses of the *Phillips* case only confirm the depth of commitment to the present liability requirements of a sufficiently developed and resolute intent and sufficiently advanced conduct.

Attempt versus the Complete Offense: The Significance of Resulting Harm

Assume for the sake of argument that Phillips and friend in fact had gone further. Assume they were stopped by police in front of a bank. If that is not enough to make attempted robbery liability clear for you, assume further they are caught just as they are pulling ski masks down over their faces while sitting in front of the bank. Presumably, on these facts, their intention is sufficiently mature and their conduct sufficiently advanced for liability for attempted bank robbery.

Should their liability in such a case of attempted bank robbery be the same as it would be for bank robbery itself—that is, the same as if they in fact had entered the bank, displayed their weapons, taken the money, and fled? A few people, and many academics, will say yes, the liability for attempted robbery ought to be the same as for actual robbery. That the police got lucky, or smart, in the interrupted-attempt case does not reduce the subjective culpability of the culprits. In fact, even the American Law Institute's Model Penal Code, which has been the blueprint in varying degrees for over two-thirds of the criminal codes in the United States, provides, generally, that attempts are to be graded the same as the offense attempted. Under that code, the outside-the-bank interrupted-attempted robbery would be as serious an offense as the took-the-money-and-ran robbery.

But this provision in the Model Penal Code is one of the most frequently rejected by state legislatures that use the code as a model. The intuition that the occurrence of resulting harm does matter is nearly universal and runs very deep among the public. Most jurisdictions grade the completed offense as more serious than the attempt, usually carrying double the statutory penalty of attempt. The next case explores our intuitions about, and the law's treatment of, resulting harm.

CAN FATHER AND DAUGHTER KILL
THE SAME MAN TWICE?

It is 1874. Joseph B. Wood's daughter, Alma, a short, slight woman in her late twenties, marries Luman Smith, a farmer in Williston, Vermont. It is Alma's second marriage. She brings to it a child from her previous marriage, Joseph B. (named after his grandfather). Luman, forty, and Alma have two children together. Luman is devoted to the children.

The relationship between Luman and Alma is not good and they have many fights. Alma leaves the home several times between 1874 and 1879. Tensions in the household are heightened by Alma's infidelity and prostitution, and by Luman's threats and sometimes violence toward Alma. In 1879 Alma again leaves Luman, the farm, and the three children.

Luman soon realizes he cannot run a farm and raise the three children by himself. The infant, in particular, requires constant attention. He goes to his estranged wife and begs her to return. She agrees, but only after he accepts several conditions. First, she is to be given her own room in the house where she can entertain guests without interruption from Luman. Second, her father is to move in with them. This arrangement helps her father and provides her with some degree of protection, if needed, as does the small revolver she has recently purchased. Finally, Luman signs most of his property over to her and agrees to allow her to use his horse when he does not need it.

After the deal is made and the property transferred, Alma nonetheless begins to plan to move west to Lincoln, Nebraska. Luman carries a good-sized dirk knife (a short, straight dagger) with him throughout the day. Fearing that Luman might use it against her, Alma steals the knife and hides it.

On October 23, just a few days after Alma and her father move back to the farm, Luman returns from a visit to the doctor in Essex Junction. His daughter Helen runs to greet him at the gate and they walk to the stable so Luman can hitch up his horse to go into town.

Joseph Wood enters the stable and objects to Luman hitching the horse, telling Luman he can no longer use it. Luman explains that the horse was not transferred to Alma with the other property, but Wood is undeterred. Before Luman can finish hitching the horse, Wood pulls a pistol on Luman, who grabs the barrel and points it away. The

A typical 1880s Vermont farm. (Vermont Historical Society)

two men struggle. Wood fires several shots at Luman but misses. Finally, Wood points the gun at Luman's abdomen and pulls the trigger. It is a lethal wound.

Would you convict Wood for the killing of Luman? If so, what amount of punishment would you impose?

no liability	☐	1 year	☐
liability but		3 years	☐
no punishment	☐	7 years	☐
1 day	☐	15 years	☐
2 weeks	☐	30 years	☐
2 months	☐	life imprisonment	☐
6 months	☐	death	☐

People's Intuitions of Justice

It is an intentional killing, murder. Most people would punish severely, although some people would view the case as less egregious than the most serious kind of murder perhaps because it is not a planned killing. Instead, it arises from the "heat of passion" of a fight.

And while Wood has no right to use force against Luman, he may mistakenly believe that he does.

Here is how the people in the survey would sentence Wood on these facts:

no liability	—	1 year	—
liability but		3 years	4%
no punishment	—	7 years	7%
1 day	—	15 years	14%
2 weeks	—	30 years	22%
2 months	—	life imprisonment	41%
6 months	—	death	11%

Mean = between 30 years and life imprisonment.

More Facts

In fact, Luman does not die immediately. The nature of the wound allows him to survive for some time and, for a period, with full mobility. Given the state of medical science at the time, however, all experts agree that he will die from the wound within a week or two due to loss of blood and infection.

Alma, hearing the gunshots, runs out of the house with her revolver hidden in her apron. As she approaches, Luman sees the gun and grabs for it, but Alma holds tight. Luman begins choking Alma. Afraid for her life, she points the revolver at Luman and fires a round into his chest. Luman staggers away. "You need not shoot again, for I am a dead man." As Luman slumps, Alma and Wood go back to what they were doing before the shooting, showing no concern or remorse.

Luman and the daughter, Helen, make it to the home of Mr. and Mrs. Josiah Thompson, a neighboring farmer. Two doctors are called. Luman's lungs begin to fill with fluid immediately from Alma's gunshot wound to his chest. He dies two days later from asphyxiation from the fluid. Experts agree that the would have died from Wood's shot to the abdomen, had he not first died from Alma's shot to the chest.

Would you impose criminal liability on Wood? If so, how much liability would you impose?

no liability	☐	1 year	☐
liability but		3 years	☐
no punishment	☐	7 years	☐
1 day	☐	15 years	☐
2 weeks	☐	30 years	☐
2 months	☐	life imprisonment	☐
6 months	☐	death	☐

People's Intuitions of Justice

If Alma had not come along, Luman would have died from Wood's shot within a week or two, and Wood would have been liable for Luman's murder. That Alma has independently killed Luman changes nothing of Wood's conduct and intention in the case. If Wood's conduct and intention are all that matter in assessing criminal liability, then nothing is different by virtue of Alma's killing. Should Wood's liability and punishment be any less because of events occurring after his conduct—Alma's killing of Luman—over which he had no control?

Most people think causing the harm does matter. The person who shoots and misses because the victim happens to bend down to tie his shoe is seen as deserving less punishment than the person who shoots and kills. Both may have engaged in the same conduct with the same state of mind, but only the latter is a murderer. Wood's case is different from this only in that the intended victim is in fact dead, but the victim was killed by another person, with no causal connection to Wood or Wood's wounding.

Here is how the people in the survey sentenced Wood when they knew the whole story:

no liability	—	1 year	4%
liability but		3 years	4%
no punishment	2%	7 years	17%
1 day	—	15 years	23%
2 weeks	—	30 years	22%
2 months	—	life imprisonment	23%
6 months	1%	death	—

Mean = 22.5 years.

If you compare this distribution of sentences to the previous one (in which Wood was thought to have caused the death), it seems that the entire distribution has shifted about one category to the left. The reduction in the mean from the first variation to the second confirms this. (The points on the penalty scale represent the typical pattern of offense grading categories in American criminal codes. A one-grade reduction, which is what we see here, typically represents a halving of the statutory penalty.)

We know Wood's intention is to shoot Luman, and that he has no justification for doing so. We know he is willing to carry through with this intention. In fact, he did. He went all the way. Indeed, he did in fact cause a lethal wound. That Luman died from Alma's shot before he could die from Wood's hardly alters Wood's subjective culpability. What could all these people be thinking who gave Wood a grade lower sentence?

The answer, of course, is that, however evil Wood's intention and however much he tried to cause Luman's death, the fact is he did not cause Luman's death. And *causing* harm is of great significance to most people in assessing blameworthiness and criminal liability.

That importance is confirmed by social science studies of the issue. One study used a jewelry store robbery as a base scenario, altering the facts to determine the effect on liability imposed by average people. The perpetrator who completes the jewelry store robbery is given an average sentence of 3.4 years. Where the same robbery is attempted but not completed, the perpetrator's sentence drops (to between 7.5 days and 1.8 years, depending on how close the robber comes to completion). Another study, using a murder scenario, found life imprisonment as the average sentence for a standard intentional killing, compared to only 9.4 years where the intended victim happened to move, causing the shooter to miss his target. In other words, the failure to actually bring about the harm or evil of the offense results in a significant "discount" off the punishment assigned for the completed offense.

In a study that used a scenario analogous to the situation in the *Wood* case, researchers found the no-causation "discount" to be less than usual, for the *Wood* case presents the most extreme case of attempt that is possible. Not only is the offender's conduct complete, but he in fact is successful at causing a lethal wound, and in fact the victim dies. The case presents the most technical of differences from the straight murder case, but that minor difference—that Wood's shot was not in fact necessary for the result of death to occur when it did—nonetheless makes a difference to people's intuition of blameworthiness. Trying to be a murderer and actually being one are simply different.

The notion of causation has strong intuitive roots with many people. To be the cause of a result, a person's action must be necessary for that result. If the result would have occurred when it did even without the person's action, then the action cannot be its cause. In this case, Luman's death would have occurred when it did *even if Wood had never shot Luman in the abdomen.* Thus, Wood's shot was not necessary for Luman's death, and therefore it is not seen as the factual cause of Luman's death. For this reason, Wood deserves less punishment.

The Law's Rules

The law tracks lay intuition on this issue. Criminal codes almost universally require that an actor's conduct be necessary for a result to occur before it can be judged a "factual cause" of that result. (Codes also require for causation that the result be sufficiently proximate to the conduct—that it be "not too remote or accidental or too dependent upon another's volitional act.") The result of this legal causation inquiry will determine whether the person is liable only for attempt or for the full offense. In Wood's case, this is the difference between attempted murder and murder. The difference is of great legal significance because attempt typically is graded at a lower level than the completed offense, and commonly is punished at half the penalty for the full offense.

The Aftermath

Later in the day of the shooting, Wood and Alma are arrested and jailed. The preliminary examination takes place on November 10 in the city court. The hearing is long and exhaustive and at the conclusion of the arguments, the judge determines that Wood and Alma must remain in custody pending a hearing by the grand jury and, if indicted, trial on the charge of murder. At the September term of the Chittenden County Court, 1880, the grand jury finds a true indictment on several counts against the two. The daughter, Helen Smith, four, among others, testifies as to the events.

Left: Burlington Police Department, which investigated the murder of Luman Smith. (Vermont Historical Society); *Right:* Chittenden County Courthouse in Burlington, Vermont, where *State v. Wood* was tried. (Vermont Historical Society)

The trial is presided over by Judge Wheelock G. Veazey.[*] The evidence at trial makes clear that "Luman died of the wound inflicted by Alma and not from that inflicted by Wood," that "there was no concert of action between them, and each acted independently, and they were therefore only responsible for their own acts respectively," and that "the wound inflicted by Wood was mortal and would in course of time have killed Luman, if he had not previously died from the wound inflicted by Alma." But the judge instructs the jury that as a matter of law, this is enough to convict Wood of murder, even though Wood's injury to Luman is not necessary for the death. The jury follows the instruction and convicts Wood of murder. Alma is also so convicted and both are sentenced to life in prison, as required by statute.

But the case is appealed to the Vermont Supreme Court, where the court notes the erroneous jury instruction regarding causation—Wood

---

[*]Veazey is a Civil War hero who led Vermont regiments in many of the battles of the Army of the Potomac, including those at Richmond and Gettysburg. In the latter, it was his maneuvering that countered Pickett's charge and won him the Medal of Honor from Congress.

cannot be liable for murder if his shot was not necessary for Luman's death—and reverses the conviction, remanding the case for a new trial.

Murder versus Attempted Murder: The Significance of Resulting Harm

If Wood is convicted of only attempted murder, he is subject to a minimum term of five years, rather than the life imprisonment required upon conviction for murder. That dramatic difference in punishment reflects the strength of common intuition on the importance of resulting harm.

That difference may seem irrational to some, but consider a world where resulting harm was ignored. There would be no offense of homicide or rape or robbery, only crimes of intentional conduct toward those ends. No offense would be defined to require actual result; all crimes would be defined simply as conduct that intended or risked the result. You drive home from a party and, as you pull into your garage, you realize what a risk you created to others by driving after drinking. In a world where resulting harm did not matter, your consciously creating a risk of death would be enough for liability equal to that for actually recklessly causing a death (manslaughter). You are no less liable because you were lucky enough on this occasion not to have killed anyone.

Such a world simply does not match the community's intuitions of justice. And a criminal law that took this view—that ignored whether or not a person actually caused the harm—would quickly lose credibility with the community. A criminal law without moral credibility can play no effective role in the public dynamic that shapes the society's moral norms. In contrast, morally credible criminal law can help develop or reinforce norms against damaging conduct—such as domestic violence, drunk driving, child abuse, or insider trading—when it criminalizes the conduct or increases the seriousness of the offense's grade or penalty. In addition, loss of moral credibility undercuts the powerful yet cheap deterrent effect that law can have by stigmatizing a violator. If criminal law has a poor reputation as a reliable authority in assessing blameworthiness, the imposition of criminal liability fails to carry a moral stigma.

But these useful powers of criminal law are possible only if the law has previously shown itself to be a reliable judge of what is truly condemnable. To adopt rules of criminal liability that conflict dramatically with community intuitions, as in ignoring the strong community sense that causing harm matters—that a murder is really worse than an attempted murder—is to undercut criminal law's moral credibility and reduce its power to stigmatize and to shape the development of community norms.

The Final Outcome

On July 5, 1881, before Wood gets his retrial, he dies. At Alma's retrial, she initially pleads guilty to manslaughter. But after the indictment is read, she changes her mind and pleads not guilty.

At the conclusion of trial, the jury finds her not guilty, accepting her claim of self-defense.

The Requirements of Criminal Liability

Together, the *Phillips* and *Wood* cases tell us something about the fundamentals of criminal liability, points on which law and common intuition generally agree. Criminal liability and punishment require, at minimum, a sufficiently developed and resolute intention and sufficiently advanced conduct toward an offense. In addition, once these minimum requirements of liability are established, the seriousness of an offense is increased if the offender actually brings about the harm or evil of the offense—whatever it be, bank robbery or death—and such an increase in seriousness translates into a higher statutory offense grade and greater punishment. While these may seem unexceptionable and commonsense lessons in the rules for assigning blame and punishment, the next case shows that the criminal law regularly violates these rules and challenges these lessons.

LIFE IMPRISONMENT FOR AIR CONDITIONING FRAUD?

William J. Rummel has had trouble holding down any kind of job. More because of laziness than inability, he has opted instead to make his living through small-time larceny and fraud. If he were good enough, check forgery might be called his specialty. But he is not and his arrests begin to pile up. As a con man, the tall and thin Rummel is inept, leaving clues like his real name and signature on receipts from stolen credit cards and on stolen checks. His legitimate skills are as limited as his criminal ones. His educational background consists of a few Dale Carnegie courses. At the age of thirty, he has no family and no friends. His parents are both alive but their health is poor and they see Rummel rarely.

On August 15, 1972, Rummel walks into Captain Hook's Lounge in San Antonio. It is a hot day and the bar's air conditioning is not working. Rummel gets an idea. He approaches the bar's owner, David Shaw, and offers to fix the air conditioner. Shaw agrees and Rummel begins his inspection. After a few minutes and a little tinkering, Rummel announces the unit needs a new compressor. Cost: $129.75, labor free. Shaw quickly agrees and writes Rummel a check for the amount payable to Rummel. Rummel leaves, cashes the check, and never returns. Shaw files a complaint with the police, who easily trace Rummel.

Rummel's offense, theft by false pretext, would normally render him liable under Texas law for a maximum sentence of between two and ten years, although violators typically are given a sentence of months, not years.

But Rummel has a criminal record. On October 20, 1959, in San Antonio he is convicted of misdemeanor theft and unlawful possession of alcoholic beverages. On the day of those convictions at the Bexar County Courthouse, he is arrested again, for unlawfully carrying a Bowie knife. He is convicted of the weapons charge on January 21, 1960, and fined one hundred dollars. On May 17, 1960, he is given three years of probation on a burglary charge. On July 25, 1963, he passes a ten dollar bad check at a Holiday Inn and on December 22, 1963, a thirty-dollar bad check. He is convicted on March 6, 1964, of two counts of swindling by check and is sentenced to thirty days in jail.

On December 16, 1964, Rummel is convicted of credit card fraud after he uses a company credit card without authority to buy two new tires for his car, worth a total of $80. He is sentenced to three years in prison, but is paroled. He violates parole on July 21, 1966, and is returned to the Department of Corrections on August 25, 1966. On February 21, 1968, Rummel is convicted of aggravated assault on a female, Penny Rummel, and is sentenced to thirty days in jail. On the day of his assault conviction, he passes a bad check for $5.61 at a Gulf service station and is convicted of swindling by check. He is sentenced to thirty days, to run consecutively with the sentence for the assault conviction.

William James Rummel in 1980. (Corbis)

On March 11, 1969, Rummel is convicted of forging a $28.36 check and is sentenced to two to four years in prison, of which he serves twenty-eight months.

What liability and punishment would you impose on Rummel for his $129.75 air conditioning fraud?

no liability	☐	1 year	☐
liability but		3 years	☐
no punishment	☐	7 years	☐
1 day	☐	15 years	☐
2 weeks	☐	30 years	☐
2 months	☐	life imprisonment	☐
6 months	☐	death	☐

People's Intuitions of Justice

While Rummel's offense on this particular occasion is not terribly serious, most people are likely to feel that he deserves more than if this were his first offense. His repeated violations have the appearance of thumbing his nose at the law and at the community's norms. The "more" he deserves for nose-thumbing may not be as much as what he deserves for the offense itself; the thumbing isn't a greater violation than the offense itself, but rather an aggravating circumstance. But the nose-thumbing does suggest some percentage increase in what otherwise would be deserved.

Here is how the people in the survey sentenced Rummel:

no liability	—	1 year	18%
liability but		3 years	29%
no punishment	2%	7 years	30%
1 day	—	15 years	7%
2 weeks	1%	30 years	—
2 months	3%	life imprisonment	—
6 months	9%	death	—

Mean = 2.8 years.

The average sentence imposed is less than three years, which is about what Rummel served for his last theft conviction. But 66 percent would impose a sentence of three years or more, which would be providing an increase over his last sentence.

Trial and Sentence

On April 10, 1973, a jury convicts Rummel of the theft. Because the value is over fifty dollars, the offense is a felony. The next day, the state presents evidence of two prior felony convictions and asks the judge to declare Rummel a habitual criminal. A habitual criminal classification authorizes a dramatic increase in the available prison term, under the theory that such is the only effective way of preventing habitual offenders from committing more offenses in the future. The declared purpose of the Texas sentencing statute is to deal "with those who by repeated criminal acts have shown that they are simply incapable of conforming to the norms of society as established by its criminal law." The prior felony offenses that qualify Rummel include the December 1964 credit card fraud and the March 1969 forgery. All totaled, the three felonies netted Rummel $233.11. Following the statute's direction, on April 26, 1973, the judge sentences thirty-year-old Rummel to life in prison without parole.

Punishing Dangerousness: Cloaking Preventive Detention as Criminal Justice

There can be little doubt that crime is a problem in the United States. While crime rates have leveled off and even fallen some, they remain dramatically higher than they were forty years ago. Today's murder rate is twice what it was in 1955. Rape rates have quadrupled, as have robbery rates. The aggravated assault rate has increased fivefold. Overall, including both rural and urban areas, the serious crime rate is four times what it was four decades ago.

Nor can there be doubt that repeat offenders are a serious part of the crime problem. One classic study of ten thousand young male offenders in Philadelphia revealed that 18 percent of the offenders committed five or more offenses, and that this group of "chronic offenders" committed 52 percent of all the group's offenses. Another study found that about 70 percent of violent crimes are committed by the same 6 percent repeat offenders.

Nor can one reasonably dispute that a society must be able to, and inevitably will, do what is necessary to protect itself from dangerous persons. Any democratic government that does not will soon lose political power.

But while the protection of society from dangerous persons is legitimate and inevitable, the use of the criminal justice system for that end, as in the Texas habitual offender statute, creates serious complications. A system that distributes liability and punishment in order to protect society from dangerous persons assigns liability and punishment differently than one that distributes liability and punishment to do justice. Not all dangerous people are blameworthy. Severely mentally ill persons and persons with contagious diseases, for example, may need detention but may not deserve punishment. Similarly, not all blameworthy persons are dangerous. The law-abiding citizen recently discovered to be a former Nazi concentration camp commandant deserves punishment even if he is no longer a danger.

A just punishment system and a protection system are very different. The former focuses on what is deserved for a past wrong, while the latter has no reason to even require one. For example, there may exist a test that reliably predicts the persons who will commit certain kinds of sexual offenses in the future. Would it be justice to "punish" persons who fail the test? Obviously not. One can debate whether some preventive measures are appropriate, but there is no ground for punishment.

It is impossible to *punish dangerousness*, of course, within the meanings of those terms. To "punish" is "to subject to pain, loss, confinement, death, etc., as a penalty for some offense or transgression"; that is, punishment focuses on *a past* crime or wrongdoing. "Dangerous" means "likely to cause injury, pain, etc.," that is, a threat of *future* harm. One can "restrain" or "detain" or "incapacitate" to prevent a future crime, but one cannot logically "punish" dangerousness.

The criminal justice system generally purports to be in the business of doing justice, giving offenders what they deserve, no more, no less. It calls itself the criminal *justice* system, not a *preventive detention* system. It describes its sanctions as *punishment*, and on this ground justifies punitive conditions of confinement.

In cases like *Rummel*, however, the system quietly shifts from a justice rationale to a protection rationale without openly admitting the change. The system keeps the "punishment" label, but uses it as a cloak for its preventionist purpose. It does not punish Rummel for what he has done; his current offense is minor (and he already has been punished for his previous offenses). Further, even taken together, his string of minor thefts and frauds would not add up to deserve life imprisonment, a punishment typically reserved for murder.

In reality, Rummel is being punished for what he is thought likely to do in the future. The currently popular "three strikes" statutes assign punishment for the same reason. Indeed, the drafters of "three strikes" laws—of which the statute in *Rummel* was one of the first—typically are explicit about their protectionist goals and rationales. They keep the "justice" label because it makes the long-term incapacitation of offenders easier, simpler, and cheaper.

A true punishment system logically can set a fixed term of imprisonment, giving no further thought to the propriety of release until the set release date arrives. The length of the imprisonment is a function of the punishment deserved for the past offense, and such deserved punishment does not change while the term is being served. In contrast, a prevention system—which justifies incarceration by a person's dangerousness—logically must periodically reconsider whether the justification for detention continues to exist, and must release the detainee as soon as he is no longer dangerous. Further, a preventive detention system might conclude, upon evaluating a case like Rummel's, that the danger of additional minor theft offenses cannot justify the deprivation of liberty—life imprisonment—that prevention would require. But such an issue is never considered under the present system because the system does not openly admit that it is in fact a system of preventive detention.

The shift to a prevention rationale also affects the proper conditions of incarceration. Imprisonment justified as deserved punishment logically can have punitive conditions. The point of the imprisonment is to impose deserved suffering (but ought not dehumanize or demean). Preventive detention, in contrast, is an intrusion on liberty that an individual suffers for our benefit. We ought to, and commonly do, treat differently the person being punished and the person involuntarily confined because of a contagious disease or civilly committed because of mental disease. For the latter prevention cases, the conditions of confinement logically should be nonpunitive. The person is already suffering a sub-stantial loss of liberty for our benefit. We logically ought to minimize the extent of the intrusion as much as is consistent with public security. That may mean not only nonpunitive conditions, but also less intrusive forms of custody, such as house detention or electronic bracelet surveil-lance if such would provide adequate security.

Further, a prevention rather than punishment rationale logically suggests that if there is something that can be done to reduce or extin-guish the detainee's dangerousness, it ought to be done at the detainee's request and at our expense. This means, for example, that a detainee ought to have an absolute right to any treatment that can reduce the need for or the extent of the loss of liberty being imposed on him.

In other words, if the system is to shift from one of punishment to one of prevention—as it does in *Rummel*—it logically must change the way it operates: provide periodic reviews, nonpunitive conditions, least intrusive restraint, and a right to treatment. The current criminal justice system typically does not.

A more serious problem with prevention cases like *Rummel* be-comes apparent when we consider it under the fundamental principles of justice we see expressed in cases like *Phillips* and *Wood*.

We are highly suspicious that Phillips is on his way to a robbery. But he has not yet gone far enough toward an offense for us to comfortably impose criminal liability and punishment. We can't punish a person for what we think they might do, we said, even if the person's intention is evident. Yet Rummel has done *nothing* toward the future offenses for which we now punish him. Indeed, he has not even thought of the of-fenses that are used as the justification for his incarceration.

One might try to argue that Rummel is different from Phillips be-cause the former, Rummel, has prior offenses and therefore is an im-portantly different case. But the minimum requirements for attempt li-ability, as expressed in *Phillips*, do not differ according to whether the person has a prior criminal record. (In fact, Phillips did have a prior record.) Phillips would have escaped attempt liability even if he had as many prior robbery convictions as Rummel had prior thefts. Similarly, Wood would have been convicted of only attempted murder, not mur-der, no matter what his prior record.

But perhaps one can argue that Rummel can be treated differently than Phillips because Rummel in fact committed an offense on this oc-casion; Phillips committed no robbery. Once one has done enough to qualify for *some* criminal liability, it might be argued, the law is then free to do as it chooses in the amount of punishment it imposes. Innocent citizens need not fear unfair criminal liability; but for lawbreakers, all bets are off.

But that harsh theory of criminal justice is inconsistent with what we saw in the *Wood* case. There, the law with strong public support took great pains to determine the proper grade that Wood's offense deserved. The only issue in *Wood* is whether he should be liable for attempted murder or murder. The facts in *Wood* present the most egregious case possible—of a person who has done everything he can do to be a murderer—yet the community and the law refuse to treat him as a murderer because his conduct does not meet the strict requirements of causation. He can be held liable only for the lower grade offense of attempt. Yet Rummel is being punished as if he had actually caused the harms of all those future offenses, offenses of which he has not yet even thought.

The law's inconsistency in this regard also is apparent in other ways. For example, the law explicitly limits the use of a defendant's prior criminal record at trial, for fear that it may prejudice the jury. We say that the defendant's liability ought to be determined solely according to the prosecution's proof of what he did on this occasion. But the prejudicial fact of prior record somehow becomes a respectable principle when the amount of punishment is being set. We say the prosecution cannot introduce a prior offense to suggest the defendant was more likely to have committed the present offense. But isn't this just what "three strikes" laws do, and worse: they use prior offenses to suggest the defendant is likely to commit a future offense, and justify life imprisonment on these predicted future offenses.

Prior record, as a predictor of future criminality, is one of the primary determinants of sentence in a preventionist system. If prevention is a legitimate ground for distributing liability and punishment, why not openly declare prior record relevant in assessing liability? Why not include prior record as an element of offenses and as a determinant of offense grade? Under the preventionist rationale, logically, in close cases, we should convict a Phillips of attempt if he has a prior record, and convict a Wood of murder if he has a prior criminal record. Yet no jurisdiction does this. Jurisdictions do not do so because no one is seriously prepared to openly offer prevention as a substitute for justice. Instead, prevention is cloaked as desert, and hides in the shadows of a system that purports to do justice.

The Appeal

Rummel appeals his case to the U.S. Court of Appeals for the Fifth Circuit, located in New Orleans. Helping to craft his own motions and arguments from the prison library, he contends that the state's one-hundred-year-old habitual offender law violates the Eighth Amendment prohibition against cruel and unusual punishment.

On March 6, 1978, a three-judge panel of the Fifth Circuit reverses his sentence as cruel and unusual. However, on December 20, 1978, the Fifth Circuit sitting as a whole for a rehearing— lawyers call it sitting *en banc*—reinstates the sentence by an eight to five vote and upholds the constitutionality of the Texas habitual offender statute. Rummel appeals to the U.S. Supreme Court, pushing his claim that the disproportionate length of his sentence compared to the seriousness of his crimes violates the Eight Amendment prohibition against cruel and unusual punishment. He also claims his attorney was incompetent. The high court agrees to hear his case, to be argued *pro bono* by Scott J. Atlas, a partner in the prominent Houston law firm of former Texas governor John B. Connally. "No jurisdiction in the United States or the free world punishes habitual offenders as harshly as Texas," Atlas writes in his brief.

The Cost of Undercutting the Criminal Law's Moral Credibility

Rummel's punishment is unfair, it was suggested earlier, because it imposes punishment far out of proportion to what he deserves for his offense. And it is unfair because, as a form of preventive detention, it fails to limit the detention to a period of continuing dangerousness, it fails to weigh the extent of the danger threatened against the loss of liberty required to prevent it, and it fails to limit the confinement to non-punitive conditions.

But perhaps more important than seeing the injustice to Rummel is to see how the injustice to Rummel is damaging to us. As noted in the discussion of the *Wood* case, the moral credibility of the criminal law is central to its ability to stigmatize and thereby deter conduct. Even more important, it is the source of the criminal law's power to influence the norms that govern people's conduct. Recent social science research has only confirmed what many have long sensed: societal norms internalized by an individual and by the individual's circle of family and friends influence the person's conduct more than the threat of official sanction.

The fact is, the perceived chances of getting caught and convicted for an offense are so low that few people obey the law out of fear of official punishment. An astounding number of serious offenses are never reported to the police—for example, 21 percent of rapes and 40 percent of burglaries—out of embarrassment, out of fear of reprisal, or in the belief that the authorities are unable or unwilling to act. For the offenses reported, clearance rates (the rates at which the police identify and arrest suspects) have been dropping steadily for decades. The nationwide clearance rate for homicide, which was 93 percent in 1955, has steadily declined to 67 percent. The rate for rape has declined from 79 to 52 percent and that for burglary from 32 to 14 percent. Further, being arrested is a far cry from being punished. The overall conviction rate among those arrested for the most serious offenses is 30 percent. Then, fewer than half of those convicted of a felony are sentenced to state prison. Finally, the median time served by those actually sentenced to a state prison ranges from 5.5 years for murder to 2.2 years for kidnapping to 1.4 years for arson.

The cumulative effect of the many escape hatches from punishment leaves a deterrent threat that looks like this: homicide offers less than a 45 percent chance of being caught, convicted, and imprisoned, rape a 12 percent chance, robbery a 4 percent chance. Assault, burglary, larceny, and motor vehicle theft are each a hundred-to-one shot. A potential offender may not be cowed by these threats.

The threat of punishment may play some role with some people, but the force of norms in influencing conduct plays a substantial role with nearly all people. The real power to enforce compliance with society's rules of prescribed conduct lies not in the threat of official criminal sanction, but in the influence of family and peers in judging each of us and our own internalized norms by which we judge ourselves.

The law is not irrelevant to these social and personal forces. Criminal law, in particular, plays a central role in creating and maintaining the social consensus necessary for sustaining moral norms. In fact, in a society as diverse as ours, the criminal law may be the only society-wide mechanism that transcends cultural and ethnic differences. Thus, the criminal law's most important real-world effect is arguably its ability to assist in the building, shaping, and maintaining of these norms. It contributes to and harnesses the compliance-producing power of interpersonal relationships and personal morality.

In addition, if the criminal law earns a reputation as a reliable statement of what the community, given sufficient information and time to reflect, perceives as condemnable, people are more likely to defer to its commands as morally authoritative in those borderline cases where the propriety of certain conduct is unsettled or ambiguous in the mind of the actor. The importance of this role should not be underestimated; in a society with the complex interdependencies characteristic of ours, an apparently harmless action can have destructive consequences. When the action is criminalized by the legal system, one wants the citizen to "respect the law" even though he or she does not immediately intuit why that action is banned. Such deference is facilitated if people believe the law is an accurate guide to what is truly immoral behavior.

Here, then, are at least two ways the criminal law can influence conduct: by discouraging conduct that it identifies as criminal and thus immoral and, less directly but more powerfully, by helping to shape community norms that condemn some conduct and not others. The criminal law's effectiveness in both these respects is to a great extent dependent on the degree of moral credibility it has achieved. With strong moral credibility, criminalization persuasively signals immoral conduct. With weak credibility, it can have little effect.

Thus, the criminal law's moral credibility is essential in the long run to effective crime control. Credibility is enhanced if the distribution of criminal liability is perceived as "doing justice," that is, if liability and punishment are assigned in ways that the community perceives as consistent with its principles of justice. Conversely, the system's moral credibility, and therefore its crime control effectiveness, is undermined by a distribution of liability that deviates from community perceptions of just desert. What effect can one expect from newspaper headlines like those generated by the *Rummel* case: "Billy Sol [Estes] Bilks Companies Out of Millions; Rummel's Fraud Totals $229.11. Estes Serving 10 Years—Rummel Gets Life."

The Final Outcome

Rummel, who has grown pale and thinner in prison, makes something of his time. In just over seven years he earns 67 hours of college credit, spends 350 hours teaching other inmates, and takes additional training in construction maintenance. His prison time passes unremarkably. Rummel is a "middle of the road type inmate," prison warden D. A. Christian says. "He don't cause any problems. He's not a ringleader or a big follower. In a prison, you know your troublemakers, your snitches. He's not any of these. He's not that violent. As a con man, he ranks low on the totem pole."

"I'm not saying I should not be punished, but why give me a life sentence?" Rummel asks an interviewer as he awaits his appeal. "If I had murdered 75 people or raped five women, something of that nature, I could see where I could become a potential threat to society. But who do I threaten? I don't threaten anybody. I don't use narcotics. I don't use alcohol to any extent."

In 1980, as the Supreme Court considers his appeal, Rummel's case begins attracting national attention from newspapers and television stations. The television news magazine *60 Minutes* airs a segment on his case in the winter of 1980. The local prosecutor's office begins to bristle under the spotlight, angered that the media portray Rummel as a mere petty thief and ignore his long history of offenses. Finally, on March 19, the Supreme Court issues its ruling and rejects Rummel's claim that his life sentence is unconstitutionally cruel and unusual because it is disproportionate to the seriousness of his offense.

But Rummel's case and the attention it generates do not go away. Less than two months after the Supreme Court upholds Rummel's sentence, U.S. District Judge D. W. Suttle orders the state to release Rummel or give him a new trial. Suttle rules that Rummel's trial attorney, William B. Chenault III, provided ineffective counsel in 1973 when Rummel received the life sentence. Noting that Chenault attempted virtually no investigation of the case before it went to trial, Judge Suttle orders Rummel released and sent back to criminal court for a new trial. The district attorney, still weary from the nationwide publicity aimed at Rummel's case, offers Rummel a deal: if Rummel pleads guilty to felony theft over fifty dollars, the state will recommend an eight-year prison sentence. That would allow Rummel, who has already served almost eight years, to go free immediately.

Even if he were retried, the theft charge he was convicted of in 1973 has been reduced by the Texas legislature to a misdemeanor, meaning the habitual offender statute no longer would require a life term and he could not be sentenced to more time than he already has served. On November 15, surrounded in court by national news media, Rummel pleads guilty to the theft offense and receives a seven-year sentence backdated to 1973. He is released from custody five hours later. "I am ready to go out and work. And I intend to stay free for the rest of my life." As of this writing, he apparently has.

Segregating Preventive Detention from Criminal Justice

The problems raised by cases like *Rummel* are not easily solved. Rummel's sentence seems dramatically more than he deserves, wildly disproportionate to the seriousness of his offense. On the other hand, a society must be able to protect itself. The criminal justice system, which deals with harmdoers, is an obvious and convenient mechanism to use to protect us from harm. But using criminal justice for prevention means that it sometimes does not do justice. And not doing justice undercuts the system's moral credibility and, thereby, its long-term crime-control effectiveness.

What is needed, perhaps, are two mechanisms: one to punish offenders for past crimes with a criminal sentence for a fixed term according to the amount deserved for the past offense, no more, no less; and another mechanism, apart from the criminal justice system, to civilly commit offenders who are shown to remain dangerous at the conclusion of their criminal sentence. That could protect the moral credibility of the criminal justice system from the taint of undeserved punishment, while insuring preventive detention. Even more important, such a preventive detention system, which openly admits its purpose and rationale, logically would give detainees the periodic review, minimum restraint, right to treatment, and nonpunitive conditions that our current scheme of criminal commitment denies.

Such a two-system scheme also would be a more honest approach, admitting openly when incarceration is preventive detention rather than deserved punishment. Without the obfuscation of our current mixed punishment-prevention system, preventive detention would have to justify itself. The public might conclude that the threat that a Rummel presents cannot justify the imposed detention.

Many states have implemented such a distinct civil detention system on a small scale, for application against sexual predators who remain dangerous at the conclusion of their prison terms.* Ironically, this effort has met a host of challenges by the ACLU and similar groups. These much-criticized "sexual predator" laws provide for the civil commitment of sexual offenders if, at the conclusion of their criminal sentence, they remain likely to repeat their sexual offenses.

Such a two-system approach permits minimum use of dangerousness considerations in criminal sentencing decisions. It relies instead on the explicit preventive-detention civil commitment process to provide any additional protection needed beyond that inherent in the criminal term. (In this respect, legislators might improve some of these statutes by making it clearer that the initial criminal sentence must be based solely on the defendant's desert, without reliance on predictions of his future dangerousness.)

If restricting civil liberties is the concern, the civil commitment approach seems preferable to that of the many states that sentence such sex offenders to life imprisonment as a preventive measure. Oddly enough, the latter scheme—life imprisonment for sexual offenders—is the safer course for states, given the current constitutional restrictions on civil commitment, which require periodic review of both continuing mental illness and dangerousness. The periodic review requirement is not applied to criminal commitment, presumably because criminal commitment is justified as punishment for a past offense.

But this simply illustrates the deceptiveness of our present system. By considering dangerousness in setting *criminal* terms, the state avoids the periodic review requirement that appropriately ought to attach whenever dangerousness is the justification for commitment. But because the commitment is labeled "criminal," and thus apparently based on blameworthiness for a *past* offense, no periodic review is thought to be required. Logic would seem to suggest that if the criminal law is not purged of its reliance on dangerousness in setting incarceration terms, the standard civil commitment requirements, including periodic re-

*At the time the Kansas statute was challenged in 1996 (and upheld as constitutional by the U.S. Supreme Court), six states had such statutes—Arizona, California, Kansas, Minnesota, Washington, and Wisconsin. Thirty-eight states filed legal briefs in support of the law, indicating an interest in such legislation.

view, ought to be applied to that additional portion of the term imposed on dangerousness grounds.

Even from an offender's point of view, opposing such civil commitment schemes seems a bit mad. If the state has the ability to provide a long prison term for the offense, such as life imprisonment, why oppose a provision that can allow the state to give a shorter term, so that only those offenders shown to be dangerous are detained longer, and then only as long as they remain dangerous? This is especially true given that the terms and conditions of such civil commitment may be better than those for a criminal life term: periodic reviews of the justification for detention, a logical claim for least restricting confinement, nonpunitive conditions, and a right to treatment (all conditions that are difficult to claim in the context of criminal commitment, where the imprisonment is supposedly deserved as punishment for a past offense).

We can rebuild the moral credibility of the criminal law by putting it back into the business of doing justice, undistorted by other functions. If protection is needed, let it be done: first, only when present dangerousness is shown; second, only in a way that minimizes the loss of individual liberties; and third, in a form that does not confuse such preventive detention with deserved punishment and, therefore, does not taint the criminal justice system's claim to be doing justice.

2

Knowing the Law's Commands

ONCE CRIMINAL LAW drafters settle on a set of rules, they must make those rules known to the people to be bound by them. That communication and education are essential if the law hopes to influence people's conduct. They also are essential if the law is to treat people fairly, for there is no fairness in punishing violation of a rule the violator could not reasonably have been expected to know. Finally, the criminal law must articulate its rules to insure that all persons, whatever their race, religion, gender, social or economic status, or other characteristic, are held to the same rules. Unwritten or vague rules invite discretion and create the potential for abuse. These, then, are the reasons for the law's commitment to what it calls the "legality principle," which requires a previously existing rule written with clarity and precision before a violation can be punished.

As the following four cases illustrate, articulating the criminal law's commands—adhering to the legality principle—is a more demanding challenge than one might expect. And the criminal law has not risen to meet it.

THE CONGENIAL CADAVER

It is 1947 near Mountain Home, Arkansas, a rural town ten miles from the Missouri border. Canna Baker, born on January 11, 1883, and her husband, Jim, seven years her senior, live on a small piece of property with a main house, some cabins and sheds, a barn, and other outbuildings. They make their living by farming and raising milk cows. Since their marriage in 1901, they also have earned income from the state by lodging, feeding, and caring for welfare paupers. They get one dollar per day for each.

Canna, or "Cannie," as she is called, is well known in the county. The dominant force in her marriage, she can hitch up and drive a team of horses as well as any man. On Saturday afternoons she does just that, running her team and wagon into town and around the Mountain Home County Courthouse Square. She wears a man's hat, bright red lipstick and rouge, and a cotton housedress with maybe a sweater or a coat. Her cotton hose is rolled below her knees. Cannie talks to everybody—long and loud.

Cannie Baker's relationship with the county welfare authorities has not been smooth. Baxter County Department of Public Welfare director Mamie Green has been in her position since 1936 and regularly objects to sending people to live with Cannie. She has heard the boarders may not be "getting the care they should have." Busy with her duties in the office, Green rarely gets out to visit the welfare wards under her care. Instead she must send visitors to check on them, usually about once every three or four months, sometimes less.

Margaret Bryant, the visitor who usually goes to the Baker home, regularly returns with grim reports, but Green has no power to move people out unless the boarders themselves request it. The few who have asked to be moved have quietly whispered their request when alone with the welfare worker. In all the years that she has been working in the welfare office, only three people have moved out. Two were boarders; the third was Cannie Baker's mother, an old-age pensioner who one day when alone with Green asked for help in getting away from her daughter.

The state pays its welfare recipients once a month, in advance, by sending a check made out to the recipient on the first of the month. When the check arrives each month, Cannie takes it to the boarder, who signs it in Cannie's presence. Cannie then endorses the check and cashes it, keeping the full amount, thirty dollars, for the coming month's upkeep. The check pays for food, rent, and a few basic necessities.

On April 2, 1947, Cannie Baker reports the death of Annie Reynolds, a welfare boarder at her house. The check for Annie's April board comes the morning of the second, but Cannie does not get it signed before Annie dies. Cannie takes the check to a local shopkeeper, Fred Burrow, who regularly cashes the checks for her. Burrow and Cannie write to the state welfare department in Little Rock, informing the state of the woman's death on April 2, and asking whether Cannie can cash the check and use the money to pay Reynolds's funeral expenses. The state refers the issue to the Baxter County welfare department and the check is held for weeks while the case is sorted out. It is ultimately decided that the state will pay the funeral expenses directly. The check is never cashed.

Ed White has been a pauper on the Baxter County welfare rolls for as long as most residents and social workers can remember. For several years he lived in nearby Cotter, Arkansas. He is well known in Cotter, largely because of his smell—a strong, rancid odor that hangs about him. Most think the smell comes from his dirty clothes; others think it is caused by his ill health and kidney trouble. In 1947 White is in his late seventies and in poor health. He decides to travel from Cotter to Mountain Home in Baxter County to find a new place to live. He stops first at the courthouse where the welfare office is located. He sleeps and putters around the courthouse as welfare workers try to figure out where to send him.

White hears from people around the courthouse that Cannie Baker takes in boarders and cares for them in exchange for their welfare checks, and asks to be sent to live at the Bakers'. Welfare workers, wary of sending boarders to the Bakers, stall. After several days and repeated requests by White, the welfare director finally agrees. A sheriff's deputy drives White out to the Baker home that afternoon. After a short conversation, Cannie agrees to take White on as a boarder for the usual one dollar a day, the thirty dollars a month being White's entire old-age assistance check.

White arrives after the first of the month, which is when the state writes its welfare checks, so Cannie does not get paid immediately for

Cannie Baker behind the plow on her farm. (*Arkansas Gazette*)

Cannie and Jim Baker in their cornfield. (*Arkansas Gazette*)

the first few weeks of the old man's lodging. Since subsequent checks pay in advance for each following month, in Cannie's mind, the state remains several weeks behind in what it owes her.

White is already in poor physical condition when he arrives at the Bakers'. His clothes are dirty and are torn so badly that he appears almost naked. His feet are black and gangrenous and he has no feeling left in them. His odor is unbearably strong and his breath so foul that Cannie refuses to get close enough to shave him. She buys him a new suit for three dollars and sixty-five cans of Saymon's Salve to treat the sores on his legs, neck, and back, which are open, infected, and oozing. A local doctor prescribes two dollars' worth of pills to fight the infections that have discolored his skin and bloated his body.

For several months White lives in one of the small cabins at the back of the Baker property, a short walk from the main house. Each day, Cannie fixes White breakfast, lunch, and dinner, although White usually eats little, sometimes just Jell-O, milk, and a bite or two of cake. The neighbors come to know him as a sickly old man who hangs around his cabin most of the day and hardly ever says a word to anyone. Because of his age, they give him the nickname "Daddy."

In late November 1948 White suffers a stroke. His sores continue to seep, infected and not responding to the medication and salves. His genitals have long since rotted and fallen off, and Cannie fashions a makeshift diaper for him.

On November 27 White dies in his cabin. Cannie discovers his body, but does not report it to the authorities or undertaker. She knows the state will not send White another welfare check until December 1. Cannie believes the state still owes her for the first several weeks of White's stay at her house. And she recalls the difficulties in trying to cash Annie Reynolds's check after Annie died. She decides she will not report White's death until after she gets his check on the first of the month, four days away.

She pulls his hat low, almost over his eyes, and sits him up in bed. During the next four days she keeps him pretty well hidden by the sheets on his bed and the hat over his face. White's body and face are swollen and discolored in spots. His legs are black, as they have been for months. His odor, getting even worse in death, naturally keeps people from coming too close, and his nontalkative demeanor surprises no one. Occasionally she moves White, so that no one gets suspicious. Sometimes she props him up in a chair in his room or on the steps of the porch to his cabin.

On Tuesday, November 30, Cannie goes into town, buys another can of salve and some new clothes, making sure to tell the shopkeeper, Henry Tipton, that she is buying them for White.

On Wednesday, December 1, Johnnie McCarty, the husband of Cannie's granddaughter, walks over to Cannie's at about eight or nine in the morning to help strain the milk taken from the cows that day. He passes by the house where White lives. The old man is sitting in a chair by the front door, but he does not move a muscle or say a word. That does not strike McCarty as unusual. White almost never says anything and hardly ever moves. Although he later wonders whether the old man was really alive, McCarty thinks nothing of it as he passes by. "I never saw a dead man sitting up," he thinks later.

The same day, Irene Schreiner, a neighbor, walks by White's cabin and sees him sitting on the steps to the porch. "How are you, Mr. White?" Schreiner asks. White does not answer and does not move, but Schreiner is not really paying attention to him and thinks nothing of it. Later Cecil Kyter, another neighbor who lives about a hundred yards from the Bakers' home, returns from work in the afternoon and goes to White's cabin between six and seven in the evening to gather some hay that he stores in another room of the cabin. While he is there, he looks in the door to White's room and sees the old man sitting on the bed. Kyter says a few words but does not get very close because of the "odor nobody couldn't hardly stand." Kyter says something about the weather and believes White responds in his usual feeble voice.

The morning mail of December 2 brings White's monthly welfare check, which Cannie signs for White, endorses, then cashes.

On the afternoon of December 2, Cannie, Johnnie McCarty, and his wife, Mary Lee (Cannie's granddaughter) travel to Cotter to see Frank Baker about buying and slaughtering a hog. Afterwards, the group goes to a movie, returning home at 10:00 P.M. Cannie asks her husband if he has checked on Ed White. He tells her he has not. Cannie says, "I'll go," lights a lantern, and walks out to White's cabin. As she approaches the cabin, she hollers "Daddy" but gets no response from inside. White is lying on the bed. Cannie runs back to the house and yells, "Jim, Daddy White's dead." Shortly after 10:00 P.M., Cannie sends Johnnie and Mary Lee McCarty to get Denver Roller, the Mountain Home undertaker.

Later in the evening Dr. S. W. Chambers, a practicing physician in Mountain Home and the county health officer, comes to the funeral home to examine White's body, which has been brought over from the cabin. The body is discolored, greatly swelled, and decomposed, but the limbs move easily, evidence that rigor mortis has already left the body. Because of the absence of rigor mortis and the advanced decomposition, Chambers believes White has been dead for at least five or six days. Dr. Gerald Pearce, another Mountain Home physician, examines the body the next day, December 3. He too concludes White has been dead for a number of days.

Cannie can be held liable for the welfare fraud, but authorities are more upset about her treatment of Ed White's dead body. Would you impose criminal liability on Cannie Baker for her handling of White's body? If so, what amount of punishment would you impose?

no liability	☐	1 year	☐
liability but no punishment	☐	3 years	☐
		7 years	☐
1 day	☐	15 years	☐
2 weeks	☐	30 years	☐
2 months	☐	life imprisonment	☐
6 months	☐	death	☐

People's Intuitions of Justice

Here is how the people in the survey sentenced Canna Baker:

no liability	5%	1 year	16%
liability but		3 years	4%
no punishment	17%	7 years	2%
1 day	5%	15 years	—
2 weeks	17%	30 years	—
2 months	19%	life imprisonment	—
6 months	15%	death	—

Mean = 6.8 weeks.

Most people seem to think Cannie Baker deserves some punishment, although the offense is not seen as a serious one. 73 percent would impose a sentence of two weeks or more. The average sentence is about a month and a half.

The Legality Principle and Its Rationales

No doubt Cannie knew her treatment of the body was wrong and probably assumed it was criminal. But in fact, Arkansas does not have on its books a statutory offense prohibiting the mistreatment of bodies. It does recognize and apply the "common law," as it is called—the uncodified judge-made law of seventeenth- and eighteenth-century England, which recognized it as a crime to "treat a dead human body indecently." Like many common law offenses, this one was vague in its terms; it did not define what did or did not constitute "indecent" treatment, but left the definition to the discretion of the judge in the individual case.

Should Cannie Baker get off because there is in fact no applicable statutory offense on the books in Arkansas, even if she thought her conduct was criminal? Most states do not allow prosecution for such uncodified common law offenses. This restriction on the government's ability to prosecute stems from what lawyers call the "legality principle," noted at the beginning of this chapter. That principle operates through a variety of legal doctrines to require a prior, written offense definition that specifically describes the prohibited conduct. The legality principle is not itself a legal rule but rather is the overarching principle used to describe a collection of related rules: the constitutional prohibition against ex post facto laws, the constitutional invalidation of vague offenses, the statutory abolition of common law offenses, and the statutory bar to judicial creation of offenses.

Imagine a legislature retroactively making certain conduct a crime, then punishing people for such conduct even though it was not a crime when they performed it. The Constitution's prohibition against ex post facto laws that prevents this obvious injustice.

Imagine driving down a main street with four friends, then hanging out at a social club. You may have just committed the now-invalidated Jacksonville, Florida, offenses of "prowling by auto" and vagrancy ("neglecting all lawful business and habitually spending time by frequenting . . . places where alcoholic beverages are sold"). The Constitution prohibits such vague offenses.

Or imagine the judge-created common law offenses of "engaging in conduct injurious to public morals," or being a "public nuisance" or "common scold." What exactly do these offenses prohibit? One may never know until after being charged with a violation and brought before a judge, who then must decide. Most jurisdictions now expressly abolish all common law offenses.

Does the offense of "delivering drugs to a minor" include a mother who, while pregnant, drinks alcohol or takes a controlled substance? Should the answer depend on what a judge decides after the fact? Is it murder—the intentional killing of a "human being"—if a person kicks a pregnant woman in the abdomen, causing the fetus to be stillborn? Most states now prohibit the expansion of an offense—such as delivering drugs to a minor or murder—to cover new situations not apparent from the language of the offense statute or contemplated by its drafters.

The reasons for having a legality principle, requiring a prior, written prohibition of sufficient clarity and precision, are quite strong. Should they provide a defense to Cannie Baker?

First, such requirements insure the possibility of fair notice of what the criminal law commands of us. Without such notice the law can hardly hope to deter prohibited conduct. And without such notice it cannot fairly impose punishment for a violation. In Cannie Baker's case, however, she probably thought her conduct was a crime, so she had actual notice, at least she believed she did. Thus, the fair notice rationale may have force in some cases but seems inapplicable here.

A second and independent rationale for the legality principle is to help minimize discretion in the application of criminal law, for with discretion comes the potential for abuse. Vague and uncodified offenses, like the common law rule in *Baker* making it an offense to "treat a body indecently," create discretion in the application of the offense by police, prosecutors, judges, and juries. The Jacksonville "prowling by auto" and "vagrancy" offenses, for example, were used by Florida officials in the late 1960s to harass interracial couples.

Discretion also reduces the predictability of law, undercutting law's value in bringing order and stability. In the *Baker* case, there is little reason to think that discretion is being abused, but the system cannot have application of the legality principle depend on such ad hoc speculation. A person abusing his or her discretion will never admit it, often will hide it, and sometimes will not realize it. Thus, the demands of legality must be applied in all cases.

One final rationale for the legality requirement of a written code is that it preserves the allocation of criminalization authority to the legislature, the most democratic branch. Vague and ambiguous statutes are de facto delegations of the criminalization authority to the judges, who must determine the contours of the offense ex post.

For all these reasons, most jurisdictions prohibit prosecution for offenses that are not defined beforehand by statute with adequate clarity and precision to give the reasonable person notice of the precise conduct that is prohibited. In most American jurisdictions, then, Cannie Baker would escape liability because, at the time of the conduct charged as the offense, there is no applicable statute in the state's criminal code that criminalizes her handling of White's body, and the old uncodified, judge-made, common law offense is an inadequate basis for criminal liability.

The Aftermath

Unlike most states, Arkansas never enacted the typical statute prohibiting the use of common law offenses. On April 18, 1949, Baxter County prosecutor Carmack Sullivan files an information and warrant charging Cannie with the offense of "treating a body indecently," a common law misdemeanor. Baker's lawyer responds by arguing that the facts in the information do not constitute a crime under Arkansas law. The court holds that the offense was recognized under English common law and, therefore, such law remains effective in Arkansas. Baker pleads not guilty to the charge.

On May 4, 1949, a twelve-man jury finds Cannie Baker guilty of the crime and sets her punishment at a $100 fine plus court costs, a total of about $250. She can pay the fine and costs or serve a day in jail for every seventy-five cents—almost a year in jail.

Baker appeals to the Arkansas Supreme Court, which delivers its opinion on October 24, 1949. The court cites English common law cases that prohibit a person charged with the care of another to neglect to bury that person's body. The court also cites an 1842 English case, *Queen v. Francis Scott*, in which a jailer refuses to release the body of a dead prisoner until the prisoner's debt for food and lodging in the jail is paid. The court concludes that Baker's conduct does constitute a crime under the common law. The judgment of conviction is affirmed.

Today

Today Arkansas still does not bar the use of common law offenses, but it has enacted a specific offense governing the mistreatment of dead bodies. Arkansas Statutes § 5-60-101, Abuse of a Corpse, provides that

> (a) A person commits abuse of a corpse if, except as authorized by law, he knowingly:
>> (1) Disinters, removes, dissects, or mutilates a corpse; or
>> (2) Physically mistreats a corpse in a manner offensive to a person of reasonable sensibilities.
> (b) Abuse of a corpse is a Class D felony.

Even under this statute, one might complain that there remains some imprecision. What conduct, exactly, would be included under the phrase "physically mistreats"? Would Cannie's posing of White's body be "physically mistreating" it? The gravamen of her offense seems more to be the disrespect her conduct shows for the body, rather than actual injury to it. But certainly the statute provides greater notice that mistreatment of a body may be a crime than did the previous vague, unwritten common law offense. At the very least, this offense is codified

Canna Baker's farm is now a modern subdivision, in which a road bears her nickname, "Cannie." (Mary Ann Messick)

and published—written down for anyone to see—rather than hidden in a hundred-year-old English case decision.

The law is not impractical. No code can be perfectly clear as to every point of possible application. But through the rules of the legality principle, the law has struck a workable and important balance between the demands of practicality and the need to give fair notice and to limit discretion. Under that balance, reflected in the law of most states, Cannie would not be held liable without some prior, written offense.

The Baker house still stands today, although the rest of the farm is now a subdivision of homes. Cannie, who died in 1950, and her husband, Jim, who died some time later, are buried at the entrance of a small cemetery near the subdivision's main road—Cannie Baker Road.

WHEN CAN AN OFFICER CARRY A GUN?

Julio Marrero of Bronx, New York, is a disabled Vietnam vet who previously worked as an undercover agent in a drug enforcement operation for Puerto Rico's taxation department. Now, in 1997, he works as a prison guard at the federal prison in Danbury, Connecticut, and is the father of six: Sonya, eleven; Hector Louis, eight; Ricardo, six; Carina, four; and Joe and Vanessa, three. (Two other children, Endira and Carlos, will be born later.)

During his time as a guard at Danbury, he has received death threats, as many guards have, including one from a recently released inmate. He regularly carries a pistol for protection, having received weapons training when he was in the military police. Marrero keeps storage space for several weapons at the Military Police Armory in Manhattan, weapons he uses for target practice at the MP firing range.

Marrero purchased his pistol from a New York City gun dealer, Eugene DiMayo, who sold it to Marrero knowing Marrero did not have a

Julio Marrero, circa 1984. (Family photo)

special New York gun permit, but believing and advising Marrero that, as a federal prison guard, Marrero did not need one. DiMayo knows several federal prison guards who similarly have bought weapons without a special New York gun permit. DiMayo explains to Marrero that "federal corrections officers" are considered "peace officers" under the New York firearms statute and "licenses are not required if proper identification is presented."

On December 19, 1977, while off duty, Marrero visits a social club at 207 Madison Street in the old section of New York City. As he enters the club, he is searched by police officer G. Dugan of the Seventh Precinct, who finds a loaded .38-caliber pistol. Marrero explains that he does not have a permit but does not need one because he is a federal corrections officer. He shows his identification badge. The police call the Danbury prison and confirm that he is a guard there. Marrero nonetheless is arrested and charges are filed. Ten days later Marrero is indicted for criminal possession of a weapon. New York law does allow "peace officers" to carry weapons, but prosecutors believe that, while a state correctional officer is a "peace officer," as defined by the New York statute, a federal correctional officer is not.

Would you convict Marrero? If so, what amount of punishment would you impose?

no liability	☐	1 year	☐
liability but		3 years	☐
no punishment	☐	7 years	☐
1 day	☐	15 years	☐
2 weeks	☐	30 years	☐
2 months	☐	life imprisonment	☐
6 months	☐	death	☐

People's Intuitions of Justice

If Marrero is right about his exemption from the offense because he is a peace officer, he will not be liable. If he is wrong, if the court reads the offense definition differently than he does, he is likely to be convicted because of the old legal maxim that "ignorance or mistake of law is no excuse." The maxim is sustained by the fear that any other rule would allow people to simply ignore the law. If ignorance were a defense, people would have an incentive to keep themselves ignorant of the law. If the law is to have meaning, it is argued, every citizen must have the duty to find out the law. They fail to do so at their own peril.

On the other hand, Marrero's mistake as to the law seems like an honest mistake, one that you or I could have made in the same situation. Does he deserve to be branded and punished as a criminal?

Here is how the people in the survey sentenced Marrero:

no liability	23%	1 year	1%
liability but		3 years	—
no punishment	53%	7 years	—
1 day	4%	15 years	—
2 weeks	11%	30 years	—
2 months	4%	life imprisonment	—
6 months	3%	death	—

Mean = about half a day.

Seventy-six percent would impose no punishment. Only 8 percent would impose punishment of more than two weeks, for what the criminal code treats as a serious offense, a felony. The average sentence is less than a day. There seems to be strong feeling that Marrero has little blameworthiness.

The Law

Assume you are Marrero. You want to carry a gun for protection, but you want to be careful and check out the law first. Luckily you don't have to go figure out what statutes govern whether you can carry a gun or not, because you have a smart friend in law school who gives you a copy of the relevant statutes. Below is what he gives you. Can you carry a gun or not?

McKINNEY'S CONSOLIDATED LAWS OF NEW YORK— PENAL LAW (1970)

§ 265.01—Criminal Possession of a Weapon in the Fourth Degree

A person is guilty of criminal possession of a weapon in the fourth degree when:

(1) He possesses any firearm, electronic dart gun, gravity knife, switchblade knife, cane sword, billy, blackjack, bludgeon, metal knuckles, chuka stick, sand bag, sandclub, or slingshot, or

(2) He possesses any dagger, dangerous knife, dirk, razor, stiletto, imitation pistol, or any other dangerous or deadly instrument or weapon with intent to use the same unlawfully against another; or

(3) He knowingly has in his possession a rifle, shotgun or firearm in or upon a building or grounds, used for educational purposes, of any school, college or university, except the forestry lands, wherever located, owned and maintained by the State University of New York college of environmental science and forestry, without the written authorization of such educational institution; or

(4) He possesses a rifle or shotgun and has been convicted of a felony or serious offense; or

(5) He possesses any dangerous or deadly weapon and is not a citizen of the United States; or

(6) He is a person who has been certified not suitable to possess a rifle or shotgun, as defined in subsection sixteen of section 265.00, and refuses to yield possession of such rifle or shotgun upon the demand of a police officer. Whenever a person is certified not suitable to possess a rifle or shotgun, a member of the police department to which such certification is made, or of the state police, shall forthwith seize any rifle or shotgun possessed by such person. A rifle or shotgun seized as herein provided shall not be destroyed, but shall be delivered to the headquarters of such police department, or state police, and there retained until the aforesaid certificate has been rescinded by the director or physician in charge, or other disposition of such rifle or shotgun has been ordered or authorized by a court of competent jurisdiction.

§ 265.02—*Criminal Possession of a Weapon in the Third Degree*

A person is guilty of criminal possession of a weapon in the third degree when:

(1) He commits the crime of criminal possession of a weapon in the fourth degree as defined in subdivision one, two, three or five of section 265.01, and has been previously convicted of any crime; or

(2) He possesses any explosive or incendiary bomb, bombshell, firearm silencer, machine-gun or any other firearm or weapon simulating a machine-gun and which is adaptable for such use; or

(3) He knowingly has in his possession a machine-gun or firearm which has been defaced for the purpose of concealment or prevention of the detection of a crime or misrepresenting the identity of such machine-gun or firearm; or

(4) He possesses any loaded firearm. Such possession shall not, except as provided in subdivision one, constitute a violation of this section if such possession takes place in such person's home or place of business.

(5) (i) He possesses twenty or more firearms; or (ii) he possesses a firearm and has been previously convicted of a felony or a class A misdemeanor defined in this chapter within the five years immediately preceding the commission of the offense and such possession did not take place in the person's home or place of business.

Criminal possession of a weapon in the third degree is a class D felony.

§ 265.20—*Exemptions*

(A) Sections 265.01, 265.02, 265.03, 265.04, 265.05, 265.10, 265.15 and 270.05 shall not apply to:

    (1) Possession of any of the weapons, instruments, appliances or substances specified in sections 265.01, 265.02, 265.03, 265.04, 265.05 and 270.05 by the following:

        (a) Persons in the military service of the state of New York when duly authorized by regulations issued by the chief of staff to the governor to possess the same, members of the division of state police, and peace officers as defined

continued

in subdivision thirty-three of section 1.20 of the criminal procedure law and persons appointed as railroad policemen pursuant to section eighty-eight of the railroad law.

(b) Persons in the military or other service of the United States, in pursuit of official duty or when duly authorized by federal law, regulation or order to possess the same.

(c) Persons employed in fulfilling defense contracts with the government of the United States or agencies thereof when possession of the same is necessary for manufacture, transport, installation and testing under the requirements of such contract.

(d) A person voluntarily surrendering such weapon, instrument, appliance or substance, provided that such surrender shall be made to the sheriff of the county in which such person resides and in the county of Nassau to the commissioner of police or a member of the police department thereof designated by him, or if such person resides in a city having a population of seventy-five thousand or more to the police commissioner or head of the police force or department, or to a member of the force or department designated by such commissioner or head; and provided, further, that the same shall be surrendered by such person only after he gives notice in writing to the appropriate authority, stating his name, address, the nature of the weapon to be surrendered, and the approximate time of day and the place where such surrender shall take place. Such notice shall be acknowledged immediately upon receipt thereof by such authority. Nothing in this paragraph shall be construed as granting immunity from prosecution for any crime or offense except that of unlawful possession of such weapons, instruments, appliances or substances surrendered as herein provided. A person who possesses any such weapon, instrument, appliance or substance as an executor or administrator or any other lawful possessor of such property of a decedent may continue to possess such property for a period not over fifteen days. If such property is not lawfully disposed of within such period the possessor shall deliver it to an appropriate official described in this paragraph or such property may be delivered to the superintendent of state police. Such officer shall hold it and shall thereafter deliver it on the written request of such executor, administrator or other lawful possessor of such property to a named person, provided such named person is licensed to or is otherwise lawfully permitted to possess the same. If no request to deliver the property is received within two years of the delivery of such property to such official he shall dispose of it in accordance with the provisions of section 400.05 of the penal law.

(2) Possession of a machine-gun, firearm, switchblade knife, gravity knife, billy or blackjack by a warden, superintendent, headkeeper or deputy of a state prison, penitentiary, workhouse, county jail or other institution for the detention of persons convicted or accused of crime or detained as witnesses in criminal cases, in pursuit of official duty or when duly authorized by regulation or order to possess the same.

(3) Possession of a pistol or revolver by a person to whom a license therefore has been issued as provided under section 400.00; provided, that such a license shall not preclude a conviction for the offense defined in subdivision three of section 265.01.

(4) Possession of a rifle, shotgun or longbow for use while hunting, trapping or fishing, by a person, not a citizen of the United States, carrying a valid license issued pursuant to section 11-0713 of the environmental conservation law.

(5) Possession of a rifle or shotgun by a person who has been convicted as specified in subdivision four of section 265.01 to whom a certificate of good conduct has been issued pursuant to section two hundred forty-two, subdivision three of the executive law.

(6) Possession of a switchblade or gravity knife for use while hunting, trapping or fishing by a person carrying a valid license issued to him pursuant to section 11-0713 of the environmental conservation law.

continued

(7) Possession, at an indoor or outdoor rifle range for the purpose of loading and firing the same, of a rifle of not more than twenty-two caliber rim fire, the propelling force of which may be either gunpowder, air or springs, by a person under sixteen years of age but not under twelve, who is a duly enrolled member of any club, team or society organized for educational purposes and maintaining as a part of its facilities, or having written permission to use, such rifle range under the supervision, guidance and instruction of (a) a duly commissioned officer of the United States army, navy, marine corps or coast guard, or of the national guard of the state of New York; or (b) a duly qualified adult citizen of the United States who has been granted a certificate as an instructor in small arms practice issued by the United States army, navy or marine corps, or by the adjutant general of this state, or by the National Rifle Association of America, a not-for-profit corporation duly organized under the laws of this state.

(8) The manufacture of machine-guns, pilum ballistic knives, switchblade or gravity knives, billies or blackjacks as merchandise and the disposal and shipment thereof direct to a regularly constituted or appointed state or municipal police department, sheriff, policeman or other peace officer, or to a state prison, penitentiary, workhouse, county jail or other institution for the detention of persons convicted or accused of crime or held as witnesses in criminal cases, or to the military service of this state or of the United States.

(9)

    (a) The regular and ordinary transport of firearms as merchandise, provided that the person transporting such firearms, where he knows or has reasonable means of ascertaining what he is transporting, notifies in writing the police commissioner, police chief or other law enforcement officer performing such functions at the place of delivery, of the name and address of the consignee and the place of delivery, and withholds delivery to the consignee for such reasonable period of time designated in writing by such police commissioner, police chief or other law enforcement officer as such official may deem necessary for investigation as to whether the consignee may lawfully receive and possess such firearms.

(b) The transportation of such pistols or revolvers into, out of or within the city of New York may be done only with the consent of the police commissioner of the city of New York. To obtain such consent, the manufacturer must notify the police commissioner in writing of the name and address of the transporting manufacturer, or agent or employee of the manufacturer who is authorized in writing by such manufacturer to transport pistols or revolvers, the number, make and model number of the firearms to be transported and the place where the manufacturer regularly conducts business within the city of New York and such other information as the commissioner may deem necessary. The manufacturer must not transport such pistols and revolvers between the designated places of business for such reasonable period of time designated in writing by the police commissioner as such official may deem necessary for investigation and to give consent. The police commissioner may not unreasonably withhold his consent.

(10) Engaging in the business of gunsmith or dealer in firearms by a person to whom a valid license therefor has been issued pursuant to section 400.00.

(11) Possession of a pistol or revolver by a police officer or sworn peace officer of another state while conducting official business within the state of New York.

(B) At any time, any person who voluntarily delivers to a peace officer any weapon, instrument, appliance or substance specified in section 265.01, 265.02, 265.03, 265.04, or 265.05, under circumstances not suspicious, peculiar or involving the commission of any crime, shall not be arrested. Instead, the officer who might make the arrest shall issue or cause to be issued in a proper case a summons or other legal process to the person for investigation of the source of the weapon, instrument, appliance or substance.

continued

(C) Section 265.01 shall not apply to possession of that type of billy commonly known as a "police baton" which is twenty-four to twenty-six inches in length and no more than one and one-quarter inches in thickness by members of an auxiliary police force of a city with a population in excess of one million persons when duly authorized by regulation or order issued by the police commissioner of such city. Such regulations shall require training in the use of the baton and instruction in the legal use of deadly physical force pursuant to article thirty-five of this chapter. Notwithstanding the provisions of this section or any other provision of law, possession of such baton shall not be authorized when used intentionally to strike another person except in those situations when the use of deadly physical force is authorized by such article thirty-five.

McKINNEY'S CONSOLIDATED LAWS OF NEW YORK ANNOTATED—CRIMINAL PROCEDURE LAW (1970)

§ 1.20—Definitions of Terms of General Use in This Chapter

Except where different meanings are expressly specified in subsequent provisions of this chapter, the term definitions contained in section 10.00 of the penal law are applicable to this chapter, and, in addition, the following terms have the following meanings:

(1) "Accusatory instrument" means an indictment, an information, a simplified information, a prosecutor's information, a superior court information, a misdemeanor complaint or a felony complaint. Every accusatory instrument, regardless of the person designated therein as accuser, constitutes an accusation on behalf of the state as plaintiff and must be entitled "the people of the state of New York" against a designated person, known as the defendant.

(2) "Local criminal court accusatory instrument" means any accusatory instrument other than an indictment or a superior court information.

(3) "Indictment" means a written accusation by a grand jury, more fully defined and described in article two hundred, filed with a superior court, which charges one or more defendants with the commission of one or more offenses, at least one of which is a crime, and which serves as a basis for prosecution thereof.

(3)-a. "Superior court information" means a written accusation by a district attorney more fully defined and described in articles one hundred ninety-five and two hundred, filed with a superior court pursuant to article one hundred ninety-five, which charges one or more defendants with the commission of one or more offenses, at least one of which is a crime, and which serves as a basis for prosecution thereof.

(4) "Information" means a verified written accusation by a person, more fully defined and described in article one hundred, filed with a local criminal court, which charges one or more defendants with the commission of one or more offenses, none of which is a felony, and which may serve both to commence a criminal action and as a basis for prosecution thereof.

(5) [See, also, subd. 5 below.] "Simplified traffic information" means a written accusation, more fully defined and described in article one hundred, by a police officer or other public servant authorized by law to issue same, filed with a local criminal court, which, being in a brief or simplified form prescribed by the commissioner of motor vehicles, charges a person with one or more traffic infractions or misdemeanors relating to traffic, and which may serve both to commence a criminal action for such offense and as a basis for prosecution thereof.

(5) [See, also, subd. 5 above.]

    (a) "Simplified information" means a simplified traffic information, a simplified parks information, or a simplified environmental conservation information.

    (b) "Simplified traffic information" means a written accusation by a police officer, or other public servant authorized by law to issue same, more fully defined and described in article one hundred, filed with a local criminal court, which, being in a brief or simplified form prescribed by the commissioner of motor vehicles, charges a person with one or more traffic

continued

infractions or misdemeanors relating to traffic, and which may serve both to commence a criminal action for such offense and as a basis for prosecution thereof.

(c) "Simplified parks information" means a written accusation by a police officer, or other public servant authorized by law to issue same, filed with a local criminal court, which, being in a brief or simplified form prescribed by the commissioner of parks and recreation, charges a person with one or more offenses, other than a felony, for which a uniform simplified parks information may be issued pursuant to the parks and recreation law and the navigation law, and which may serve both to commence a criminal action for such offense and as a basis for prosecution thereof.

(d) "Simplified environmental conservation information" means a written accusation by a police officer, or other public servant authorized by law to issue same, filed with a local criminal court, which being in a brief or simplified form prescribed by the commissioner of environmental conservation, charges a person with one or more offenses, other than a felony, for which a uniform simplified environmental conservation simplified information may be issued pursuant to the environmental conservation law, and which may serve both to commence a criminal action for such offense and as a basis for prosecution thereof.

(6) "Prosecutor's information" means a written accusation by a district attorney, more fully defined and described in article one hundred, filed with a local criminal court, which charges one or more defendants with the commission of one or more offenses, none of which is a felony, and which serves as a basis for prosecution thereof.

(7) "Misdemeanor complaint" means a verified written accusation by a person, more fully defined and described in article one hundred, filed with a local criminal court, which charges one or more defendants with the commission of one or more offenses, at least one of which is a misdemeanor and none of which is a felony, and which serves to commence a criminal action but which may not, except upon the defendant's con-

sent, serve as a basis for prosecution of the offenses charged therein.

(8) "Felony complaint" means a verified written accusation by a person, more fully defined and described in article one hundred, filed with a local criminal court, which charges one or more defendants with the commission of one or more felonies and which serves to commence a criminal action but not as a basis for prosecution thereof.

(9) "Arraignment" means the occasion upon which a defendant against whom an accusatory instrument has been filed appears before the court in which the criminal action is pending for the purpose of having such court acquire and exercise control over his person with respect to such accusatory instrument and of setting the course of further proceedings in the action.

(10) "Plea," in addition to its ordinary meaning as prescribed in sections 220.10 and 340.20, means, where appropriate, the occasion upon which a defendant enters such a plea to an accusatory instrument.

(11) "Trial." A jury trial commences with the selection of the jury and includes all further proceedings through the rendition of a verdict. A non-jury trial commences with the first opening address, if there be any, and, if not, when the first witness is sworn, and includes all further proceedings through the rendition of a verdict.

(12) "Verdict" means the announcement by a jury in the case of a jury trial, or by the court in the case of a non-jury trial, of its decision upon the defendant's guilt or innocence of the charges submitted to or considered by it.

(13) "Conviction" means the entry of a plea of guilty to, or a verdict of guilty upon, an accusatory instrument other than a felony complaint, or to one or more counts of such instrument.

(14) "Sentence" means the imposition and entry of sentence upon a conviction.

(15) "Judgment." A judgment is comprised of a conviction and the sentence imposed thereon and is completed by imposition and entry of the sentence.

(16) "Criminal action." A criminal action (a) commences with the filing of an accusatory instrument against a defendant in a

continued

criminal court, as specified in subdivision seventeen; (b) includes the filing of all further accusatory instruments directly derived from the initial one, and all proceedings, orders and motions conducted or made by a criminal court in the course of disposing of any such accusatory instrument, or which, regardless of the court in which they occurred or were made, could properly be considered as a part of the record of the case by an appellate court upon an appeal from a judgment of conviction; and (c) terminates with the imposition of sentence or some other final disposition in a criminal court of the last accusatory instrument filed in the case.

(17) "Commencement of criminal action." A criminal action is commenced by the filing of an accusatory instrument against a defendant in a criminal court, and, if more than one accusatory instrument is filed in the course of the action, it commences when the first of such instruments is filed.

(18) "Criminal proceeding" means any proceeding which (a) constitutes a part of a criminal action or (b) occurs in a criminal court and is related to a prospective, pending or completed criminal action, either of this state or of any other jurisdiction, or involves a criminal investigation.

(19) "Criminal court" means any court defined as such by section 10.10.

(20) "Superior court" means any court defined as such by subdivision two of section 10.10.

(21) "Local criminal court" means any court defined as such by subdivision three of section 10.10.

(22) "Intermediate appellate court" means any court possessing appellate jurisdiction, other than the court of appeals.

(23) "Judge" means any judicial officer who is a member of or constitutes a court, whether referred to in another provision of law as a justice or by any other title.

(24) "Trial jurisdiction." A criminal court has "trial jurisdiction" of an offense when an indictment or an information charging such offense may properly be filed with such court, and when such court has authority to accept a plea to, try or otherwise finally dispose of such accusatory instrument.

(25) "Preliminary jurisdiction." A criminal court has "preliminary jurisdiction" of an offense when, regardless of whether it has trial jurisdiction thereof, a criminal action for such offense may be commenced therein, and when such court may conduct proceedings with respect thereto which lead or may lead to prosecution and final disposition of the action in a court having trial jurisdiction thereof.

(26) "Appearance ticket" means a written notice issued by a public servant, more fully defined in section 150.10, requiring a person to appear before a local criminal court in connection with an accusatory instrument to be filed against him therein.

(27) "Summons" means a process of a local criminal court, more fully defined in section 130.10, requiring a defendant to appear before such court for the purpose of arraignment upon an accusatory instrument filed therewith by which a criminal action against him has been commenced.

(28) "Warrant of arrest" means a process of a local criminal court, more fully defined in section 120.10, directing a police officer to arrest a defendant and to bring him before such court for the purpose of arraignment upon an accusatory instrument filed therewith by which a criminal action against him has been commenced.

(29) "Superior court warrant of arrest" means a process of a superior court directing a police officer to arrest a defendant and to bring him before such court for the purpose of arraignment upon an indictment filed therewith by which a criminal action against him has been commenced.

(30) "Bench warrant" means a process of a criminal court in which a criminal action is pending, directing a police officer, or a uniformed court officer, pursuant to paragraph b of subdivision two of section 530.70 of this chapter, to take into custody a defendant in such action who has previously been arraigned upon the accusatory instrument by which the action was commenced, and to bring him before such court. The function of a bench warrant is to achieve the court appearance of a defendant in a pending criminal action for some purpose other than his initial arraignment in the action.

continued

(31) "Prosecutor" means a district attorney or any other public servant who represents the people in a criminal action.

(32) "District attorney" means a district attorney, an assistant district attorney or a special district attorney, and, where appropriate, the attorney general, an assistant attorney general, a deputy attorney general or a special deputy attorney general.

(33) "Peace officer." The following persons are peace officers:
  (a) A police officer;
  (b) An attendant, uniformed court officer or an official of the supreme court in the first and second departments;
  (c) An attendant, uniformed court officer or other official attached to the county courts of Nassau and Suffolk counties;
  (d) A marshal, clerk or attendant of a district court;
  (e) A clerk, uniformed court officer or other official of the criminal court of the city of New York;
  (f) A uniformed court officer or an official of the civil court of the city of New York;
  (g) An attendant, clerk or uniformed court officer of the family court;
  (h) An attendant, or an official, or guard of any state prison or of any penal correctional institution.
  (i) A parole officer in the department of correctional services;
  (j) A harbor master appointed by a county, city, town or village;
  (k) An investigator of the office of the state commission of investigation;
  (l) Onondaga county park rangers;
  (m) An officer or agent of a duly incorporated society for the prevention of cruelty to animals and children;
  (n) An inspector or investigator of the department of agriculture and markets;
  (o) An employee of the department of taxation and finance assigned to enforcement of the tax on cigarettes imposed by article twenty of the tax law by the commissioner of taxation and finance;
  (p) An employee of the New York City finance administration assigned to enforcement of the tax on cigarettes imposed by

section D46-2.0 of the administrative code of the city of New York by the finance administrator;

(q) A constable or police constable of a city, county, town or village; or a bay constable of the town of Hempstead;

(r) Suffolk county park rangers;

(s) A probation officer;

(t) The sheriff, under-sheriff and deputy sheriffs of New York City;

(u) Long Island railroad police.

(34) "Police officer." The following persons are police officers:

(a) A sworn officer of the division of state police;

(b) Sheriffs, under-sheriffs and deputy sheriffs of counties outside of New York City;

(c) A sworn officer of an authorized county or county parkway police department;

(d) A sworn officer of an authorized police department or force of a city, town, village or police district;

(e) A sworn officer of an authorized police department of an authority or a sworn officer of the state regional park police in the office of parks and recreation;

(f) A sworn officer of the capital police force of the office of general services;

(g) An investigator employed in the office of a district attorney;

(h) An investigator employed by a commission created by an interstate compact who is, to a substantial extent, engaged in the enforcement of the criminal laws of this state;

(i) The chief and deputy fire marshals, the supervising fire marshals and the fire marshals of the bureau of fire investigation of the New York City fire department;

(j) A sworn officer of the division of law enforcement in the department of environmental conservation;

(k) A sworn officer of a police force of a public authority created by an interstate compact;

(l) [See, also, par. (l) below] Long Island railroad police.

(l) [See, also, par. (l) above] An employee of the department of taxation and finance assigned to enforcement of the tax on cigarettes imposed by article twenty of the tax law by the

continued

commissioner of taxation and finance for the purpose of applying for and executing search warrants under article six
hundred ninety of this chapter in connection with the enforcement of such tax on cigarettes.

(34)-a. "Geographical area of employment." The "geographical area of
employment" of certain police officers is as follows:

(a) New York state constitutes the "geographical area of employment" of any police officer employed as such by an
agency of the state or by an authority which functions
throughout the state;

(b) A county, city, town or village, as the case may be, constitutes the "geographical area of employment" of any police
officer employed as such by an agency of such political subdivision or by an authority which functions only in such political subdivision; and

(c) Where an authority functions in more than one county, the
"geographical area of employment" of a police officer employed thereby extends through all of such counties.

(35) "Commitment to the custody of the sheriff," when referring to an
order of a court located in a county or city which has established
a department of correction, means commitment to the commissioner of correction of such county or city.

(36) "County" ordinarily means (a) any county outside of New York
City or (b) New York City in its entirety. Unless the context requires a different construction, New York City, despite its five
counties, is deemed a single county within the meaning of the
provisions of this chapter in which that term appears.

(37) "Lesser included offense." When it is impossible to commit a particular crime without concomitantly committing, by the same
conduct, another offense of lesser grade or degree, the latter is,
with respect to the former, a "lesser included offense." In any case
in which it is legally possible to attempt to commit a crime, an attempt to commit such crime constitutes a lesser included offense
with respect thereto.

(38) "Oath" includes an affirmation and every other mode authorized
by law of attesting to the truth of that which is stated.

(39) "Petty offense" means a violation or a traffic infraction.

(40) "Evidence in chief" means evidence, received at a trial or other criminal proceeding in which a defendant's guilt or innocence of an offense is in issue, which may be considered as a part of the quantum of substantive proof establishing or tending to establish the commission of such offense or an element thereof or the defendant's connection therewith.

Give up? You probably read a few paragraphs and skipped to here because the language of the law is so user-unfriendly. But this is what Marrero faced.

Even after being given the relevant statutes, as you have them above, first-year law students usually need an hour or so to sort out the answer. And they usually get the wrong answer, at least "wrong" in the sense that it is different from the answer reached by the New York Court of Appeals, New York's highest court, when it decided Marrero's case.

At Trial

At trial Marrero pleads not guilty. The prosecution claims that Marrero violated section 265.02(4) of the Penal Law, a class D felony. They concede he would be exempt from such an offense under section 265.20(A) if he were a "peace officer," as defined by section 1.20 of the Criminal Procedure Law. Under section 1.20, a "peace officer" includes, among other persons, any "guard of any state prison or of any penal correctional institution." But prosecutors read the word "state" as applying not only to the immediately following word, "prison," but also to the later phrase, "any penal correctional institution." Thus Marrero, as a guard at a federal institution, is not a "peace officer" and therefore not exempt from the offense.

But the trial court disagrees with this reading of the statute and agrees with Marrero's interpretation that the word "state" modifies only the word "prison" immediately following it, and does not modify the phrase "any penal correctional institution." The judge dismisses the charge on May 3, 1978.

The prosecution appeals. On December 11, 1979, in a three to two vote, the appellate division, reverses the trial court's dismissal. A majority of the court conclude that, when read in its entirety and when harmonized with other sections of the law, the statute does not exempt federal prison officers. The case is sent back to the lower court for trial.

At Trial Again: Ignorance or Mistake of Law Is No Excuse

When the case comes back to trial court on remand, Marrero argues in his defense that he should be acquitted, even if he interpreted the statute incorrectly, because he made a reasonable mistake in reading the somewhat misleading statute. Other fellow officers and teachers at the prison read the statute as he did. So did the gun seller. Indeed, so did the trial judge and two of the five appellate judges. Thus, of the six judges who have heard the case so far, half have agreed with Marrero's interpretation of the law! Given the complexity of the statute, does not this level of disagreement among judges itself suggest that Marrero's "mistake" is not only reasonable but, indeed, predictable?

But the trial court (a different judge this time, Judge Hornblass) follows the old maxim "Ignorance or mistake of law is no excuse." Marrero is forbidden to offer his mistake theory to the jury as a defense.

At trial Marrero is convicted. On July 9, 1982, he is sentenced to a three-year suspended sentence and a five-hundred-dollar fine. He appeals. The appellate division again rules against Marrero and upholds his conviction, this time without issuing a written opinion.

The state's highest court, the New York Court of Appeals, issues its judgment on April 2, 1987, almost ten years after the offense. The court concludes that public policy encouraging knowledge of and adherence to the law weighs against providing a defense for a reasonable mistake of law. Marrero's judgment of conviction is affirmed on a four to three vote.

Acquitting the Bakers but Convicting the Marreros?

Criminal liability for Marrero may seem harsh, given the facts of the case. But, perhaps more to the point, liability may seem genuinely puzzling in light of the law's treatment of cases like *Baker*. How can the law let off a Baker (the rule in most states, Arkansas excepted), even if she believes her conduct is unlawful, but convict a Marrero, even if he reasonably believes his conduct is lawful? A misleading statute, like that in *Marrero*, provides as little notice and is as open to abuse, disparity in application, and unpredictability as a vague common law rule, like that in *Baker*.

This is not to deny that the legality principle is important. Its application in *Baker*, despite Baker's obvious blameworthiness, shows the importance we properly give to it. Baker must be let off, even if she thought what she was doing was criminal, in part because fair notice is not possible under a vague common law offense. But if the possibility of fair notice is so important to us that we will let Baker off, how can we convict Marrero when a misleading statute leads him and others to reasonably believe his conduct is not criminal?

The simple truth is that the law is inconsistent in the concern it shows for fair notice. It regularly excludes from liability blameworthy offenders in order to compel government to provide prior, written, specific definitions of what the criminal law commands, but then fails to exculpate blameless violators who make reasonable mistakes in interpreting statutes that the government has left ambiguous and misleading.

No doubt the practical concerns for potential abuse are in good faith. But it seems clear that one can construct a narrowly defined mistake defense that protects against abuse. New Jersey is the one state that has a general defense for a reasonable mistake of law, and there is not rampant abuse of it. Indeed, there is no evidence that it has ever been used, perhaps because it is so demanding in what it requires. It appears to require that a person pursue "all means" to determine the law. Frankly, the reasonable person would never do this.

While the New Jersey defense statute may be too demanding to be effective, its existence does show that not every mistake of law defense would lead to abuse. The challenge for code drafters is to fashion a defense provision that strikes a proper balance between the potential for abuse and the need to acquit blameless defendants. The most effective means of achieving this balance may be to shift the burden of proof of the defense to the defendant and to require the defendant to prove the defense by clear and convincing evidence. Thus, a defendant could gain the defense only if he or she was able to persuade a jury by clear and convincing evidence that a reasonable person in the defendant's situation would have made the same mistake the defendant made. This leaves little room for abuse—juries are not likely to be persuaded unless the defendant has clear facts to show his or her blamelessness—but the Marreros of the world could meet this requirement and escape liability.

Communicating the Criminal Law's Commands

Cases like *Baker* and *Marrero* also reveal another kind of failure of the criminal justice system: while the law holds us to an unerring standard of knowing the law, it does nothing to help the average person learn the law. There are no courses in high school teaching young adults the commands of the criminal law, nor television shows or newspaper columns reminding older adults. Studies of prospective jurors, for example, show that people in fact know little of the law they are presumed to know. Worse, even after they are instructed in the law using the applicable statutory language, jurors typically still have poor comprehension of it. The conclusion of the jury experts is that jury instructions should be given in "plain meaning" language. Several researchers have developed special styles for writing jury instructions that increase comprehension.

But what is the fairness of such special efforts to educate the jury to judge a defendant who has no similar opportunity for such special education before the offense? It is not plain-meaning jury instructions that are needed, but plain-meaning criminal codes. There is every reason to think that such codes and public comprehension of them are well within the reach of current drafting techniques.

People do not revolt at the trap the law sets for them—in legally presuming they know the law that a reasonable person could not—because people assume they do know the criminal law: the law criminalizes what it is that people think is highly condemnable. But empirical studies and cases like *Baker* and *Marrero*, as well as others that we will see, make clear that the law's rules and people's intuitions commonly diverge.

The Outcome

Because of his felony conviction, Marrero loses his job and is barred from further work in law enforcement or corrections. (The nightclub at 207 Madison Street, where the arrest occurred, is now a Mexican restaurant.)

The legislature never fixes the statute of which Marrero is convicted. Today its language is as misleading as it was at the time of Mar-

Formerly a social club, now a Mexican restaurant, 207 Madison Street was where Julio Marrero was arrested on December 19, 1977. (Photograph by the author)

rero's case. Exempt from gun possession offense are "correction officers of any state correctional facility or of any penal correctional institution." Is a guard at a nonstate "penal correctional institution" exempt from the offense under the second clause?

Without a reasonable mistake of law defense, the state has little incentive to clarify its laws. Unlike the escape of a Baker from liability, which commonly prompts legislative action in order to prevent others from a similar escape, the imposition of undeserved liability presents no similar societal danger. One would have hoped that convictions of the blameless would provide as much legislative incentive for action as do escapes from justice.

Legality in Omission Offenses

The legality principle is at the heart of the next case as well. Its concern for fair notice is greatest when criminal law goes beyond simply prohibiting conduct and requires a person to affirmatively act, on pain of criminal liability for failure to act. Indeed in one case, *Lambert v. California*, the Supreme Court seems to suggest that the demands of notice in the context of affirmative duties to act are so important that the absence of notice of a duty may be an unconstitutional violation of substantive due process. Lambert was a convicted felon who did not report to the police within five days of arriving, as a Los Angeles ordinance required. The Supreme Court reversed Lambert's conviction because the state had not given reasonable notice of this duty to report, just as most states would bar liability of Baker for the unwritten crime of "treating a body indecently."

Indeed, affirmative duties to act are themselves something rare in American law, even when properly and clearly defined. Perhaps this is a legacy of the American pioneering spirit of self-sufficiency and independence, or perhaps a product of the American suspicion of government and its intrusion into the lives of its citizens. Whatever the reason, American law typically is hesitant to create an affirmative duty to act and, when it does so, it demands close adherence to the legality principle's call for a clear, prior, written statement of exactly what is required.

NEGLECTING MOM ... TO DEATH

It is 1984. Ray Edwin Billingslea lives in a small two-story Dallas, Texas, house owned by his mother, ninety-four-year-old Hazel Billingslea. The arrangement saves him the cost of rent, utilities, and living expenses. Fifty-year-old Ray has lived with his mother for the past twenty years. He has held menial jobs on and off but does not now work.

Hazel Billingslea's granddaughter, Virginia, who is the daughter of Ray's sister, Katherine Jefferson, also lived at Hazel's house but moved out soon after she graduated from high school. Tired of being sexually harassed by Ray, she gets a judge to grant a peace bond, or injunction, against Ray to make him leave her alone. But Virginia stays close to her grandmother for the next several years, living fifteen blocks away in the same Dallas neighborhood. She does shopping for her and brings her

Hazel Billingslea's house in Dallas, in which her son, Ray, now lives. (Joel Sauer)

candy during her regular Saturday visits. But Ray runs the house his mother owns and does not get along with the granddaughter.

In March 1984 Hazel's health takes a downturn and she becomes confined to her bed. For reasons unknown, Hazel's arm and jaw are broken, but Ray does not take the elderly woman to the hospital.

In recent weeks Virginia has not seen her grandmother, frequently getting turned away at the door by Ray, who tells her that his mother is "asleep" and cannot be disturbed. Virginia persists and tries to reach her by telephone but is twice threatened by Ray to "keep your god-damned mother-fucking ass out of my and my mother's business."

Frustrated, Virginia calls her mother, Katherine, who moved to Albuquerque, New Mexico, years earlier. After talking to her daughter, Katherine calls the Dallas social service Department with her suspicions that Ray is mistreating their mother. The social service office reports the complaint to Velma Mosley of the Adult Protective Services Section of the Department of Human Resources. Mosley, two police officers, and a police social services worker go to investigate the complaint, but when they arrive, Ray refuses to let them inside because, he says, it is too late at night.

The next day, April 24, 1984, they return but when they get to the Billingslea home, Ray meets them in the front yard and objects to their entry into the house. After much discussion, he acquiesces. Once inside, the group is overwhelmed by the strong, rancid odor of rotting flesh. Ray begins to berate the officers, demanding to know what "you mother-fuckers are doing in my house." The police officers and the social worker find their way upstairs to Hazel's bedroom. The elderly woman is lying in bed. "Oh, please help me," she says when she sees the social worker. Mosley pulls back the sheets to examine her and finds her naked from the waist down and in great pain. The smell of feces and rotting flesh is overpowering. She has bed sores on her buttocks and thighs, which are filled with maggots. One of the officers vomits from the sight and the smell. Paramedics are called.

The paramedics and social worker attempt to dress Hazel, to cover her nakedness, but she is in too much pain to be moved. The social worker vomits. The paramedics place a plastic bag over her—usually used as a body bag—to cover her and to contain the odor and maggots. She screams in pain as the paramedics move her to the stretcher. One of the paramedics vomits. Eventually, they get the elderly woman into an ambulance and take her to the hospital.

A doctor examining Hazel discovers that she has lost most of her muscle to deterioration, and confirms that maggots are eating away at her bedsores. The doctors x-ray her and discover broken bones. Hazel is disoriented and unable to feed herself. Her inner thighs are covered by second-degree burns and blisters from lying in pools of urine. The doctor believes her bedsores have taken four to six weeks to develop.

Earlier attention would have prevented the injuries to her; even after the deterioration, earlier medical treatment could have reversed it. But it is determined that, in her present condition, nothing can be done for Hazel other than to administer large doses of antibiotics and painkillers.

When told that his mother requires medical care, Ray Billingslea responds, "Who will pay the utility here [at the house]?"

On May 5, 1984, eleven days after she is found by authorities, Hazel Billingslea dies. Ray continues to live in his mother's house after her death.

What liability and punishment, if any, would you impose on Ray for failing to care for his mother?

no liability	☐	1 year	☐
liability but		3 years	☐
no punishment	☐	7 years	☐
1 day	☐	15 years	☐
2 weeks	☐	30 years	☐
2 months	☐	life imprisonment	☐
6 months	☐	death	☐

People's Intuitions of Justice

Most people who read these facts think Ray deserves criminal liability and punishment. They conclude that by his failure to care for his mother, who was providing him with free lodging, he seriously injured or perhaps killed her.

no liability	1%	1 year	4%
liability but		3 years	10%
no punishment	1%	7 years	20%
1 day	—	15 years	30%
2 weeks	—	30 years	15%
2 months	1%	life imprisonment	14%
6 months	—	death	4%

Mean = 14.2 years.

The most common sentence people impose, and the average sentence, is about fifteen years; 83 percent give seven years imprisonment or more. There seems to be a consensus that this is a serious crime and Ray is fully blameworthy for it.

The Charge

Prosecutors charge Ray Billingslea under Texas Penal Code section 22.04, causing injury to a person older than sixty-five, which carries penalties almost as severe as those for homicide. The statute, which originally applied only to injury done to children, now makes it a crime to "intentionally, knowingly, recklessly or with criminal negligence" cause serious bodily injury to a person over sixty-five or under fourteen. The prosecutors charge that Hazel could not physically secure medical care for herself and that Ray caused such injury to his mother by failing to obtain aid for her.

Ray claims he had no legal duty to care for his mother. The state responds that even if the statute does not explicitly impose on Ray an affirmative duty to provide care, the duty exists through common law. The indictment alleges that Ray Billingslea voluntarily assumed the care of his mother, who was unable to care for herself, and thereby prevented others from caring for her, which, the state argues, is sufficient to create a duty by Ray to care for her.

The Law's Reluctance to Impose Duties

American legislatures are generally reluctant to create affirmative duties. Only one state, Vermont, creates a general duty to aid a stranger in danger, even if the person's life can be saved with little inconvenience and no risk.* To the extent that the law creates duties, they tend to be applicable only to people who undertake special activities, such as dangerous activities, that justify special regulation. For example, a person may have a duty to get a driver's licence if they wish to drive a car. A person may have a duty to check the age of a customer if they sell alcohol. A person hired as a lifeguard may have a duty to try to rescue a swimmer in danger. In these instances, a person commonly is given notice of the special duties that come with the activity, when they are licensed or trained for the activity, as in the state's driver education manual, for example. At the very least, the special nature of the activity may signal that a special duty may accompany it.

In *Billingslea*, the prosecutors concede that Texas does not have a statutory duty of children to care for their elderly parents. The prosecutors claim, however, that there is a common law duty of care created when one voluntarily assumes care and thereby discourages others from providing it. But as we saw in *Baker*, most states frown on using the unwritten common law as grounds for imposing criminal liability, for such law fails to give adequate notice and commonly is vague. Such weaknesses are all the more problematic when liability is based not on an act, but on a failure to act, as here. Indeed, the Texas statute author-

*Rhode Island and Wisconsin have more limited duties to rescue a stranger.

izing liability for an omission expressly requires a *statutory* duty. A duty recognized only at common law is legally insufficient.

On the other hand, the state does have a special offense that punishes injury to an elderly person and provides severe penalties. The prosecutor argues that the statute should be interpreted as creating a statutory duty on which liability for an omission can be based.

The Outcome

On August 28, 1986, a Dallas County jury convicts Billingslea on a charge of injury to an elderly person. Texas is one of the few states to allow jury sentencing, if the defendant elects it. The jury sentences Billingslea to ninety-nine years in prison.

Billingslea's attorney, Deke Austin, vows to appeal the conviction because he believes the court has erred in interpreting the statute as imposing an affirmative duty on Ray to seek aid for his mother. The statute criminalizing causing injury to an elderly person only prohibits harmful *conduct*, he claims; it does not create an affirmative duty to act. Since there is no statutory duty requiring Billingslea to provide care for Hazel, Ray's omission to do so cannot be criminal.

Less than a year later, on July 16, 1987, the Dallas Court of Appeals overturns Billingslea's conviction. It holds that Texas law does not explicitly require children to care for their elderly parents and that the "injury to an elderly person" statute might be read to create such a duty but also might be read not to. Consistent with the legality principle, any ambiguity in an offense definition must be resolved to the benefit of the defendant. (Lawyers call this the "rule of strict construction" or "rule of levity.") With no duty to care for his mother, Billingslea cannot be held criminally liable for neglecting her. "Although the facts in this case are extreme, and the conduct of [Billingslea] reprehensible, the evidence is insufficient" for criminal liability, the court writes in its opinion.

"I guess you can just let your parents lay there and rot," says Norman Kinne, first assistant Dallas County prosecutor. The state's Court of Criminal Appeals upholds the lower appellate court's decision, noting that limited liability for omissions "is firmly rooted in the evolution of Texas criminal jurisprudence." Criminal liability, the court says, requires notice to individuals as to what they may and may not do, an element absent in omission crimes when no legal duty exists. Billingslea is released. Liability for his mother's injuries and death is barred.

Today

Prompted by Billingslea's escape from liability, the state has revised its "injury to an elderly person" statute to make explicit that a duty of care is created once someone voluntarily undertakes control and care and thereby discourages help by others.

Most states still do not criminalize a failure to care for a parent, even if the person is living in the parent's house. (Twenty-two states still have no law requiring children to provide any support to their indigent parents.) Thus, a case like *Billingslea* would end in the same result in most states today.

Ray Billingslea still lives in Dallas, in his mother's house, with his two sons, Elvis, thirty-one, and Bubba, twenty-eight.

Striking the Proper Balance between Legality and Justice

Billingslea is much like *Baker*. Legality trumps blameworthiness. That we are willing to let so despicable a person as Billingslea escape liability is only a testament to the depth of our commitment to the principle of legality.

It is significant that the unfortunate result in *Billingslea* prompted a correction of the law's weakness. This seems the proper accommodation of the tension between the demands for legality and justice. The occasional offender will escape justice but, with legislative vigilance and correction, the law over time will improve.

But compare this to the legislative inaction in *Marrero*. One again might conclude that acquitting a blameworthy person is more energizing for reform than convicting a blameless person. If improper acquittals rather than improper convictions get legislative attention, then the best way for the criminal law to refine itself is to recognize a reasonable mistake of law defense, which would give a defense to people like *Marrero*. If blameworthy offenders begin escaping justice under the defense, by taking advantage of an ambiguous or misleading statute, we can guess it will prompt corrective legislative action.

If we can suffer the escape of the guilty Bakers and Billingsleas to further the fair notice of the legality principle, then we certainly should

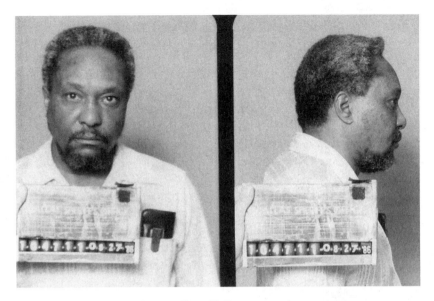

Ray Billingslea. (Dallas County Sheriff's Department)

rejoice in the acquittal of the innocent Marreros when it achieves the same end—encouraging the legislature to provide greater opportunity for fair notice.

FINDERS KEEPERS, LOSERS WEEPERS?

It is Monday night, July 19, 1993, in the Massachusetts town of Winchendon, sixty miles from Boston near the New Hampshire line. Winchendon is a typical small town, with a population of six thousand. Many residents commute to Boston for work, but Winchendon has retained its small-town atmosphere and its small-town economy. Most people would be considered middle-class and few live luxuriously. Paying the bills each month is a full-time concern for nearly everyone.

Linda Ruschioni, a plaque maker, and her husband, Ricci, a firefighter, live with their son Ricci, Jr., eleven, daughter Randi, ten, and daughter Traci, eight. This night, Linda and Traci go to the Family VideoLand store to rent a movie. They pick out a comedy, *Death Becomes Her*, and get in line to pay for the movie. They are a few minutes behind Dudley P. Haney, another Winchendon resident they will soon know much better.

Linda Ruschioni pays for the movie and leaves with her daughter in tow. As they walk across the parking lot, Traci spots something on the ground. There are no cars around and no people. She bends down and picks up two instant Twin Spins lottery tickets. The tickets are from a new game started a week earlier by the Massachusetts Lottery Commission. They cost $2 each and have the potential to pay from $1 to $20,000.

Traci yells, "Mom. Come here!" and hands her the tickets. Linda examines the tickets and sees that they are not scratched off. No one seems to be around looking for the tickets, so she puts them in her pocketbook, intending to play them later. Later that night, as Traci, her sister, and a friend watch the movie, Linda remembers the tickets and has Traci scratch them off. One of them is a $4 winner. The other scores $10,000, a 144,000-to-1 shot!

Linda cannot believe it. She grabs the children, packs them in the car, and heads for the nearest lottery dealer, a convenience store a few minutes from her house. Seconds later she is in the store, jumping up and down as the children watch from the car. The clerk at the store verifies that both tickets are legitimate winners. Only the lottery commission itself can pay a $10,000 prize. Elated, Linda goes home.

The next morning Linda, Ricci, and Traci show up at the lottery commission's regional office in Worcester and present the $10,000 ticket. Linda tells the commission agent that her daughter found the ticket in a parking lot. Smiling and charmed by the child, the employee tells her that Traci is too young to cash the ticket, but it is perfectly okay for Linda to sign it and take the prize. After taxes, the ticket pays $6,700. The commission determines that the winning ticket came from a book distributed to the Beverage Barn in Winchendon, next door to Family VideoLand.

Amazed by her daughter's good luck and thinking it a wonderful story, Linda calls the local television station and tells them of Traci's find. The news station loves the story and airs it on the evening broadcast: the little girl who finds a $10,000 lottery ticket! Happy endings for all. Other Boston stations and newspapers pick up the story, with national coverage close behind. The *Good Morning America* program soon calls, and Linda goes on television.

Traci Ruschioni, eight, holds a copy of the winning lottery ticket at home in Winchendon, Massachusetts. (John Bohn, *Boston Globe*)

After paying a dentist bill and car insurance and splurging on a freezer, a new cage for Traci's birds, and a bicycle for Traci's sister, the Ruschionis plan to use the money to go back to Disney World, where they vacationed the year before.

The Law

Unknown to the Ruschionis at the time, a Massachusetts statute requires persons finding property worth over $3 to turn it in to the local police station. The true owner may reclaim the property within one year; otherwise it becomes the property of the finder. Another provision makes it a crime—a form of larceny—to "unlawfully convert" the property of another to one's own use. The Ruschionis' conversion of the tickets to their own use is "unlawful" because it is in violation of their affirmative duty to turn the property in at the police station. The two tickets they find have a face value of $4, already over the statutory limit of $3, but in fact are worth much more, of course, $10,004. At the time they "convert" the property to their use by cashing the tickets, however, the Ruschionis are unaware of their statutory duty to turn in lost property. The Ruschionis hear of the law only during the *Good Morning America* appearance.

"I didn't know about the law, of course not. Nobody knew it," Ricci Ruschioni later explains. "How many times has anybody walked down the street or found some change in a phone booth or found a few dollars on the street? How many of these people in the world would go back and give it to the police department? Most people would do what we did. You put it in your pocket and walk away."

Should Linda and Ricci Ruschioni be criminally liable for converting the lost ticket to their own use? If so, what amount of punishment would you impose?

no liability	☐	1 year	☐
liability but no punishment	☐	3 years	☐
		7 years	☐
1 day	☐	15 years	☐
2 weeks	☐	30 years	☐
2 months	☐	life imprisonment	☐
6 months	☐	death	☐

Ignorance of Law an Excuse?

Given how reluctant the law traditionally is to create duties—for example, a duty of a child to care for an elderly parent, a duty to help a stranger in danger—one may be surprised to see it create a duty in a matter such as this, where life or limb is not at stake. If the government is willing to create a duty to take a lost $3 to the police station, why not a duty to kick a life preserver to a drowning man?

It may be the moral thing to do to make some effort to find the owner, but is it criminal not to? Many people would disagree that even common morality requires turning in the tickets. A time-honored maxim is "Finders keepers, losers weepers." On the other hand, others may feel that the large amount at stake makes the maxim inapplicable.

The duty here is all the more surprising because it is not tied to a special activity, such as driving a car, selling liquor, or being a lifeguard, which might justify the intrusion and help give notice that an affirmative duty exists. The duty created here applies to every person.

Do you have a similar duty in your state to try to find the owner or to turn in lost property? Most people won't know the answer to that question. But they may be criminally liable if they have such a duty and fail to perform it.

Even conceding that there is a duty in Massachusetts, the Ruschionis may correctly point out that they did not know of it. If they had known of it, they presumably would not have encouraged the publicity they did. Should their ignorance of their duty be an excuse?

People's Intuitions of Justice

Here is how the people in the survey sentenced Linda Ruschioni:

no liability	27%	1 year	—
liability but		3 years	—
no punishment	56%	7 years	—
1 day	5%	15 years	—
2 weeks	8%	30 years	—
2 months	3%	life imprisonment	—
6 months	1%	death	—

Mean = less than half a day.

Even for a ticket worth $10,000, 83 percent of the people would impose no punishment. And the average liability imposed is a symbolic amount, less than half a day imprisonment. Even though Linda failed to perform her legal duty, there seems to be a general sense that her failure ought to be excused, just as many people thought Julio Marrero ought to be excused for his mistake as to the gun possession law.

The Aftermath

No charges are brought against the Ruschionis. Police Chief Steven Thompson says he, too, did not know of the duty to turn in lost property, which suggests that not too many people in Winchendon have been turning in lost property at the local police station. "That's not something I was aware of. There are a lot of conflicts here. I don't think [the Ruschionis] have committed a crime," he says. Even after the existence of the lost property statute is revealed, neither police nor prosecutors institute criminal proceedings.

The Problem of Discretion

Most people will think that justice has been done in this case, that blameless persons were properly spared criminal liability. And I agree. But note that this result was achieved only through the exercise of discretion by the authorities in the system. To reach the right result, they had to refuse to follow the law as written. The difficulty with such a resolution is that such discretion is an unreliable and dangerous mechanism on which to rely. Ricci Ruschioni is a firefighter, one of the "in" crowd in a small town. (He is soon after promoted to fire captain.) Is it clear that there would have been no charges if he had been the town's gadfly or boisterous drunk, or of an ethnicity or religion viewed as foreign or inferior?

Recall that official discretion did not operate to save Julio Marrero. The prosecutors there may have had different values or may have been in a different situation. Or a host of other things might explain why an exception was made for Ruschioni but not for Marrero, although both reasonably believed their conduct was not criminal. (Indeed, some will argue that the Ruschionis' conduct is at least unethical if not illegal, which might not be said of Marrero's.)

But whatever the reason for the difference in treatment, the fact is that relying on discretion to determine the imposition of criminal liability makes the law unpredictable, creates the potential for abuse of discretion, creates the potential for disparity in the treatment of similar cases, and fails to give fair warning as to the real rules of conduct and liability. In other words, discretion undercuts all the good reasons for adhering to the legality principle.

A codified defense for a reasonable mistake of law was not needed in the *Ruschioni* case because the authorities essentially provided such a defense informally. But the absence of such a codified defense has a real cost, for it forces the authorities to ignore the law to reach the right result, and official lawbreaking of any sort can undermine the law. It undercuts the law's moral credibility, for the legal officials themselves seem to be conceding that the law does injustice. One can wonder what kind of signal that sends, and what kind of confidence in the law that creates.

Instead of conflicting with legality interests, the recognition of a mistake of law defense can advance them. To recognize such a defense is to provide an incentive for lawmakers to make the law known. The more effectively communicated the law, the more difficult it will be for a person to persuade a jury that ignorance of the law was reasonable.

Without such a reasonable-mistake-of-law defense, each instance of such official disregard for the law creates confusion about the status of the law. What other laws can be similarly ignored? Is there now a duty in Winchendon to turn in the lost property, or not? Is the law to be obeyed in the future or not?

In fact, the prosecutors' disregard of the law in the *Ruschioni* case had significant effects beyond the issue of criminal liability for the Ruschionis. The authorities' disregard was taken, not surprisingly, to void all aspects of the law, and that introduced an entirely new set of complications.

Same Facts, Different Perspective

Dudley Haney is not a big gambler. But just about every week, when he is in a convenience store or gas station, he tries his luck with the state's instant scratch-off lottery tickets. He doesn't buy much, usually just a couple of tickets. Most weeks, he takes the tickets home to his wife and they scratch them off together. On this occasion, Haney stops by the Beverage Barn in Winchendon. He parks his car in the parking lot, which is shared by two businesses, the Beverage Barn and the Family VideoLand. It is between 6:00 P.M. and 7:00 P.M. on Monday night, and traffic in the parking lot is light. Haney enters the Beverage Barn with some returnable bottles and presents them to the clerk. While he waits for his refund, he decides to try a couple of tickets from the new game, Twin Spins, and three tickets from an older game, Royal Flush. The store's clerk and business manager, David Johnson, tears two tickets off the strip of Twin Spins hanging behind the counter and hands them to Haney. Haney pays for his tickets, stuffs them in his right pants pocket, and leaves the store.

After leaving the Beverage Barn, Haney returns to his car to retrieve his broken VCR, which he plans to have repaired at VideoLand. They are running a special where they check out a customer's VCR and give a free estimate of the repair cost. Haney brings his VCR in along with the remote control, which he jams in his right pocket, waiting in line for a few minutes. (Linda and Traci Ruschioni will get in the same line a few minutes later.) When it is his turn, he sets the VCR down on the counter and waits for the clerk to enter his information into the computer. Before he leaves, Haney pulls the remote control out of his pocket and hands it to the clerk. Haney exits the store and starts to walk toward his car.

As Haney fishes for his keys, he realizes he has lost his Twin Spins tickets. The bigger Royal Flush tickets are still in his pocket. Bewildered at having lost something he had just a few minutes earlier, Haney checks all his pockets and the ground around where he is standing, thinking they could have fallen out as he reached for his keys. When he doesn't find them, he checks his car.

It occurs to Haney that he may have left the tickets in the Beverage Barn or that they might have fallen out before he left the store. He walks the twenty paces back to the barn and asks Johnson, the clerk, if he has seen the tickets. Johnson says no, but since it is slow in the store at the time, he agrees to come out and help Haney search. They will not find anything. The Ruschionis have already found the tickets and left.

Johnson and Haney begin searching the entire parking lot, figuring the tickets might have blown away from the spot where they were dropped. Together the two wander around the parking lot scanning the ground as if they are looking for a lost contact lens. Haney retraces his steps into the video store and asks the clerk and a few customers if they have seen the lottery tickets. None have. After a while, Haney and Johnson give up and Haney goes home, thinking the tickets are gone forever.

After Johnson returns to his counter at the Beverage Barn, he checks the strip of Twin Spins and sees that the last two tickets purchased—by

Dudley Haney lost the tickets found by Traci Ruschioni. (John Bohn, *Boston Globe*)

Haney, since no one else has come in during the search—are numbered 116 and 117, which he later learns include the $10,000 winner.

After the Ruschionis tell the media about their good luck, a camera crew from Channel 4 visits the parking lot and store where the tickets were found. Ray Sirois, the owner of the video store, talks to the news crew and remembers that Dudley Haney had come back into the store looking for two lottery tickets he had lost. He checks his computer and sees that the Ruschionis checked out a movie a few minutes after Haney dropped off his VCR. Sirois, who has seen Haney around town and knows him as a customer, gets his phone number from the store computer and calls Haney's home. As the story airs, Haney, a youth counselor with a degree in psychology who works for a social service agency, Metro-Boston Community Service Network, is still at the office. Haney's wife, Wanda, answers and Sirois tells her about the television crew and the winning ticket. Haney's wife recalls her husband telling her about losing the two tickets that he had bought at the Beverage Barn.

Wanda calls her husband at work and tells him about the Ruschionis' find. After some investigation it becomes clear that the tickets found by the Ruschionis are the ones Haney lost. After some discussion with his wife, Haney decides to call the Ruschionis. He talks to the father, Ricci, and tells him that he lost the two tickets his daughter found and that he can prove that they are his. He asks if they can talk over what to do about the ticket winnings. He is told that the Ruschionis' view is "Finders keepers, losers weepers."

Haney is somewhat surprised by the response, and thinks to himself, "Wow. That's a real nice 'city' attitude versus a 'small town' attitude. Tough luck to the person who lost it." The Ruschionis feel that the law, making it a crime not to return anything worth $3 or more, is out of date and absurd. Ricci Ruschioni, a lieutenant in the local fire department, says, "I think the law is very vague. Three dollars back in 1820 is like $300 today. There's no one who would convict someone of that law today."

Haney isn't sure what to do. He decides to contact the Lottery Commission and file a claim for the $10,000. The commission denies his claim. They have already paid the winnings to the Ruschionis.

Haney finds out from friends and a lawyer that a Massachusetts state law requires the return of lost property to its owner. The statute that requires finders to turn in lost property also provides that "If, within . . . one year after the finding of lost money or goods, the owner appears and pays all reasonable expenses incurred by the finder in keeping such goods . . . and in complying with this chapter, he shall have restitution of the money [or] goods." Despite the statute, the Ruschionis refuse to give Haney any of the ticket proceeds.

Haney calls the Winchendon police to report the loss and asks that they pursue its return. The police refuse to get involved. Haney isn't interested in having the Ruschionis prosecuted but does want his winnings. "It's very clear. These are state laws, and the state didn't apply its own laws."

Haney, concerned about maintaining his relationship with people in the small town, does not pursue the matter further.

Regarding his refusal to return the ticket, Ricci Ruschioni tells a reporter, "I defend my actions 125 percent. We didn't do anything wrong, and we sure don't feel guilty. Certain people are using the media to try and make certain people feel guilty, and it's not working."

The Virtues of Legality

It seems only fair that the Ruschionis not be held criminally liable for failing to perform a legal duty—turning in found property at the police station—of which they and most other people were unaware. But the way this result was reached—through official disregard of the law—only served to encourage further disregard. The Ruschionis were only following the lead of the police and prosecutors when they disregarded the statute's direction to return the lost property to its owner, Haney. Such lawlessness is a hidden cost of a criminal justice system's reliance on official discretion to do justice.

A better approach would be to formally recognize a defense for reasonable mistake or ignorance of law. Prosecutors then need not disregard the law; they need only apply it in order to allow the Ruschionis an escape from criminal liability. And instead of seeing prosecutors disregard the law, the Ruschionis would have been saved by it. In this setting, they might well have been less inclined to disregard the law when the owner, Haney, asked for his property back.

We benefit much from the predictability, uniformity in application, protection from abuse, and fair notice that the legality principle gives to law. The alternative system to the "principle of legality" is the "principle of analogy," as used in the former Soviet Union. In that somewhat extreme form, offenses were broadly defined—"conduct against the national interest" was a crime—and the state could impose criminal liability in the absence of a specific criminal statute, simply by showing an analogy between the conduct and some existing offense. The principle of analogy creates a world in which power resides in the officials who administer the law, rather than in the law itself. That kind of official discretion no doubt could have usefully avoided the escape from justice of blameworthy people like Baker and Billingslea. But we reject this world, and prefer the rule of law to the rule of men. In *Ruschioni*, we see the lawlessness of official discretion on a small scale, although its sting for those hurt may be as real. On a larger scale, law without legality allows the law to become a weapon of oppression of citizens by government or a mechanism of personal power of officials.

Finishing the Story

Two months after the lost lottery ticket controversy, a reporter covering a special election at the Central Street Fire Station in Winchendon loses his wallet. He calls the station. Ricci Ruschioni tells him no one turned it in, but offers to go outside and look for it in the parking lot. He spends several minutes looking for it despite heavy rain, finally finds it, and notifies the relieved reporter. The good deed is reported in the local paper.

The Ruschionis never make it to Disney World, as they had planned. The pressure of the media attention—and the ongoing debate among their neighbors about their personal ethics—strains their marriage and they separate, and remain separated today.

Dudley Haney soon after gets a hit on the Twin Spins and wins $400.

3

Can Committing a Crime Be
Doing the Right Thing?

OUR JUDGMENTS OF justice frequently are complex. We may agree
that conduct is wrong and ought to be prohibited and that violations of
the prohibition ought to be punished. Yet we also may agree that there
are some situations in which violations of the law are not wrong, ought
to be permitted, and in fact are the right thing to do—something we are
happy to have done in similar situations in the future.

Is the criminal law capable of defining these special circumstances
when normally criminal conduct is to be tolerated, even encouraged?
The law attempts to do so through its formulation of "justification defenses." As the following three cases illustrate, the criminal law has developed some impressive insights in defining justifications, but also is
blind to some serious problems.

ESCAPING THE PRISONERS

John Charles Green is nineteen years old, five feet nine inches tall, and
155 pounds. He has never known his father, and was separated from his
mother as a child and placed in various foster homes. He does not know
where any of his relatives are.

Green is convicted of burglary in the circuit court of Adair County,
Missouri, on November 1, 1966, and sentenced to three years imprisonment. The Department of Corrections receives him on November 4,
1966, and a month later he enters the Missouri Training Center for Men,
a medium-security prison in Moberly, Missouri.

The Missouri Training Center has a population of about six hundred inmates. Most of the inmates are second offenders over twenty-
five years old, a number of whom are serving life terms. On the night
shift, two guards are assigned to each of the two buildings. Each

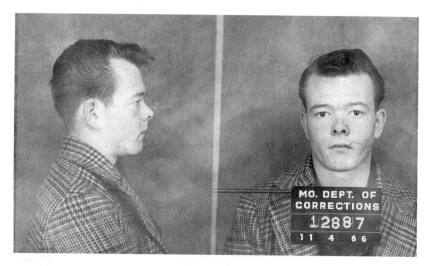

John Charles Green. (Missouri Department of Corrections)

Aerial view of the Missouri Training Center for Men at Moberly. (Missouri Department of Corrections)

building houses three hundred inmates, celled in four separate wings. The prison has three case workers, each serving about two hundred inmates. There is one nurse and one chaplain. No "jailhouse lawyers" are allowed. No legal services for indigent inmates are provided. The library contains only a set of the Missouri statutes.

It is commonly known that same-sex rapes occur in the prison. The Missouri Training Center has a procedure for dealing with complaints by one prisoner against another. Upon complaint to a guard, the guard may take no action or may pass the complaint on for investigation. A prisoner may complain directly to the prison administration, bypassing the guards, by sending a note through the prison mail. But such "snitch-kites," as they are known, frequently are examined by prisoners working in the prison mail system. Most prisoners are hesitant to use snitch-kites for fear of retaliation. Prison policy does not permit investigation of complaints or transfers unless the victim divulges the name of his assailant. Usually the prisoner is left among his fellow inmates during the investigation, unless the guard witnesses the alleged assault. If an attack is investigated and confirmed, the victim can be given protective custody in "the hole," normally used to discipline prisoners.

A few days after his arrival, on December 16, 1966, Green appears before the disciplinary board for fighting, the result of fending off sexual advances by other prisoners. On January 2, 1967, after lights out, two men pick the lock on Green's cell, a practice that is easily and commonly done. One man is about Green's size. The other is approximately six feet tall and two hundred pounds. Green yells for a guard, but the guard on duty is separated from the wing by a heavy door and does not respond. Green tries to push the first man aside but the second man grabs him, holds a knife to his throat, and threatens to stab him if he does not "cooperate" with them. Green then submits to rape by both men.

Several minutes after the assailants leave, Green slits his own arm in order to get removed from the inmate population, then goes for a guard. He is taken to the prison hospital, where he is kept for several days. Green speaks with Donald Hartness, the assistant superintendent of treatment, reports what happened, and asks to be moved so he can avoid further attacks. Green refuses to name his attackers for fear that he will be killed. Hartness tells him he must resolve his own problems and suggests that he go back and fight it out. Over his objections, Green is returned to his old cell and situation.

Several days later, again after lights out, three men pick Green's lock and enter his cell. Green attempts to run but is knocked out. He wakes up later with anal pain and discovers "grease" in his anal area. Realizing he has been raped again, he feigns having swallowed glass so that he can talk to an official without the other inmates knowing, and asks a guard to hospitalize him.

The next day Green is brought before the disciplinary board, charged with self-destruction. The disciplinary board is composed of A. H. Baldwin (the assistant superintendent of custody), Hartness, and a guard. Green describes the assaults and asks for protective custody. He again refuses to give his attackers' names. Baldwin tells Green the best that he can do is to arrange a wing change. He advises Green to "fight it out, submit to the assaults, or go over the fence." The board assigns no punishment for the violation charged. The superintendent of the center, Edward Haynes, reviews the hearing's record and approves Green's cell change to an adjoining wing.

When Green is moved to the new wing, he is taunted by other prisoners. He also is propositioned for sex by a guard named Petre. He reports this to Captain Chapman, and the guard is transferred.

At noon on April 14, 1967, five inmates come to Green's cell and tell him they will come for him that night to gang rape him and that he will be their "punk" (a person who plays the female role in male same-sex activity) for the remainder of his time in prison. They threaten to seriously injure or kill him if he does not cooperate.

As with his old cell, the lock in Green's new cell can easily be picked. Because his past reports have been futile, Green decides not to tell authorities of the threat of gang rape, but instead to escape. Around 6:00 P.M. that day, he quietly escapes.

Green climbs over the fence near the powerhouse on the west side of the institution and walks down a railroad track for a short distance, across several fields, and along the highway.

At the 10:00 P.M. bed check, he is discovered missing and a search begins.

About 4:00 A.M., north of the nearby town of Yates, Green comes across a car in the driveway of William Wagner, Jr. The keys are in the car, so he starts the engine and begins maneuvering the car out of the driveway, but with some difficulty. Wagner, awakened by the engine, yells at him from the house, and Green jumps out and runs off. Wagner notifies the police. Early that afternoon, Trooper Roy Robinson

The administrative staff of the Missouri Training Center for Men at Moberly in the 1960s, from left: Major Wilbur Morgan, Donald Hartness, Jerry Heming, Lew Walker, Superintendent Edward Haynes, Vern Baker, John Kozlowski, and Ernest McNealy. (Missouri Department of Corrections)

Edward Haynes, *left,* and A. H. Baldwin, *right,* Moberly prison officials. (Missouri Department of Corrections)

An album cover for the Prodigals, a Moberly prison choir that won national broadcasting awards during 1964 and 1965. (Earl Clayton Grandstaff)

Basketball team at Moberly prison. (Missouri Department of Corrections)

comes across Green sitting beside the road looking at a highway map. He takes Green into custody without incident and returns him to Moberly.

Green is charged with escape. Would you convict? If so, what amount of punishment would you impose?

no liability	☐	1 year	☐
liability but		3 years	☐
no punishment	☐	7 years	☐
1 day	☐	15 years	☐
2 weeks	☐	30 years	☐
2 months	☐	life imprisonment	☐
6 months	☐	death	☐

The Law's Rules

The exceptions to the law's prohibitions—defined in the law's "justification defenses"—include such doctrines as self-defense and law enforcement authority. Justification defenses like self-defense—defense of property, defense of others, and, in some jurisdictions, a special defense of habitation—allow the use of defensive force to resist unjustified aggression. Justification defenses like law enforcement authority authorize aggressive conduct, such as the authority given to prison guards, soldiers, and executioners, when such is necessary to protect or advance a specific societal interest.

The common theory underlying all justification defenses allows a person to violate a criminal law prohibition if, by doing so, the person avoids a greater harm, tangible or intangible. We allow police officers to use force, which would normally constitute criminal assault, to effect an arrest. The law justifies such force because using it allows capture of the suspect at hand and, more generally, allows effective operation of the criminal justice system. Similarly, we allow a person to kill another in self-defense because it saves the intended victim's life and, more generally, discourages unjustified aggression. This general theory of justification is made explicit in the general justification of "lesser evils" (or "necessity"), which authorizes criminal conduct not already covered by another, more specific justification defense if it avoids a greater harm. It is the general justification defense of lesser evils that Green may attempt to claim as a defense to the escape charge.

Justification defenses applicable here have two central requirements. First, the conduct must be *necessary* to avoid an unjustified threat of harm. Thus, if one can successfully avoid the threat by using nondeadly force, then deadly force is not justified. If one can avoid the threat in complete safety by simply walking away, then one has no right to kill another in self-defense—the so-called "retreat exception" to the authorization of deadly force in self-defense.

The second requirement of justification defenses is that the violation must cause less harm than it avoids, the so-called *proportionality* requirement. Typically, the relative balance of the conflicting harms is clear. One cannot lawfully shoot someone to prevent the person from stepping on one's toe. Where the balance of harms is not clear, it is the view of society that controls, frequently expressed in legislative action, not the personal opinion of the violator. One cannot use a lesser evils defense to interfere with a nuclear power plant or the armed forces draft system, for example, as some have tried to do, if the legislature has approved the criticized activity, thereby striking the balance of interests in favor of the activity. In the absence of such a legislative predetermination, it is for the judge or jury to balance the harm avoided against the harm caused.

In the *Green* case, the use of force against the attackers is not much of an option for Green, who is smaller, younger, and outnumbered. Green's resistance would have resulted only in greater injury to himself, as his attackers warned him. Instead of using force, Green avoids the threatened rape by escaping, which seems like a less serious harm than the threatened gang rape, thereby satisfying the *proportionality* requirement. And the escape does seem to have been *necessary*, in that Green had no other, less harmful means to protect himself. At first glance, then, Green would seem to satisfy the general requirements of a "lesser evils" justification defense.

The Trial and Sentence

On November 22, 1967, an information is filed in the circuit court of Randolph County charging John Charles Green with felonious escape. Joan Krauskopf from the ACLU represents Green. The state brings in a well-known Kansas City attorney as a special prosecutor. Trial begins in the circuit court on April 21, 1969. Both sides agree to trial by judge, without a jury.

Green claims that his escape was justifiable because of the unconstitutional conditions of his confinement and because of the necessity to avoid death or severe physical harm. The court concludes that "unwholesome" conditions, even though shocking, are no justification for escape and thus such evidence cannot be introduced at trial.

On April 23, 1969, the circuit court of Randolph County convicts Green of felonious escape. He is sentenced to three years in the state penitentiary.

The Defense's Problems

Two complications seem to stand in the way of Green getting a justification defense. First, the formulation of justification defenses at common law traditionally required that the threat be "imminent." If a person threatens to go home, get his gun, return, and shoot you, you generally are not permitted to use force against him at the moment of his verbal threat. If he in fact returns with his gun, he then presents an imminent threat and you can use force to defend.

The "imminent threat" requirement presents a problem for Green because he escaped before the attackers actually showed up to rape him. His reason for not waiting, of course, was that if he did wait, it would be too late to avoid his attackers. His only chance of protecting himself was to act before it was too late, to act before the threat of rape was imminent.

A second complication for Green is that the danger of same-sex rape in prison is well known. David Blackwell, the former head of Missouri's corrections system and later St. Louis County sheriff, says that rape is "not condoned as part of the punishment of an inmate, but it's a byproduct of incarceration." (At the time of Green's trial, which attracts some publicity, prison officials begin installing bolts on the *inside* of the cell doors.) The well-known nature of the problem means that, presumably, the legislature knew of the danger of rape in prison when it defined the offense of escape. As noted above, a lesser evils defense must look to the legislature's balancing of the competing harms, not the individual offender's. By not creating an exception for threatened rape in its escape prohibition, the legislature might be taken as expressing a view that the threatened harm of rape is not sufficiently great to justify the offense of escape. Better to suffer the rape than to permit escape.

The unfortunate frequency with which prison rape occurs also adds to the practical complications for authorities in allowing escape. Studies estimate that 290,000 men are raped by other men in prison each year. (This is almost twice the number of women in the country raped each year.) And many experts argue that the statistics are conservative because few men in prison are willing to report being sexually victimized. Studies have estimated that 10 percent of all prisoners are sexually assaulted; some estimates are higher. (Green is typical of the prisoner most likely to be raped: small, young, and white.) Thus, to allow escape upon a threat of rape would be to authorize escape on a frequent basis, which no doubt would play havoc with prison security.

On Appeal

On appeal to the Missouri Supreme Court, Green argues that the conditions of his imprisonment gave rise to a "defense of necessity," which he should have been allowed to present to a jury. Escape was the only means he had of protecting himself; the prison administration had already demonstrated its inability or unwillingness to protect him. To deny him such a defense would, among other things, be a violation of due process and would subject him to cruel and unusual punishment.

The majority opinion of the court, written by Justice Fred L. Henley, rejects these arguments. The court holds that Green had no right to a necessity defense. He could have avoided the threatened assault by reporting the inmates' names to authorities, who then could have brought disciplinary action or criminal prosecution. Further, Green did not escape while being pursued by the attackers; thus the threatened harm was not "imminent."

Justice Robert E. Seiler dissents. He concludes that Green lacked options other than escape and was "confronted with a horrific dilemma, not of his making." Seiler notes that if Green had waited until he was being pursued, it would have been nearly impossible for him to escape the attack. Further, Green couldn't protect himself by reporting to authorities the names of the inmates because he would have been killed or injured in retaliation. In any case, he could not protect himself from the latest threat because the mechanism for this, a "snitch-kite," would take several days to reach authorities. If he told a guard of the planned attack, the physical structure of Moberly insured that others would hear and brand him a "snitch," and he would be "good as dead right then." Given the particular facts of the case, Judge Seiler concludes that Green should have been permitted to submit a necessity defense to the jury.

On September 13, 1971, the Supreme Court of Missouri affirms the decision of the circuit court of Randolph County in an eight to one decision. The supreme court orders Green to be immediately delivered to the Department of Corrections in Jefferson City, Missouri, to serve his three-year sentence for felony escape. A petition to the U.S. Supreme Court is denied on April 17, 1972.

That same year, a lawsuit is filed by a group of sixty-two Moberly inmates, claiming that, "If [a prisoner is] timid appearing or youthful, he is immediately surrounded . . . , assaulted, raped and robbed of his personal belongings." They also claim that prison guards do nothing to prevent the attacks.

People's Intuitions of Justice

This is how the people in our survey sentenced Green:

no liability	27%	1 year	9%
liability but		3 years	4%
no punishment	38%	7 years	2%
1 day	3%	15 years	—
2 weeks	7%	30 years	—
2 months	1%	life imprisonment	—
6 months	10%	death	—

Mean = 6.2 days.

Nearly three-quarters of the people imposed no more than essentially symbolic punishment (of two weeks or less) for what is a serious felony. There appears to be a shared intuition among most of the group that Green's situation justified his escape.

The Green Case under the Criminal Law of Other States

The Model Penal Code, promulgated by the American Law Institute (the closest thing to a U.S. "national academy" for law), reformulates justification defenses by dropping an "imminent threat" require-ment in favor of a requirement that *the response* to the threat *be immedi-ately necessary*. The advantage of this modern formulation is that it con-tinues to require a person to delay using force where appropriate—you still cannot shoot the person who threatens to go home and get his gun, until he returns—but it allows a person to act before it is too late. Green, for example, must delay breaking any law as long as possible—he can act only when it is "necessary" to do so—but when that time comes, he can act even if the threat is not imminent. The point of the Model Penal Code's useful reformulation is that it is the timing of the *response* that is most important—it must be "necessary"—not the timing of the *threat*.

Many jurisdictions have followed the lead of the Model Penal Code on this issue, but many others have not. Those that continue to follow the old "imminent threat" requirement will continue to deny a defense in cases like Green's.

Recall that Green had a second problem, beyond the "imminent threat" requirement: the apparent legislative predetermination that known prison conditions, such as rape, could not be grounds for a lesser evils (necessity) defense to escape. The general rule is a good one: the balance of interests in a lesser evils defense must be that of the soci-ety, as expressed by the legislature, not that of the individual violator. To provide otherwise would allow a person to break the law whenever it conflicts with an interest the individual thinks more important.

But application of this rule to cases like Green's seems misguided. First, can it really be true that the Missouri legislature believes that the harm caused by escape is greater than the harm of a gang rape? What seems more likely is that the legislature never thought about this issue, even when it drafted the escape offense. Or, if legislators did think about the issue, they assumed it would be settled by administrative ac-tion to give better protection from rape (or perhaps by a general lesser evils justification defense for those inmates still left unprotected).

But even if it were reasonable to speculate that the legislature thought about the issue and determined that escape should not be tol-erated and that prison officials simply should work to reduce the inci-dence of rape, that does not end the inquiry. Whatever the expectation of the legislature, the facts are clear that Green, for one, was being raped and nothing was being done to prevent future attacks. It would be only a barbaric society that would tolerate such victimization on the grounds of administrative convenience. The prison officials took complete control of Green's life, including his means of protecting himself. If they then failed to give him adequate protection, how can he be denied the right to take on the task himself, as best he can?

A system that allowed such rapes to continue and simultaneously denied the victim a legal right to protect himself would make it difficult to distinguish the criminal justice system from the criminals. Such a system would demean us all and would trash the law's claim to moral authority. Before we allow such a result, it seems wise, at the very least, that the law not speculate about legislative intention. When denying a defense to someone like Green would be so patently unfair and the consequences so appalling, the law ought to require the legislature at least to be very clear in its statement of the balancing of harms. If the legislators are anything like the people in our survey, they will enthusiastically confirm that an escape like Green's avoids a greater harm and that such a person ought to have a defense. (And if they fail to come to this conclusion, their view may well raise constitutional issues.)

Some jurisdictions do not recognize any lesser evils defense, such as Arizona and Kansas (and others have technically recognized a lesser evils defense but never granted it, as in Ohio, Rhode Island, and New Mexico).

Other jurisdictions recognize such a defense in the occasional case but have failed to codify the court-made defense: California, Connecticut, Florida, Indiana, Iowa, Maryland, Massachusetts, Minnesota, Mississippi, Montana, Nevada, North Carolina, South Carolina, South Dakota, Tennessee, Utah, Vermont, Virginia, and Washington. This failure to codify leaves the defense's requirements less clear and subject to ex post change by the courts. Further, nearly all court-made formulations of the defense follow the traditional common law rule, requiring an "imminent threat," which, recall, is problematic.

The Final Outcome

From the Randolph County Jail, where he was transferred for his trial for escape, Green writes to *Playboy* magazine, which is in the midst of a prison reform campaign. In his letter, entitled "The Sodomy Factories," published in the September 1969 issue, he tells of his repeated rapes and the prison officials' lack of response.

A year later, on September 24, 1970, Governor Warren E. Hearnes commutes Green's sentence for escape. He is released on October 9,

1970, having served one year and twenty-nine days of the three-year sentence for escape. He heads for Chicago, where he has been offered a job as an apprentice printer for *Playboy* magazine.

A year after the Missouri Supreme Court denies Green's appeal, a proposed new Missouri criminal code includes a codified lesser-evils justification defense based in large part on the Model Penal Code. The revised code is passed in 1977 and becomes effective on January 1, 1979. The defense formulation does not follow the Model Penal Code suggestion that the "imminent threat" requirement be dropped. But the code's official commentary suggests that the "imminent threat" requirement be interpreted broadly to depend not only on the interval of time before the threatened injury but also on the "circumstance of the particular fact situation." While this seems an awkward and unreliable alternative to the Model Penal Code formulation, Green might well have been able to get a defense under current Missouri law.

KILLING FOR APPLES

It is early November 1918. Conditions in Germany are difficult because of the past four years of World War I. Due to the emphasis on industrial war production, ill-advised agricultural policies, and the Allied embargo, food shortages and rising prices have been a continuing problem. Morale is low. Malnourishment is common. The shortages and price rises prompt protests and strikes, and occasionally even riots. A revolution starts with a mutiny at the naval base at Kiel on November 3 and spreads to the civilian populace, culminating in the abdication of the kaiser on November 10, 1918. The next day, World War I comes to an end as Germany surrenders.

While 1919 brings peace, it does not bring stability. In January 1919 food prices are 2.6 times higher than they were in 1913, before the war. The country endures the failed Spartacist Revolt in January, in which left-wing socialists, mostly workers and former soldiers, try to take over Berlin but are crushed by volunteer units loyal to the social democratic government. In April local communists attempt to create a republic in Munich, but this also ultimately fails. The food shortages, price rises, and the accompanying protests continue. By December 1919, food prices are 4.5 times higher than in 1913.

Soldiers and civilians crowd around two moving vans thrown across a Berlin street as a barricade against the movement of Spartacist forces. (Archive Photos)

Looting of shops in one of the poorer sections of Berlin. For several days the German capital was at the mercy of plundering mobs. Circa 1923. (Archive Photos)

Divisions between the urban and rural regions have existed for some time and are exacerbated by the food shortages. Urban residents resent that rural dwellers have more food. Farmers resent the government price controls, perceived as examples of governmental bias favoring urban interests. One writer describes the situation this way:

> Thefts of farmers' crops by a hungry urban population provide country dwellers with all the proof they need of the dangerous and depraved nature of the inhabitants of Germany's cities. Such thefts reach epidemic proportion in the aftermath of the War. An undernourished urban population, which has suffered for years from inadequate food-rations and extortionate black-market prices for food, make self-service expeditions into farmers' fields, as the ability of the police . . . to control lawbreaking plummets.*

This is the situation facing Johann Schlicht, the owner of a fruit orchard in Reindorf, of the Bavarian region. The police are wholly ineffective at stemming recurring thievery. Schlicht tries passive means of protecting his livelihood, such as fences around the orchard, but all measures prove ineffective. It becomes clear that the only effective means of protection will be the force of arms.

Neither the thieves nor Schlicht need the fruit to avoid starvation. The thieves want food without having to pay the normally inflated prices. Schlicht depends on the fruit to make a living and support his family.

Schlicht holds watch at night, sitting in a shed amidst his fruit trees. He is accompanied by his dog and armed with a loaded rifle. In the early morning, two men sneak into the orchard and begin stealing fruit from the trees. Schlicht shouts at them to drop the fruit and threatens to shoot. They nonetheless begin running away with the fruit. As the only means left to him to prevent the thievery, Schlicht fires buckshot in their direction and seriously injures one of them, who is lucky he is not killed.

Schlicht is charged with intentional assault. He notes that law enforcement authorities have proven completely ineffective at stemming

*Richard Bessel, *Germany after the First World War* (Oxford: Clarendon, 1993), 215.

the thefts and that his less harmful attempts at protecting his fruit have all failed. His injury of the thief was the only means available to him to protect his property.

Would you convict Schlicht for his assault of the thief? If so, what amount of punishment would you impose?

no liability	☐	1 year	☐
liability but		3 years	☐
no punishment	☐	7 years	☐
1 day	☐	15 years	☐
2 weeks	☐	30 years	☐
2 months	☐	life imprisonment	☐
6 months	☐	death	☐

The Law's Rule

As a society, we value the right to hold private property, as did German society in 1919. But we also value the lives of persons, even thieves. Thus, cases like this present a conflict in interests that the law must resolve.

Generally, American criminal law authorizes a person to use force that otherwise would be criminal if such force is *necessary* to protect against unjustified aggression, as discussed in the *Green* case. The effect of this "necessity" requirement is to allow use of some defensive force but to limit it to the minimum needed. Thus, the law lets neither interest be sacrificed if both interests can be preserved and some lesser interest sacrificed. If an owner can protect his fruit with a shout and the threat of a club, then he cannot legally use a gun. But the necessity requirement does not resolve Schlicht's dilemma. Less serious protective measures, short of a gunshot, have proven ineffective.

In addition to the necessity requirement, the law imposes a proportionality requirement, as noted in *Green*, which permits a person to cause only such harm as avoids a greater harm (in the broadest sense of "harm," tangible or intangible). The *Schlicht* case presents a difficult conflict of interests: should the law sacrifice the owner's right to hold personal property, or should it risk sacrificing a human life? Does the threat to the right to hold private property, a real problem in chaotic 1919 Germany, and the need to oppose unprovoked and unjustified aggression outweigh the harm of endangering a thief's life?

The Trial and Appeal

At trial, Schlicht claims a defense of necessary defensive force (called *Notwehr*). After reviewing the evidence, the trial court concludes that Schlicht used justifiable force to regain the fruit, that there was "no other means" than firing the shot that would stop the thieves and regain the property. Schlicht is acquitted.

Unlike their counterparts in the United States, German prosecutors can appeal an acquittal, and in this case they do so. On appeal, the prosecutors argue that the defendant used excessive defensive force because the fruit in question was not a sufficiently significant interest to allow him to endanger the lives and health of the fleeing persons. Thus, they claim, he sacrificed a greater interest to advance a lesser.

The German Supreme Court disagrees. "If the defendant fired the shot in order to protect his property and the fruit, and if the defendant had no other equally effective means to this end, then this is a case of permissible defense against an imminent attack against property and possession." A person in the right, the court concludes, need not give in to a person in the wrong. The lawful owner need not sacrifice his interests for those of the thief. The court dismisses the appeal, thereby affirming the defendant's acquittal.

One can see the logic and appeal of the court's conclusion: right ought to triumph over wrong. A lawbreaker ought not to expect the law's protection. Indeed, this was the theory of our own early practice of "outlawry": a person who broke the law put themselves outside the protection of the law, which meant that they were open prey for any who chose to attack them.

Further, to give a thief legal protection would empower thieves. By creating a situation in which the owner's only means of defense is deadly force, thieves could make an owner legally obliged to turn over his or her goods. Recognizing such "thieves' rights" might well encourage lawlessness.

But the fact is that most civilized societies now reject the German court's view, as current German law probably does. The generally accepted rule requires some degree of proportionality in the use of defensive force, specifically prohibiting the use of deadly force in defense of property. Under the current view, human beings have rights—and their lives have value—even if they have broken the law's rules. The law authorizes the killing of an aggressor if necessary to save the life of an innocent victim, but not to save property.

People's Intuitions of Justice

As one might expect, the conflicting principles—"Right ought not to triumph over wrong" and "All human life, even that of a lawbreaker, is of value and merits protection"—produce some disagreement in how the *Schlicht* case should be resolved. This is how the people in our survey sentenced Schlicht:

no liability	29%	1 year	6%
liability but		3 years	6%
no punishment	16%	7 years	1%
1 day	3%	15 years	—
2 weeks	8%	30 years	—
2 months	15%	life imprisonment	—
6 months	16%	death	—

Mean = 2.6 weeks.

Twenty-nine percent of our survey people agree with the old German view, in support of no criminal liability. But the remainder thought that some criminal liability and punishment were due. Of those who impose liability, most impose little or no punishment, suggesting that Schlicht's violation of the proportionality requirement is to them either blameless or excusable. Only 29 percent imposed a sentence of six months or more for a serious assault that risked death. In the next chapter we will see that people typically take this kind of gentle view of those who make mistakes in defending against unjustified aggression, as when a battered wife kills her sleeping husband. The law sometimes takes this view as well.

Another Look at Ignorance of the Law

Before leaving the *Schlicht* case, however, consider another important issue it raises, a matter on which current law does not appear so thoughtful. Recall the concern of the "legality principle," expressed in the cases of the previous chapter, that the criminal law give fair notice of what it commands of people. In the context of justification defenses, the law's approach is problematic. The law's rules of conduct for justification defenses do not announce the general requirements of necessity and proportionality, as one might expect. Instead, they enforce a hoard of special rules.

Assume you are an apple orchard owner. You are told that two men are stealing apples from your orchard, not far from your house. You recently heard of a neighboring farmer being held criminally liable for using deadly force to protect his fruit, so your plan is only to confront the thieves and scare them away, intending to use nondeadly force if necessary. But when you appear, the thieves are not cowed by your threats. (They too have heard of the neighboring farmer's liability for using deadly force.) When you start to use nondeadly force by throwing rocks at them, they come after you. You retreat to your barn, where you have a pitchfork and other deadly implements. What force can you use against them?

We know from the previous chapter that every person is presumed to know the law, but we also know that this is an unreasonable presumption. So assume here what the law seems to assume in every case, that you just happen to have a criminal code in the barn waiting for your ready reference.

You check the table of contents and determine the governing sections. Typical American criminal code provisions relevant to the situation are reproduced below. What force can you lawfully use against the attacking thieves? Can you fight them? Need you retreat from the orchard altogether and leave them to take your apples? If you can use force against them, can you use deadly force? The thieves are banging on the door. Here is what the criminal code tells you:

AMERICAN LAW INSTITUTE'S MODEL PENAL CODE

§ 3.06—Use of Force for the Protection of Property

(1) Use of Force Justifiable for Protection of Property. Subject to the provisions of this Section and of Section 3.09, the use of force upon or toward the person of another is justifiable when the actor believes that such force is immediately necessary:

    (a) to prevent or terminate an unlawful entry or other trespass upon land or a trespass against or the unlawful carrying away of tangible, movable property, provided that such land or movable property is, or is believed by the actor to be, in his possession or in the possession of another person for whose protection he acts; or

    (b) to effect an entry or re-entry upon land or to retake tangible movable property, provided that the actor believes that he or the person by whose authority he acts or a person from whom he or such other person derives title was unlawfully dispossessed of such land or movable property and is entitled to possession, and provided, further, that:

        (i) the force is used immediately or on fresh pursuit after such dispossession; or

        (ii) the actor believes that the person against whom he uses force has no claim of right to the possession of the property and, in the case of land, the circumstances, as the actor believes them to be, are of such urgency that it would be an exceptional hardship to postpone the entry or re-entry until a court order is obtained.

(2) Meaning of Possession. For the purposes of Subsection (1) of this Section:

    (a) a person who has parted with the custody of property to another who refuses to restore it to him is no longer in possession, unless the property is movable and was and still is located on land in his possession;

    (b) a person who has been dispossessed of land does not regain possession thereof merely by setting foot thereon;

(c) a person who has a license to use or occupy real property is deemed to be in possession thereof except against the licensor acting under claim of right.

(3) Limitations on Justifiable Use of Force.

(a) Request to Desist. The use of force is justifiable under this Section only if the actor first requests the person against whom such force is used to desist from his interference with the property, unless the actor believes that:

   (i) such request would be useless; or

   (ii) it would be dangerous to himself or another person to make the request; or

   (iii) substantial harm will be done to the physical condition of the property which is sought to be protected before the request can effectively be made.

(b) Exclusion of Trespasser. The use of force to prevent or terminate a trespass is not justifiable under this Section if the actor knows that the exclusion of the trespasser will expose him to substantial danger of serious bodily harm.

(c) Resistance of Lawful Re-entry or Recaption. The use of force to prevent an entry or re-entry upon land or the recaption of movable property is not justifiable under this Section, although the actor believes that such re-entry or recaption is unlawful, if:

   (i) the re-entry or recaption is made by or on behalf of a person who was actually dispossessed of the property; and

   (ii) it is otherwise justifiable under paragraph (1)(b) of this Section.

(d) Use of Deadly Force. The use of deadly force is not justifiable under this Section unless the actor believes that:

   (i) the person against whom the force is used is attempting to dispossess him of his dwelling otherwise than under a claim of right to its possession; or

   (ii) the person against whom the force is used is attempting to commit or consummate arson, burglary, robbery or other felonious theft or property destruction and either:

      (1) has employed or threatened deadly force against or in the presence of the actor; or

      (2) the use of force other than deadly force to prevent the commission or the consummation of the crime would expose the actor or another in his presence to substantial danger of serious bodily harm.

(4) Use of Confinement as Protective Force. The justification afforded by this Section extends to the use of confinement as protective force only if the actor takes all reasonable measures to terminate the confinement as soon as he knows that he can do so with safety to the property, unless the person confined has been arrested on a charge of crime.

(5) Use of Device to Protect Property. The justification afforded by this Section extends to the use of a device for the purpose of protecting property only if:

    (a) the device is not designed to cause or known to create a substantial risk of causing death or serious bodily harm; and

    (b) the use of the particular device to protect the property from entry or trespass is reasonable under the circumstances, as the actor believes them to be; and

    (c) the device is one customarily used for such a purpose or reasonable care is taken to make known to probable intruders the fact that it is used.

(6) Use of Force to Pass Wrongful Obstructor. The use of force to pass a person whom the actor believes to be purposely or knowingly and unjustifiably obstructing the actor from going to a place to which he may lawfully go is justifiable, provided that:

    (a) the actor believes that the person against whom he uses force has no claim of right to obstruct the actor; and

    (b) the actor is not being obstructed from entry or movement on land which he knows to be in the possession or custody of the person obstructing him, or in the possession or custody of another person by whose authority the obstructor acts, unless the circumstances, as the actor believes them to be, are of such urgency that it would not be reasonable to postpone the entry or movement on such land until a court order is obtained; and

    (c) the force used is not greater than would be justifiable if the person obstructing the actor were using force against him to prevent his passage.

The thieves have broken in the door, but you realize that there are other relevant code provisions to be consulted. You retreat to the hayloft for further study:

§ 3.04—Use of Force in Self-Protection

(1) Use of Force Justifiable for Protection of the Person. Subject to the provisions of this Section and of Section 3.09, the use of force upon or toward another person is justifiable when the actor believes that such force is immediately necessary for the purpose of protecting himself against the use of unlawful force by such other person on the present occasion.

(2) Limitations on Justifying Necessity for Use of Force.

    (a) The use of force is not justifiable under this Section:

        (i) to resist an arrest which the actor knows is being made by a peace officer, although the arrest is unlawful; or

        (ii) to resist force used by the occupier or possessor of property or by another person on his behalf, where the actor knows that the person using the force is doing so under a claim of right to protect the property, except that this limitation shall not apply if:

            (1) the actor is a public officer acting in the performance of his duties or a person lawfully assisting him therein or a person making or assisting in a lawful arrest; or

            (2) the actor has been unlawfully dispossessed of the property and is making a re-entry or recaption justified by Section 3.06; or

            (3) the actor believes that such force is necessary to protect himself against death or serious bodily harm.

    (b) The use of deadly force is not justifiable under this Section unless the actor believes that such force is necessary to protect himself against death, serious bodily harm, kidnapping or sexual intercourse compelled by force or threat; nor is it justifiable if:

        (i) the actor, with the purpose of causing death or serious bodily harm, provoked the use of force against himself in the same encounter; or

(ii) the actor knows that he can avoid the necessity of using such force with complete safety by retreating or by surrendering possession of a thing to a person asserting a claim of right thereto or by complying with a demand that he abstain from any action which he has no duty to take, except that:

(1) the actor is not obliged to retreat from his dwelling or place of work, unless he was the initial aggressor or is assailed in his place of work by another person whose place of work the actor knows it to be; and

(2) a public officer justified in using force in the performance of his duties or a person justified in using force in his assistance or a person justified in using force in making an arrest or preventing an escape is not obliged to desist from efforts to perform such duty, effect such arrest or prevent such escape because of resistance or threatened resistance by or on behalf of the person against whom such action is directed.

(c) Except as required by paragraphs (a) and (b) of this Subsection, a person employing protective force may estimate the necessity thereof under the circumstances as he believes them to be when the force is used, without retreating, surrendering possession, doing any other act which he has no legal duty to do or abstaining from any lawful action.

(3) Use of Confinement as Protective Force. The justification afforded by this Section extends to the use of confinement as protective force only if the actor takes all reasonable measures to terminate the confinement as soon as he knows that he safely can, unless the person confined has been arrested on a charge of crime.

The thieves are coming up the ladder to where you are hiding in the hayloft, but you are unsure of the application of the provisions you have read. Of particular importance, you realize, are the following statutory definitions:

§ 3.11—Definitions

In this Article, unless a different meaning plainly is required:

(1) "unlawful force" means force, including confinement, which is employed without the consent of the person against whom it is directed and the employment of which constitutes an offense or actionable tort or would constitute such offense or tort except for a defense (such as the absence of intent, negligence, or mental capacity; duress; youth; or diplomatic status) not amounting to a privilege to use the force. Assent constitutes consent, within the meaning of this Section, whether or not it otherwise is legally effective, except assent to the infliction of death or serious bodily harm.

(2) "deadly force" means force which the actor uses with the purpose of causing or which he knows to create a substantial risk of causing death or serious bodily harm. Purposely firing a firearm in the direction of another person or at a vehicle in which another person is believed to be constitutes deadly force. A threat to cause death or serious bodily harm, by the production of a weapon or otherwise, so long as the actor's purpose is limited to creating an apprehension that he will use deadly force if necessary, does not constitute deadly force;

(3) "dwelling" means any building or structure, though movable or temporary, or a portion thereof, which is for the time being the actor's home or place of lodging.

Don't lose your place as your head bounces off each ladder rung as the thieves drag you down from the loft.

(By the way, the applicable rules are that, first, the farmer can defend against unlawful force. The thieves' attack is unlawful. Second, he cannot use force that risks death in defense of property but he can use it to defend himself against serious bodily harm. The thieves may well be threatening serious bodily harm. Finally, on these facts, the farmer need not retreat before using deadly force.)

■

Is the law being silly? Other than the dozen criminal law professors over age fifty who have taught these code sections enough times to actually know them from memory (not me), to whom is it the code drafters are speaking when they set out these rules of conduct? Of course people can't apply these rules in the situations in which they are applicable, yet the law expects people to do so and holds them criminally liable if they don't.

Committing an offense is sometimes doing the right thing. The law has done well in this difficult area by devising the necessity and proportionality requirements to balance the interests in conflict. Yet the law fails to take advantage of the simplicity of these concepts when it drafts wildly detailed provisions that few if any people could hope to follow in the intense situations in which the provisions commonly apply.

THE RIGHT DEED FOR THE WRONG REASON

Motti Ashkenazi, a thin thirty-year-old man from a poor, crime-ridden South Tel Aviv neighborhood, is strolling along a crowded Tel Aviv beach on a hot Friday afternoon in June 1997. A drug addict and petty thief who was just released from detention after bungling a car burglary, Ashkenazi has been thinking for a while about getting off drugs and putting his life together. But the going has been tough, even with the support of his family.

As he walks, he sees that someone has left a black backpack unattended by the sidewalk. Ashkenazi watches the bag for some time. When no one is watching, he picks up the backpack and quickly leaves, pleased by his good fortune. Without opening the backpack, he walks down nearby Geula Street to a rundown apartment building and slips inside. There in the stairwell, he unzips the backpack to inspect his loot. What he finds is a clock with wires connected to a cookie tin, with loose nails surrounding the contraption. Ashkenazi quickly realizes he has just stolen a terrorist's bomb.

Panicked but in control, he runs to the nearby Savoy Hotel and tells the reception desk clerk what he found. The clerk calls the police. The bomb squad arrives in minutes and starts trying to deactivate the bomb, now on the stairs at the entrance to the building. Meanwhile, Ashkenazi stands outside the building, keeping the street clear of passersby, and

Ashkenazi pointing to the spot where the knapsack was found. (Woltson/Maariv)

warns a group of children to stay away. Police halt traffic in the area and evacuate residents from the neighboring buildings. The bomb squad finds that the bomb is packed with nearly three kilograms of explosives. After an hour's work, they use a robot to shoot the backpack in a way that neutralizes the bomb.

Police officers search the nearby crowded beach for more bombs but find none. Considering the amount of explosives and the number of people in the area where the bomb was planted, police estimate that the bomb would have killed many in a major terrorist attack.

During the police activity, Ashkenazi slips away. But because he is well known to the police, detectives easily track him down for questioning. At first, Ashkenazi lies to police and tells them he found the backpack in the apartment building stairwell where he had gone to urinate, but later confesses to having stolen the backpack from the beach.

Would you convict Ashkenazi for his theft of the backpack? If so, what amount of punishment would you impose?

no liability	☐	1 year	☐
liability but		3 years	☐
no punishment	☐	7 years	☐
1 day	☐	15 years	☐
2 weeks	☐	30 years	☐
2 months	☐	life imprisonment	☐
6 months	☐	death	☐

Disagreement in the Law

Ashkenazi's mistake is the opposite of Schlicht's, the owner of the fruit orchard: Schlicht thought his conduct was objectively justified, when in fact it was not. Ashkenazi thinks his conduct is not objectively justified, when in fact it is.

Cases like Ashkenazi—the unknowingly justified person—reveal a fundamental dispute about justification defenses. Why is a justification

Police disarm the terrorist bomb Ashkenazi brought from the crowded beach. (Moti Kimchi/Ha-aretz Daily)

defense given? Is it because the person's conduct in fact avoids a greater harm, and the law is happy to have it done in a similar situation in the future? Or is a justification defense given because the person has the right motivation—because he reasonably *believes* that his conduct is justified? The question is, in other words, is a justification defense given because the person performed the right *deed*, or because the person acted for the right *reason*?

Legal scholars disagree, but in many situations this theoretical disagreement has little practical effect. Commonly, a person believes his conduct avoids a greater harm and in fact it does. And where a person mistakenly believes he is justified, as in *Schlicht*, the person is likely to get a defense (of some sort) under either approach. Under the "reasons" approach, he would get a justification defense because he reasonably *believes* he is justified. Under the "deeds" approach, the person may not get a justification defense, but nonetheless may get an excuse defense— he is blameless and ought not to be liable because the reasonable person would have made the same mistake. (Justification defenses claim the conduct was right; excuse defenses admit the conduct was wrong but claim that the person is blameless for performing it. The next chapter examines excuse defenses.) But whether the defense is given a justification defense (under the "reasons" approach) or an excuse defense (under the "deeds" approach), the end result is the same: little or no liability.

But the case of the unknowingly justified person, as in *Ashkenazi*, presents a situation in which the two approaches to justification defenses give very different results. The "reasons" approach would deny a justification defense because Ashkenazi does not believe his conduct is justified—he is unaware he is saving lives when he steals the backpack. The unknowingly justified person has no defense and is fully liable.

The "deeds" approach, in contrast, would give a justification defense. Stealing the backpack is a lesser harm than causing the many deaths that otherwise would have resulted. Ashkenazi might have some, reduced liability under the "deeds" approach, for *attempting* to steal the backpack unjustifiably. An attempt to commit an offense, as we know from chapter 1, typically is punished at a lower level than a successful offense. But while Ashkenazi's bad intention deserves punishment—which is what attempt liability punishes—his conduct itself is justified and ought not to be grounds for liability, so says the "deeds" approach.

This, then, is the practical difference between the two approaches. Which is right? Should Ashkenazi be punished as any other thief, with no defense or mitigation for having unknowingly saved lives (the "reasons" view)? Or should he have a justification defense for his theft, and liability limited to that for an attempt, if any at all (the "deeds" view)?

People's Intuitions of Justice

Here is how the people in our survey sentenced Ashkenazi:

no liability	23%	1 year	—
liability but		3 years	—
no punishment	47%	7 years	—
1 day	6%	15 years	—
2 weeks	14%	30 years	—
2 months	7%	life imprisonment	—
6 months	2%	death	—

Mean = two-thirds of a day.

More than two-thirds of the people impose no punishment whatever. Only 9 percent impose punishment of more than two weeks. Theft is not a terribly serious offense, but, especially given Ashkenazi's prior criminal record for such thefts, it seems likely that his current theft offense would garner more than two weeks imprisonment, unless our subjects are taking account of the lives he saved.

Our subjects, then, seem to take a "deeds" view of justification, which avoids or mitigates liability and punishment if the conduct avoids a greater harm, even unknowingly. This conclusion is supported by other empirical studies of lay intuitions on the issue.

The Outcome

Ashkenazi sees the incident as a turning point in his life and says he hopes his effort repays his country for his past misdeeds. "All I want to do is try to rehabilitate myself," he says. "I have never

Ashkenazi being kissed by his mother for saving lives. (Avigail Uzi/*Yedioth Ahronoth*)

served my country so maybe now I have repaid my debt to society by saving lives." He believes God saved him from the bomb exploding because he prays. He also thinks that, had he not been on drugs at the time, he probably would have just run away when he discovered the bomb.

The police decide not to charge Ashkenazi with the theft and, in addition, allow him a generous plea bargain in another case pending against him. Some people see Ashkenazi as a hero. But he also becomes a bit of a comic hero, lampooned on a late night Tel Aviv talk show for his "good deed." The talk show host imagines a drugged-out Ashkenazi invited to meet with the president and being reimbursed for the income he lost when the backpack did not contain the valuables he thought it did.

A Terrorist's Right to Resist the Thief?

Ashkenazi's generous plea bargain and hero status may be a bit over the top, but the decision not to prosecute Ashkenazi for the backpack theft is well grounded in current Israeli law, which follows the "deeds" approach in its formulation of justification defenses. Conduct is justified if it in fact avoids a greater harm. (However, Ashkenazi could have been prosecuted for attempted theft under Israeli law and, in that respect, the decision to bring no charges to trial is more generous than the law itself provides.) Israeli law, then, is consistent with the lay intuitions of the people in our survey.

American law is not. Most U.S. jurisdictions follow the "reasons" approach in formulating their justification defenses: they give a justification defense if and only if the person "reasonably *believes*" the justifying circumstances exist. Thus, Ashkenazi would get no defense, and would be liable for the full offense with no weight given to the lives he saved. (An American prosecutor might choose not to prosecute for theft—thereby reaching the better result—but such dependence on prosecutorial discretion is an unreliable solution and can create its own problems of lawlessness, as discussed in connection with the *Ruschioni* case.)

Beyond its conflict with lay intuitions of the principles of justice, the "reasons" approach of American law is problematic for another reason. Recall from the earlier discussions in this chapter that a person has a right in law to defend against "unjustified" aggression. Thus, a person has no right of self-defense against the force used to make a lawful arrest, and no right of defense of property against a lawful repossession. This is the rule that was central to the answer to your question as you cowered in the barn, at the end of the previous case. You can use deadly force to defend against the *unjustified* attack of the thieves. (You cannot use deadly force to defend property, but your nondeadly rock throwing is justified). Thus, they cannot lawfully resist your justified stone-throwing. Thus, their chasing you into the barn is *unjustified*, which then creates in you a right to use defensive force against them to protect yourself. And since they now threaten you with serious harm, not just your property, you can use deadly defensive force.

In other words, the right of self-defense can shift during an encounter. To act *unjustifiably* is to lose that right to the other person, who then gains a right to defend against the unjustified force.

It is this dynamic in the defenses of justification that illustrates the problem with the "reasons" formulation of justification defenses prevalent in the United States. By denying a justification defense to people like Ashkenazi—because he does not "believe" his conduct is justified—American law puts him in a disfavored status that allows others to lawfully resist him. By classing Ashkenazi's theft as "unjustified," American law allows the terrorist who planted the bomb, for example, to forcefully prevent Ashkenazi from taking away the backpack!

Thankfully, such situations do not commonly arise, but cases like *Ashkenazi* reveal a flaw in the American formulation of justification defenses that ought to be fixed before it does matter. Preferable is a "deeds" formulation of justification defenses, as used in Israeli law or that of a handful of states.

The more important point illustrated by cases like *Ashkenazi* is that criminal law ought to, but frequently does not, correspond to the principles of justice reflected in the shared intuitions of the community. The criminal law presents itself as trying to do justice, and it gains the support of the community, and sometimes acquiescence of criminals, because of this reputation. But each time it adopts a rule that conflicts with community views of justice, it incrementally undercuts its moral credibility. If it is to maintain its moral authority, and all of the practical benefits that flow from that, it must avoid conflicts with community intuitions of justice whenever possible.

Today

After the bomb furor dies down, the police send Ashkenazi to a drug rehabilitation center, Gesher Ha-Ziv. He has been an addict for fifteen years, has tried rehabilitation centers many times, but has never succeeded. "But this time I decided to suffer in order to stop suffering," he later explained. He is at the rehabilitation center for a year.

After his release, he does not go back to his prior life. Friends from his drug past soon begin coming to him for advice on getting off drugs. He admits, however, that he is still a beginner at his new path in life.

Ashkenazi does house painting and renovation. His former celebrity status helps get some jobs, but many people are unwilling to hire him because they know he was an addict. When his landlord finds out, she changes the locks on her apartment. "It is very hard and humiliating, but . . . if I had gone back [to my old life], I only would have punished myself. I have a once-in-a-lifetime chance, and I don't want to blow it. I wouldn't get another chance like this."

A year after his release, Ashkenazi is still drug free.

4

Can Doing the Wrong Thing
Ever Be Blameless?

SOMETIMES PEOPLE DO things that are clearly wrong—both prohibited and unjustified—but something about them or their situation
makes it difficult to blame them. We would have preferred that they not
have done what they did, and we hope others will not do such a thing
in similar situations, but justice is served by forgoing punishment of
this particular offender on this particular occasion. The job of defining
when a defense will be given in such cases is performed by what the law
calls "offense culpability requirements" and "excuse defenses."

As will become apparent from the four cases that follow, it is a job
that presents the greatest problem now facing criminal law. Too lenient
a rule means blameworthy offenders will escape the punishment they
deserve. Too demanding a rule means blameless offenders are punished or offenders are punished more than they deserve. Both kinds of
errors are failures of justice. Both kinds of errors can undercut the criminal justice system's reputation for doing justice, a reputation that turns
out to have important practical benefits in fighting crime. Yet, as the following cases illustrate, both kinds of errors are common in current
American criminal law. But the cases also suggest that in many respects
the criminal law has made great progress in the past four decades in
cracking this troublesome puzzle.

LOVING, KILLING PARENTS

Twenty-four-year-old Walter L. Williams left school after the sixth
grade. He works as an unskilled laborer and largely has stayed out of
trouble except for an arrest for public drunkenness. Bernice J. Williams
is four years younger and did not finish high school. By the time she
turns twenty she has two children, the younger a boy named William

Joseph Tabafunda. Both Walter and Bernice are well below normal in intelligence. They live in King County, Washington.

In June 1968 Bernice marries Walter, who assumes responsibility for Bernice's two children even though he is not their natural father. William has just had his first birthday. Both parents work during the day, so Walter's eighty-five-year-old mother cares for the children while the parents work.

On September 1, 1968, the parents realize William is sick. He is crying most of the time and will eat very little. When he does eat, he usually cannot keep the food down. His cheeks begin to swell. The swelling goes up and down but never disappears. The Williamses believe that the infant is teething or has a toothache. They give him aspirin but do not take him to the doctor.

Over the next few days William's condition visibly worsens. The couple notice that his cheek is fully swollen and has turned a red or purplish-red color. He also runs a high fever, much higher than the mild temperature associated with teething. Moreover, they notice a peculiar odor coming from his cheek and mouth. They discuss taking the boy to a doctor, but believe that doctors and dentists would not pull a tooth when the mouth is as swollen as it is. They decide not to seek help. Walter Williams has himself experienced bad toothaches and abscesses. He does not think the boy is in serious danger, even without medical treatment. The parents continue to give William aspirin.

Part of their hesitation to seek medical care stems from their fear that a doctor might see the swollen and discolored cheek and think that they are neglecting or abusing the child. They fear that Child Welfare might take away both their children. Both parents are Shoshoni. Government social workers actively intervene in many Native American families in the 1960s. More than a quarter of all Native American children are separated from their families and placed in non–Native American foster homes. Sometimes this results from social workers mistaking Native American culture, which may emphasize child care by members of the extended family, for neglect.

On September 12, 1968, William Tabafunda dies of pneumonia. An autopsy reveals that an abscessed tooth was allowed to develop into an infection of the mouth and cheeks, eventually becoming gangrenous. Because the child could not eat, he also became malnourished, weakening his resistance. These conditions produced severe pneumonia and ultimately his death.

CERTIFIED COPY OF DEATH CERTIFICATE

WASHINGTON STATE DEPARTMENT OF HEALTH — BUREAU OF VITAL STATISTICS
CERTIFICATE OF DEATH 7856

DECEASED — NAME: William Joseph Tabafunda
SEX: Male
DATE OF DEATH (MONTH, DAY, YEAR): September 12, 1968

RACE: Indian
AGE — LAST BIRTHDAY (YEARS): —
UNDER 1 YEAR (MOS., DAYS): —
DATE OF BIRTH (MONTH, DAY, YEAR): 4/31/1967
COUNTY OF DEATH: King

CITY, TOWN, OR LOCATION OF DEATH: Maury Island (Vashon)
INSIDE CITY LIMITS: No
HOSPITAL OR OTHER INSTITUTION — NAME: In cabin on Larson's Farm

STATE OF BIRTH: Wash.
CITIZEN OF WHAT COUNTRY: USA
MARRIED, NEVER MARRIED, WIDOWED, ENGAGED: —
SURVIVING SPOUSE: —

SOCIAL SECURITY NUMBER: None
USUAL OCCUPATION: Infant
KIND OF BUSINESS OR INDUSTRY:

RESIDENCE — STATE: Wash.
COUNTY: King
CITY, TOWN, OR LOCATION: Maury Island (Vashon)
INSIDE CITY LIMITS: No
STREET AND NUMBER: Cabin on Larson's Farm

FATHER — NAME: Tabafunda
MOTHER — MAIDEN NAME: Bernice Jean Tabafunda

INFORMANT — NAME: KING COUNTY CORONER CASE NO. 3491
MAILING ADDRESS: 100 Crockett Street, Seattle, Wash. 98103

PART I. DEATH WAS CAUSED BY:
(a) Bronchopneumonia
(b) Abscess of both cheeks with
(c) Dental caries and osteomyelitis of mandible — wks

PART II. OTHER SIGNIFICANT CONDITIONS:
DIED WITHOUT MEDICAL ATTENDANCE
AUTOPSY: yes
IF YES WERE FINDINGS CONSIDERED IN DETERMINING CAUSE OF DEATH: yes

CERTIFICATION — CORONER: a pp. 3:00 AM approx 10:00 AM 9/12/68 did 3:00 A.M.

CERTIFIER — NAME: G. E. Wilson, M.D.
DEGREE OR TITLE: M.D PATHOLOGIST
DATE SIGNED: 9/13/68

MAILING ADDRESS — CERTIFIER: 100 Crockett Street, Seattle, Wash. 98103

BURIAL, CREMATION, REMOVAL: burial
CEMETERY OR CREMATORY — NAME: Vashon Cemetery
LOCATION: Vashon, Washington
Sept. 14, 1968

FUNERAL HOME — NAME AND ADDRESS: Island Funeral Service P.O.Box 492 Vashon, Wash. 98070

REGISTRAR SIGNATURE: D.N. Litman M.D.
DATE RECEIVED BY LOCAL REGISTRAR: SEP 17 1968

AMENDED BY AFFIDAVIT
DATE 1-16-69
NO. 2a,b,c,d,e,f,g

DOH 01-003 (8/96)

Certified copy of William's death certificate.

134

CERTIFIED COPY

State of _Washington_

County of _King_ }ss.

AFFIDAVIT
FOR CORRECTION OF A RECORD

I hereby swear that the record of {birth death} number _7356_ for _William Joseph Tabafunda_

who {wasborn died} to _____ (Name of father) and _____ (Maiden name of mother)

in the city of _Maury Island_ county of _King_

on _September 12, 1968_ (Date) is incorrect or incomplete as follows:

The record now shows:	The true facts are:
20a, b, c, d, e, f & g. - Blank	20a. Homicide
	20b. ? 8-30-68 et seq
	20c. Unknown
	20d. Failure to render medical care.
	20e. No 20f. Home
	20g. Maury Island, Rural, King Co., Wn.

I further swear that I represent the {child deceased} as _Chief Pathologist_ (Parent, attorney, etc.)

and that I have the consent of all parties concerned in stating these true facts. I further declare that if the corrected certificate is questioned, I will assume the responsibility of furnishing proof of the corrected item to the questioning agency.

Signed _____ (Affiant)Gale E. Wilson, M.D.

Address _100 Crockett St., Seattle, Wn. 98109_
King Co. Courthouse, Unit #2

Subscribed and sworn to before me this _16th_ day of _January_ 19 _69_

S. F. No. 6064—OS—(Rev.)—7-61

Notary Public in and for the State of Washington,

Residing at _Seattle_

DOH 01-003 (8/96)

Correction of William's death certificate to show "homicide" conclusion.

Bernice and Walter are much saddened by the loss. Both felt a great deal of love and affection for the child.

Gale Wilson, the chief pathologist for King County, determines that the infection leading to death had been present for at least two weeks. If medical care had been obtained anytime before the final week, it would have saved the child's life. During the critical period when William's life could have been saved, the odor from the gangrene would have been strong, an unavoidable signal that the child suffered from more than a toothache and that medical attention was needed. The Williamses knew the boy was sick and that a doctor was available. They were financially and physically able to take the boy to the doctor and were aware of his symptoms. The symptoms were such that it would have been obvious to any reasonable parent that medical attention was needed.

On October 3, 1968, Bernice and Walter Williams are charged with manslaughter for negligently failing to supply seventeen-month-old William with necessary medical attention, for the lack of which he died. They plead not guilty and the case is tried without a jury on January 13, 1969.

Would you convict? If so, what amount of punishment would you impose?

no liability	☐	1 year	☐
liability but		3 years	☐
no punishment	☐	7 years	☐
1 day	☐	15 years	☐
2 weeks	☐	30 years	☐
2 months	☐	life imprisonment	☐
6 months	☐	death	☐

■

There is no question that Bernice and Walter Williams did not intend their child's death. On the contrary. They very much wanted their child to live and were genuinely concerned about his well-being. But that in itself does not resolve the issue of criminal liability. The law punishes both intentional killings, typically as murder, and unintentional but culpable killings, usually as manslaughter or negligent homicide. Unintentional but culpable killings, such as recklessly or negligently causing death, are condemnable and do deserve punishment. Should the Williamses be criminally liable for unintentionally causing their child's death by failing to get aid?

Not every sign of sickness in a child requires a doctor's visit. Proper parenting requires medical attention only for serious threats to health. What is serious and what is not often is a matter of judgment, not unlike the decisions a person makes in many other contexts of daily life, as in driving a car. All driving creates a risk of some degree to other persons and property. Only certain kinds of driving under certain conditions—such as driving forty-five miles an hour through a residential neighborhood with narrow streets—create an *unreasonable* risk of causing death. Was it an improper risk the Williamses created when they failed to seek medical aid?

Given the circumstances—their baby had been sick for a week with a temperature, swelling, discoloration, and a putrid smell, and he had not been eating—a parent should have sought medical aid. The Williamses were wrong not to do so. It seems clear they created an improper risk.

But neither does this resolve the issue of criminal liability. Doing something wrong, or wrongfully failing to do something one should, even if death results, does not in itself mean the person deserves criminal liability. A person may do the wrong thing, yet nonetheless be blameless for it. A father rushing his burned child to the hospital may be wrong to leave the stove burner on. Even if the burner starts a fire that burns down the apartment building, we may conclude that the father's mistake was blameless. Any one of us in his situation might have been similarly distracted. The criminal law ought to punish only culpable mistakes.

Should the Williamses be criminally liable for their mistake? Into which group do the Williamses fall: culpable or nonculpable risk takers?

At Trial

At trial the prosecution points out that, unlike murder or other crimes of intention, manslaughter in Washington state requires only a showing of negligence, unreasonable risk taking. Further, the required negligence "is a concept which deals, not with the defendant's state of mind, but with the objective circumstances of his situation." Thus, even if the parents were not subjectively aware of the unreasonable risk they were taking with their son's life, the prosecutor argues, they ought to be liable for manslaughter because they failed to meet the standard of care of a reasonable parent. Whether because of their limited intelligence or something else (perhaps fear of Child Welfare intervention), the parents created an unreasonable risk of death that they ought not have.

In response, the defense argues that the parents did not know the baby was as sick as he was and would have acted differently had they known. Their failure to seek aid was primarily the result of their ignorance and lack of education, and they ought not to be punished for being ignorant and uneducated. Criminal law ought to punish only those who have chosen to act improperly or have chosen to fail to do that which is their legal duty.

The Law's Challenge

Was the Williamses' ignorance or disregard of the risk to their baby criminally culpable?

On the one hand, the facts suggest that any reasonable parent, seeing the signs of increased swelling, prolonged fever, discoloration, being exposed to the putrid smell, and knowing the baby had not eaten for some time, would have realized the clear need for aid and the risk inherent in failing to get it.

On the other hand, the limited abilities and education of these parents meant that they genuinely might not have understood the seriousness of the danger. (Further, even if they had some sense of danger, they feared that taking the child to the doctor risked having their children taken away from them.)

By what standard should they be judged? That of the reasonable parent with normal education and intelligence? If so, they are likely to fail in the comparison and have their failure judged criminal. The reasonable parent with normal education and intelligence would have sought aid.

Or should they be judged by the standard of the reasonable parent *with similar limited abilities and education? (And with similar fears of having their children taken away?)* If that is the standard of reasonableness, one may conclude the Williamses acted reasonably, given their situation.

The issue of the standard to be used—a purely objective, reasonable person standard or a standard individualized to take account of the particular characteristics of the person at hand—is one of the most important in criminal law. What factors ought the law to take into account in judging a person's blameworthiness? Yet the issue is one on which there is much confusion and disagreement.

To use a fully individualized standard means that few people will be convicted of anything. We see glimpses of this problem in the hot debate over the "abuse excuse," as in the Menendez brothers and other cases. Taken to an extreme, a fully individualized standard would take account of an offender's demonstrated bad-temperedness, for example, and would judge his conduct "reasonable," and therefore noncriminal, if a person of similar bad-temperedness would have committed the same offense in the situation.

At the other extreme, a purely objective standard—as the prosecution in the *Williams* case proposes—seems to equally miss the mark of doing justice. If a person genuinely is too unintelligent or uneducated to be able to meet the demands of the objective "reasonable person" standard, it is hard to see the moral blameworthiness of such a failure. Imposing criminal liability on such a person is simply punishing the person for being unintelligent or uneducated. Admittedly, bad-temperedness ought not to be taken into account, but there are many other personal characteristics affecting a person's capacities that are beyond a person's control, that clearly ought to be taken into account if justice is to be done.

The central question, then, is how can we determine in a principled way which characteristics ought to be permitted to individualize the objective standard in judging reasonableness and which ought not?

There are clear cases of both sorts. Bad-temperedness ought not to be taken into account. As clearly, the law should take account of a person's mental retardation, or the fact they are in shock from just seeing their child badly burned. But once we go beyond these clear cases, we need some kind of principle to explain and segregate the in-between cases, which are much more numerous. If the Williamses are of slightly below average intelligence, how much below the norm must they be for their reduced intelligence to be taken into account? Should their limited education be taken into account? (Would your view be different if they had had an opportunity for more education but had rejected it, as many teenagers today do?)

Should we take into account their desire to hide their baby's condition for fear of having him taken away? No doubt they believed that he was better off staying with them than being taken by state authorities. But could they use this as justification to disregard an existing threat to his health, even the lesser threat to health that they did perceive? Should their conduct be judged by the standard of the reasonable, poorly educated and below-normal intelligence parent distrustful of authority? Or does such an approach edge too much toward a subjective standard under which too few people would receive the punishment they deserve?

Criminal law theory presently has no principled answers to these central questions.

The Outcome

At the conclusion of the trial, the court finds no excuse for the Williamses' not taking their baby to the doctor. The judge concludes the couple were negligent and, because of their negligence, the child died. Walter and Bernice Williams are convicted of manslaughter on March 10, 1969.

On appeal, the defendants contend that the manslaughter statute requires "willful . . . misconduct" and, because of their ignorance, their failure to get medical aid was not willful. The court of appeals agrees that good parents do not need to call the doctor for every toothache. The issue, according to the court, is whether "a person of reasonable prudence" would have recognized the need to call a physician in time to save the baby's life. The court applies a strictly objective test: "If the conduct of the defendant, *regardless of his ignorance*, good intentions, and good faith, fails to measure up to the conduct required of a man of reasonable prudence, he is guilty of ordinary negligence because of his failure to use 'ordinary caution.'" Not surprisingly, the court then concludes that the Williamses are liable for manslaughter and affirms their conviction.

People's Intuitions of Justice

What criminal liability and punishment, if any, should Bernice and Walter have for William's death? Here is how the people in the survey sentenced the Williamses:

no liability	10%	1 year	21%
liability but		3 years	12%
no punishment	27%	7 years	7%
1 day	—	15 years	3%
2 weeks	3%	30 years	1%
2 months	4%	life imprisonment	1%
6 months	9%	death	—

Mean = 3.2 months.

Thirty-seven percent of the people would impose no punishment, but 45 percent would impose a substantial punishment of a year or more in prison. That reflects a high degree of disagreement, one of the highest of all our cases. It appears that laypersons, like the criminal law scholars, may be unsure of how to evaluate the Williamses' blameworthiness.

Adjudicating Blameworthiness versus Announcing Rules of Conduct

The disagreement among our survey subjects over the proper result in the *Williams* case may stem in part from a structural flaw in our criminal justice system. We ask the criminal law to perform two sometimes contradictory functions: judging the punishment the Williamses deserve, if any, and announcing to others the law's rules of conduct for future use.

Assume we conclude that what the Williamses did was wrong—that parents ought to seek medical aid in such circumstances or face criminal charges for their failure to do so—but also conclude, on balance, that the Williamses' blameworthiness is not enough to merit the condemnation of criminal conviction and punishment. What are we to do? To acquit the Williamses risks undermining the rule of conduct that the law wants to announce vigorously to parents: that they must be vigilant in guarding their children's health. But to convict the Williamses is to impose liability on defendants who do not deserve it.

The current system, which forces a verdict of either "guilty" or "not guilty," simply does not let us send the more complex message we think appropriate: to condemn the conduct but not the defendant. We want others to know that, while these defendants will not be punished because of special excusing conditions, all parents are put on notice that such failing normally will result in criminal liability.

Under the current verdict system, which does not let us distinguish the conduct from the person, it is no surprise to see disagreement as to the proper verdict, as different people pick differently between two unattractive options: either imposing undeserved punishment or undercutting the rule of conduct that parents must vigorously guard the health of their children.

The Sentence

At sentencing, each of the Williamses is given a sentence of three years, but to be deferred indefinitely if certain conditions are met. In other words, they get a sentence of probation.

The best our system can do with its current verdict system is something like what the *Williams* court did: hold the defendants criminally liable but impose essentially no punishment. This is an attempt to reaffirm the rule of conduct yet minimize the extent of undeserved punishment.

But this compromise approach ultimately fails on both counts. For some people, a probationary sentence may be seen as a suggestion that the parents did nothing too wrong. At the same time, the approach can brand a blameless person a criminal—an injustice that incrementally undercuts the moral credibility of the criminal law. A better approach is a verdict system that would allow the decision maker to more clearly condemn the conduct but excuse the offender. More on that later in the chapter.

The next case generated the highest level of disagreement of any case in our survey. You will see that it raises some of the same fundamental problems as *Williams*, but in what seems at first to be a very different context.

KILLING A SLEEPING ABUSER

It is August 1981. Janice Leidholm, forty-two, and her husband, Chester Leidholm, forty-five, live on a farm about thirteen miles from Washburn, North Dakota, near the Missouri River. The couple, who have been married for twenty-three years, have five adult children. The youngest two, Sandra and Neil, are ages twenty and twenty-one. Sandra still lives at home, as does Neil, who sleeps in an old converted bus parked on the property. The older three are married and live on their own in Washburn. The Leidholms live and support themselves off the farm and off money Chester earns when he takes an occasional construction job at area power plants.

The Leidholms' marriage is a bleak affair dominated by alcohol abuse by both Janice and Chester and physical abuse by Chester of Janice. At times, his beatings leave her black and blue for three or four days. When the pain is too much to bear by herself, she goes to her daughters' homes in the morning and has them rub her badly bruised back. During one of the beatings, Chester sits on top of her and strangles her, stopping only as she begins to lose consciousness. The beatings are regularly followed by apologies and Chester's promises never to hit her again. To hide the bruises, Janice often wears long-sleeved dresses. She seeks medical treatment only for the worst beatings.

Many people try to help Janice leave Chester, even if for a brief respite. One daughter gives Janice money to visit her brother in Chicago, which she does, but then she returns. Another time, Janice appeals to Chester's brother Lloyd, who talks to Chester about the violence. Janice tries to convince Chester to go with her to a marriage counselor. She also several times calls the sheriff's office about getting into a shelter. More than once, Janice tries to kill herself; on one occasion she stabs herself with a kitchen knife. When Janice's children try to step in to stop the beatings, Chester warns them against interfering in the marriage.

On the night of August 6, 1981, Janice spends the day at home while Chester drives to the nearby town of Underwood to pick up some parts for the combine. He returns about 4:30 P.M. slurring his words and smelling of liquor. He is still angry from a previous argument over his suspicions that Janice is having an affair. A while later, the two leave for a gun club picnic at a park in Washburn. Chester gives Janice the silent treatment on the way to the picnic, which he does frequently when he is upset.

Janice and Chester drink heavily at the picnic and both become drunk. They begin to argue, this time about new friends Janice has begun seeing, a young couple from Dunseith, a small North Dakota town near the Canadian border about 120 miles away. Chester is also

Chester and Janice Leidholm (left) at their daughter Kathy's wedding, July 18, 1981, nineteen days before Janice killed Chester. (Family photo)

upset because he thinks his wife is paying too much attention to a man at the picnic. As the picnic winds down, Janice says she wants to stay in town with her daughter Laurie, but Chester insists that she come home. Afraid of being alone with Chester, Janice convinces her daughter Sandra, who has joined them at the picnic, to come home with them rather than stay with her sister Laurie as she planned.

Chester and Janice fight constantly on the trip home. Chester accuses her of spending too much time with the man at the party. Janice reminds him of an affair he had with another woman. She says she wants to return to Washburn to spend the night at Laurie's home. Chester again refuses, but this time in his anger, he reaches across to the passenger side door, opens it, and with the truck moving at forty-five miles an hour tries to push Janice out. Sandra, who is sitting between the two, pulls her mother back in and closes the door. Sometime later, Janice says she wants to get out and tries to open the door while the truck is moving. Sandra pulls her back in. Chester tells Janice to leave in the morning if she wants to.

When they arrive home just after midnight, they discover a problem with the water system. Sandra checks around the house to find the problem. Fearing her parents may try to drive while intoxicated, Sandra checks the family cars for keys and removes the ones she finds. The argument between Chester and Janice continues. Janice goes into the house and tries to call a deputy sheriff she knows for help, but Chester pushes her to the floor. Each time she tries to stand and get to the phone, he pushes her back to the floor. Chester is now shouting and Janice is crying.

Janice walks out of the house to get away from Chester, but Chester, who is bigger, catches up with her and throws the 5'1", 150-pound Janice to the ground. During the fight, Chester takes away her wedding rings and tells her she is a drunk and does not deserve to be married anymore. Chester begins to tire and insists they go into the house and go to sleep. When Janice refuses to go with him, he picks her up and drags her inside.

Chester Leidholm enjoying a cigarette on July 19, 1981, eighteen days before he was killed in his sleep. (Family photo)

In the living room the argument continues. They argue about their drinking. They talk about divorce. There is discussion about her moving to Minot the following week to live with her daughter Wanda. Eventually Chester goes to bed, while Janice remains in the living room. Later Chester comes into the living room and tells her to go to bed. She does not. Chester comes back to the living room, picks her up, drags her across the floor into the bedroom, and throws her onto the bed. She eventually removes her clothes, puts on her nightgown, and lies in bed next to him.

Sometime before 1:00 A.M. Chester falls asleep. Janice, lying beside him, is still awake. She slips out of bed, goes to kiss Sandra goodnight, and then heads for the kitchen. Although Sandra has tried to hide all the knives out of fear that her mother might try again to hurt herself, Janice finds a butcher's knife and walks back to the bedroom, careful not to wake Chester. As he sleeps, Janice stabs Chester twice in the right side of his chest. Chester struggles out of bed and crawls to the living room. He calls Sandra and when she comes to the top of the stairs, Chester screams, "Get Neil. Mom stabbed me." Sandra runs to him and helps him sit down on the couch, then rushes to get her brother, who is sleeping in the old bus parked on the property.

Neil and Sandra return to the house to find their father lying on the floor bleeding, with the knife on the floor beside his head. Neil puts his hand over the wound to try to stop the bleeding and cradles his father's head in his arms. In a matter of minutes, Chester dies from loss of blood and shock.

Janice calls her brother-in-law Roy Leidholm and tells him, "Roy, I just killed Chester." Janice tells him to call an ambulance, which he does. It is now 1:15 A.M. and her next call is to the deputy sheriff she knows. She tries to tell him that she killed her husband, but she is nearly hysterical and her words come out in unintelligible sobs. Finally she manages to tell him just to come out to the farm but for what he does not know. Janice calls information to get the sheriff's number. She calls him and manages to tell him she killed her husband.

Paramedics pronounce Chester dead when they arrive. Janice tells a paramedic, "I couldn't take it anymore."

As she waits for deputies to arrive, Janice washes up and changes clothes. Deputies arrest Janice at 3:30 A.M. and charge her with first-degree murder.

■

Would you convict Janice Leidholm for killing her husband? If so, what amount of punishment would you impose?

no liability	☐	1 year	☐
liability but		3 years	☐
no punishment	☐	7 years	☐
1 day	☐	15 years	☐
2 weeks	☐	30 years	☐
2 months	☐	life imprisonment	☐
6 months	☐	death	☐

The Law's Challenge, Again

Unlike the *Williams* case, there is no question here that Janice Leidholm had the culpable state of mind required for homicide. It was her intention to cause the death of Chester at the time she stabbed him. The issue here is whether, despite her intention to kill, Janice should have a defense or mitigation.

As to self-defense, it is difficult for Janice to argue that she meets the defense's objective requirements. Chester's aggression had passed; a threat no longer existed. Her killing seems aggressive rather than defensive. Even if a threat had remained, she had available to her other, less harmful means of defending herself. She could have called the sheriff before she killed Chester, rather than after. She could have gotten a ride into town from her daughter and spent the night there. Even better, she could have left Chester permanently, as she had many chances to do in the past. Chester would not have gone after her. (He had not pursued her when she left on previous occasions.) While divorce can be painful, one would think it less painful than the beatings Janice suffered. In any case, if Janice refuses to leave Chester, she hardly can claim that the only way she has to avoid future beatings is to kill him as he sleeps.

Chester has done condemnable things, indeed criminal things, but, as we saw in the *Schlicht* apple orchard case, the law values even the life of a lawbreaker. A person's life can be taken justifiably only if it is the only way to defend against a threat of death or serious bodily injury from that person. If Janice had killed Chester while he was beating her, or when he was about to beat her, she might make a self-defense claim. But to kill Chester while he sleeps is to foreclose that possibility.

But, as in the *Williams* case, it does not follow that every wrongdoing is blameworthy. The psychotic aggressor, the coerced embezzler, and the surreptitiously doped driver all may perform wrongful acts—acts in violation of the criminal law's rules of conduct—but nonetheless may be exculpated if other conditions explain and excuse their wrongful conduct. Even conditions short of an excuse may support some mitigation in punishment.

Under what conditions should a person's wrongful conduct be excused? How are we to judge whether a wrongdoer is to be fairly blamed? When might a person be undeserving of an excuse but nonetheless merit a mitigation? Those are the questions to which both the *Williams* and *Leidholm* cases address themselves.

The Aftermath

Unable to meet the $30,000 bail, Janice remains in jail after pleading innocent at her arraignment. Bail later is reduced to $1,000. She posts that amount and remains free while awaiting trial.

The week after her arrest, Janice's defense attorney asks that she be sent to a state hospital for a psychiatric examination. The court sends Janice to Jamestown State Hospital for thirty days to determine if she is competent to stand trial. Nurses there observe many bruises on her arms, legs, and back, as well as scars, carbuncles, and other bruises that appear to be older than the more recent ones. It also appears that her upper left arm had been broken at some time. The psychiatrist's report indicates that Janice suffers from "depressive neurosis," probably caused by the abuse her husband inflicted on her. She is ruled fully able to assist her counsel in the preparation of her defense and therefore is held competent to stand trial.

On January 13, 1982, her murder trial begins amid heavy local publicity. The judge refuses a defense request to move the trial and begins selecting a twelve-person jury from a pool of seventy. Janice's four daughters and son testify that her husband beat her severely and frequently throughout their marriage.

Battered Spouse Syndrome

While it may be clear that Janice was not in fact justified in killing Chester as she did, the law generally allows an excuse for mistaken justification if a person honestly and reasonably *believes* that she is justified, that is, if a reasonable person would have concluded the same thing in the same situation. Did Janice Leidholm honestly and reasonably believe that killing Chester was truly immediately necessary for her protection, that she could not have protected herself through some less harmful conduct? Many people will find this hard to believe under the circumstances. It is hard to see how a sleeping victim can require immediate killing. But Janice's situation is more complicated than may first appear.

Modern psychological sciences have found a common pattern of cognitive dysfunction among persons subjected to repeated beatings, a pattern of dysfunction commonly labeled "battered spouse syndrome" or "battered woman syndrome." Common effects include a tendency to overestimate the extent and immediacy of a threat and a tendency to underestimate one's ability to successfully defend against or escape from the threat. The condition generally is associated with low self-esteem and a "learned helplessness." The batterer is seen as more powerful and the subject as more vulnerable than is in fact the case.

Battered spouse syndrome is not itself a defense. Nor does it create the kind or degree of mental dysfunction necessary for an insanity defense. Rather, it serves the more limited role of helping persuade a jury that a defendant might well have honestly believed her use of force was immediately necessary to protect herself from serious bodily injury or death. In other words, it helps persuade a jury that the defendant had the state of mind required for a defense or mitigation of mistake as to self-defense.

There are often exaggerated claims about battered spouse syndrome. Sometimes the syndrome is used as a general anti-male vehicle to promote a political agenda. For example, the syndrome is often a centerpiece of a radical feminist legal program of pressing the pardon or release of women in prison for killing their male mates.

Despite the exaggerations and abuses, the scientific evidence does suggest that a history of battering can cause some degree of distortion in perceiving and analyzing one's situation: exaggerating the extent and immediacy of the threat and underestimating one's ability to escape or defend in nondeadly ways. Of course, these distortions in thinking do not always occur. But where they do, they may establish a state of mind central to a claim of mistaken self-defense.

The Trial

The systematic battering that Janice suffered at the hands of Chester is undisputed at trial. A defense psychiatrist testifies that such a pattern of battering can cause the effects of battered spouse syndrome. It remains somewhat unclear whether Janice, in particular, suffered the effects of distorted perception that battered spouse syndrome can cause, but she might very well have.

The issue is moot, however, because the court refuses a defense request for an instruction directing the jury to take account of the effects of battered spouse syndrome in evaluating whether Janice reasonably believed her use of deadly force was immediately necessary. The judge instructs the jury instead that, to give a defense, the jurors must find Janice's belief objectively reasonable. The jury is told to consider whether a reasonably cautious person would believe it necessary, in such circumstances, to kill as Janice had.

To no one's surprise, the jury is unable to find that it was objectively reasonable to believe the killing necessary, and therefore the jury is unable to give Janice an excuse of reasonably mistaken self-defense. On January 31, 1982, after a three-week trial, the jury returns a guilty verdict. (Janice is found guilty of manslaughter, rather than murder—manslaughter includes the killing of another that would be murder but is committed "under the influence of extreme emotional disturbance.")

Janice is sentenced to five years in prison. Three years of the sentence are suspended. The judge grants a stay of the sentence pending appeal.

The Matters Relevant to Justice

Suffering from battered spouse syndrome is not itself enough to qualify for self-defense. A sufferer might have a tendency to exaggerate the threat and to minimize her defensive options, yet still know enough to know that her killing was not necessary. That is, a person must not only suffer the dysfunction, but also must honestly believe that deadly force is immediately necessary. Further, if she is to get a full excuse, her belief must be *reasonable*, given her situation.

But while the effect of the syndrome is limited, it seems clear that the trial court is wrong to have the jury ignore the possible presence of battered spouse syndrome that would distort the defendant's perceptions and thinking in ways highly relevant to a claim of mistaken self-defense. Given her situation, including the effects of battered spouse syndrome, did Janice reasonably believe she had to kill Chester to protect herself? (Even if her belief was not entirely reasonable, did she honestly believe it was necessary, and, if so, doesn't this make her blameworthiness significantly less than that of a murderer with no such belief?)

As we saw in the *Williams* case, there is much confusion and controversy over the proper standard of "reasonableness." Should it be entirely objective—what the ordinary reasonable person would have done—or should it be entirely individualized or subjective? Or should it be partially individualized, taking account of some of the characteristics of the present defendant, but not all of them?

In the *Leidholm* case, the issue comes up in determining whether Janice's belief in her need for immediate use of deadly force is reasonable. Under a purely objective standard her belief certainly is not reasonable. A reasonable person would not have thought it necessary for self-defense that she kill her husband while he slept. But if the effects of her battered spouse syndrome are taken into account—if the reasonable person standard is individualized to judge her conduct against that of the reasonable person suffering battered spouse syndrome to the same extent as she—then her belief might be judged reasonable, given her situation.

The Appeal

On appeal, the North Dakota Supreme Court reverses Janice's conviction and remands the case for a new trial. The court holds that the trial judge's refusal to give a self-defense instruction based on a subjective standard of reasonableness is reversible error. The jury must, the court holds, consider whether a reasonable person in the defendant's situation, including the effects of her battered spouse syndrome, would have similarly believed the killing necessary. The key question, according to the court, is not whether a reasonably cautious person would have thought lethal force necessary, but whether a reasonably cautious person with the mental and physical traits or disabilities of the defendant would have thought it necessary. On remand for retrial, the trial court is told to direct the jury to put itself in the defendant's shoes, with the defendant's experiences, physical characteristics, and psychological traits, and determine as best it can from that perspective whether the defendant acted reasonably in self-defense.

The All-or-Nothing Disagreement

The Supreme Court of North Dakota seems to have done the right thing with regard to Janice Leidholm. It hardly seems just to ignore her possible cognitive dysfunction in judging the reasonableness of a belief that her killing of Chester was necessary. It is true that, on remand for retrial, a jury might evaluate her situation and the effects of her battered spouse syndrome and still conclude that her killing of her husband was not reasonable, even for someone suffering her distorted perception. But it seems clearly wrong to refuse to let the jury take account of her dysfunction, which was a predictable result of Chester's beatings.

If the jury does conclude on retrial that her belief in the immediate necessity for killing was honestly held but was unreasonable—called imperfect self-defense—Janice would not get a complete excuse but would get a mitigation from murder to a less serious offense, perhaps manslaughter or even the still less serious offense of negligent homicide (depending on whether they find her belief recklessly held or only negligently held).

Not all states allow such a mitigation for an honest but unreasonable belief. Many states, including Alabama, Arizona, California, Illinois, New Jersey, New York, and Texas, require the defendant's belief be reasonable. If it is unreasonable—either reckless or negligent—the defendant gets no mitigation or defense, but rather is held liable for the full offense, murder.

This seems a questionable policy. A person who is reckless or negligent in believing her deadly force is necessary admittedly is blameworthy and deserves punishment. But it seems difficult to accept that such a person is as blameworthy as the person who kills with no claim of self-defense—the cold murderer.

On Remand

On remand, under a plea agreement, Janice agrees to plead guilty to manslaughter, for which she would serve no more than a year in prison, with three months of the sentence suspended and credit for the time she already spent in jail waiting release on bail. But the trial judge is not bound to give the one-year sentence of the plea agreement. He exercises his discretion to give only a sentence of probation, a one-year sentence suspended. Thus, Janice need serve no time in prison.

People's Intuitions of Justice

The plea bargain to which the prosecutor agreed on remand is consistent with a verdict of manslaughter or negligent homicide, for which a year's imprisonment would have been a possible sentence, if perhaps a lenient one. The trial judge's outright release of Janice is more consistent with an outright acquittal. The people in our survey, as a group, imposed an average term of nine months, although there is much disagreement among the group.

Here is how the people in the survey sentenced Janice Leidholm:

no liability	10%	1 year	13%
liability but		3 years	18%
no punishment	11%	7 years	14%
1 day	—	15 years	16%
2 weeks	—	30 years	5%
2 months	1%	life imprisonment	4%
6 months	6%	death	—

Mean = 1.4 years.

This case prompted more disagreement among our survey participants than any other case. Twenty-one percent give no punishment. Thirty-eight percent give a substantial mitigation, a sentence between two months and three years for an intentional killing. Thirty-nine percent give a substantial sentence, seven years to life imprisonment.

The group probably disagreed over whether Janice honestly believed the killing was immediately necessary and, if she did, whether that belief in fact was reasonable from her distorted perspective.

But another source of the disagreement may be the structural problem inherent in our current verdict system first noted in the context of the *Williams* case. Our current verdict system does not let juries send the message they may want to send, and instead forces them into one of two bad choices. In this case, the jury might have wanted to send this message: What Janice did was wrong. It was a violation of the rules of conduct. Others in her situation in the future ought not to do what she did. But she ought not to be punished, or punished as much, for her wrongful conduct because the effects of the battered spouse syndrome she suffered made it easier for her to honestly mistake the immediate need for the killing.

But under our present verdict system, a jury must announce either "guilty" or "not guilty," and both of these options are problematic. To find Janice "not guilty," or even to give her a mitigation, might be taken by some as approval of her conduct, which we in fact seek to disapprove. But to disregard the possible excusing or mitigating conditions, to return a verdict of "guilty," is to impose liability and punishment that are not deserved. Given the imperfect alternatives, it is easy to see how people disagree as to the proper verdict, even if they agree on the facts.

A better approach would be to recognize several verdict options. At the very least, a jurisdiction could allow these four verdicts: (1) "not guilty"; (2) "justified violation" (where a killing in fact is objectively justified—Chester is about to kill Janice and she kills him in self-defense); (3) "blameless violation" (or "wrongful conduct but excused offender") (where a killing occurs under a reasonable mistake as to self-defense, for example); and (4) "guilty." The availability of a "blameless violation" (or "wrongful conduct but excused offender") verdict would allow a jury to acquit for a reasonable mistake as to self-defense without worrying that its verdict might be taken to condone such conduct in the future.

The Law's Unmet Challenge

While many people may feel that the *Leidholm* case ended with a proper result—mitigation to manslaughter—the North Dakota Supreme Court's opinion in the case creates interesting problems for the future. The court adopted an entirely subjective standard of reasonableness, in which a decision maker must take account of all "physical and psychological properties peculiar to the accused" and the jury must "place itself as best it can in the shoes of the accused." As discussed in *Williams*, this use of a purely subjective standard creates serious dangers that undeserving offenders will be acquitted. Why should juries be required to take account of an offender's bad-temperedness, for example, or other objectionable "psychological properties peculiar to the accused"?

Imagine that the Leidholm story had played out differently, that Chester in his drunken and jealous rage had beaten Janice to death. Can he now claim that the reasonableness of his conduct (in deciding whether he has the required culpability for murder or manslaughter, as was the issue in *Williams*) must be judged from the point of view of a person in a similarly drunken and jealous state? What if he could show that most of the men in his family commonly were in such a drunken and jealous state? If so, such a state and such conduct are as predictable and "reasonable" for him as Janice's killing under battered spouse syndrome would have been for her.

The North Dakota Supreme Court would have been better served if it had relied on more narrow and careful reasoning that established the relevancy of battered spouse syndrome in judging the reasonableness of a person's belief in self-defense, but left to other cases the determination of what other conditions might properly be taken into account in individualizing the reasonable person standard.

Astonishingly, this most fundamental question—how is the law to judge the reasonableness of a violator's conduct—is one for which law has no clear answer. The law has not yet been able to define what characteristics and conditions of a defendant ought to be taken into account and which ought not. To leave this critical determination undefined is to invite all of the vices that the legality principle, discussed in chapter 2, seeks to avoid: potential for abuse of discretion, inconsistency in application among similar cases, unpredictability, and instability. Past advances suggest that some day criminal law theorists will be able to do better, but now they can only struggle.

THE PEDOPHILE WITHIN

In 1975 Barry Kingston is hired by James Forman and his wife, Diedre Forman, to run their spa in Brighton, England, the Unit One Sauna. Three years later the Formans move to Cyprus, leaving Kingston to run

Barry Kingston in the late 1970s, when he was employed at the Unit One Sauna. (Barry Kingston)

the spa on his own. The Formans' absence allows Kingston a great deal of independence with a pleasant job. He meets and befriends many of the spa's customers. On at least one occasion one of the customers gives him some sexually explicit material that the customer no longer wants, most of it dealing with young men and teenage boys.

In 1987 the Formans return from Cyprus. Mr. Forman then spends most of his time at a house in France, which the couple have just purchased. Mrs. Forman remains in England, becoming active in the running of the spa. She eventually becomes disenchanted with Kingston and fires him. Kingston files an unfair dismissal claim and is given a substantial award, £12,000, by an industrial tribunal.

The Formans are concerned that Kingston knows a great deal about their business and tax dealings and fear that he may report this information to authorities. Kevin Penn, a Brighton resident and acquaintance of Kingston, is aware of the situation. Penn has a reputation for money-making schemes, especially of the questionable sort. He offers to allay the Formans' fears of Kingston by providing them with something they can use to blackmail him. After a few false starts, he devises a workable plan and the Formans pay him £1,500.

Penn learns that Kingston has an interest in young men and teens, revealed by his magazine preferences. While he does not know of any previous involvement of Kingston with a young man, Penn plans to drug Kingston and, in that state, to use Kingston's latent desire to entice him into a compromising situation that he can record for blackmail purposes.

Penn notices a group of local surfers, all approximately fifteen years old, who he thinks may be of use in his plot. He approaches one of the boys, James Bullock, about Bullock's buying from Penn a used surfboard or helping Penn sell it. They agree Penn and the boys will meet at the Black Horse Pub, a local tavern. At the tavern, Penn quickly changes the subject to photography. Penn, who is carrying a high-quality camera, tells the boys they can make a lot of money by posing for photographic sessions. The boys see little reason not to make the easy money. Penn arranges to take a few amateurish photos, and encourages the boys to continue posing for him in the future. He is particularly interested in Bullock and Darren Child, who he thinks are the most attractive looking of the group. In order to set the stage for the blackmail session with Kingston, Penn has the boys pose several more times during the next month and a half for him and for a professional photographer, Andrew McLean, an acquaintance of Penn. None of the photos are overtly sexual. During some of the shoots, the boys drink with Penn or smoke cannabis. When McLean is alone with the boys, he warns them "to be careful in your dealings with Penn, as he is always short of money and looking for schemes to get rich quick."

In November 1990 Penn is ready to go ahead with the blackmail session. He calls Kingston and arranges to have him stop by his apartment later that evening. He then meets Darren Child at the Black Horse Pub and invites him to come to his apartment to pick up an old stereo. Child and Penn take a taxi to Penn's home. Penn offers a glass of lager beer, which Child happily accepts. They go into Penn's bedroom and sit on the bed and smoke cannabis. Cannabis normally does not make Child sleepy, but Penn has laced the lager with triazolam and temazepam. The first is a "sedative-hypnotic primarily used to relieve insomnia"; the second is "used as a sedative and hypnotic." Both can cause drowsiness, impairment of judgment, and loss of memory. The boy soon passes out. Penn removes the boy's clothes and positions him on the bed, lying on his back with his head on the pillow.

Kingston soon arrives, as planned. Penn offers him some coffee that he has laced with sedatives. He adjusts the dosage so that, unlike Child, Kingston will not pass out but instead will have only impaired judgment and loosened inhibitions.

Once the drugs begin to take effect, Kingston says, "I don't know why, am I falling asleep?" Suspicious, Kingston asks Penn, "Have you put something in my coffee?" Kingston is increasingly groggy but still conscious and aware of what is going on. Penn leads him to the bedroom, where he presents the boy lying naked on the bed and invites Kingston to have sex with him, which Kingston does. Penn audiorecords the episode and takes photographs.

When the boy awakens the next morning he remembers nothing from the night before. Kingston only remembers waking up in his own home the next morning. Soon after, Penn sells the negatives and the audiotape to the Formans. Mrs. Forman arranges a meeting with Kingston and informs him that she possesses incriminating photos and tape. She explains to him that if he does anything to hurt the Formans' interests, they will give the material to his new employer, the Department of Social Services. For reasons that are unclear, perhaps to discredit an uncooperative Kingston, Mrs. Forman several months later gives their evidence to the police. Both Penn and Kingston are charged with indecent assault on a minor. Penn is also charged with drugging the boy.

Experts conclude that Kingston would not have committed the sexual offense if he had not been drugged by Penn, but that Kingston was aware of what he was doing and knew it was wrong, and, while his capacity to control his conduct was impaired, he had not completely lost his ability to control his conduct at the time of the offense.

Should Kingston be held criminally liable for sexual assault of the boy? If so, what amount of punishment would you impose?

no liability	☐	1 year	☐
liability but		3 years	☐
no punishment	☐	7 years	☐
1 day	☐	15 years	☐
2 weeks	☐	30 years	☐
2 months	☐	life imprisonment	☐
6 months	☐	death	☐

Kingston can claim that the intoxication did have some effect on him. Indeed, he can make an even stronger claim: he would not have committed the offense but for Penn's drugging him. That argument has a powerful appeal to it, for it makes the situation look like Penn, not Kingston, caused the assault. Is the drugging enough to exculpate Kingston?

There is little doubt that Penn ought to be liable for a whole host of offenses—drugging the boy, drugging Kingston, and perhaps causing Kingston to sexually assault the boy. But that does not resolve the question of Kingston's liability for the sexual assault. Several people may be liable for the same offense. Both the paid murderer and the person who pays him are liable for a murder. Criminal liability is personal. The focus for each defendant is on what he did and thought.

Taking into account Penn's conduct, should Kingston be liable for the offense? Were the effects of Kingston's involuntary intoxication such that he deserves an excuse?

The Law's Rules

The criminal law recognizes that a wide variety of disabilities may cause conditions that properly excuse a person for doing something admittedly wrongful. Mental illness, coercion from another person, immaturity, or, as in this case, involuntary intoxication can cause a person to lose control of his conduct or to fail to appreciate the physical or legal nature of the conduct. Most jurisdictions recognize these four conditions as a possible basis for excuse, and sometimes recognize a variety of others, such as epileptic seizure, somnambulism (sleepwalking), hypnosis, or physiological dysfunction resulting from brain disease, hormone imbalance, or a variety of other causes.

There is general agreement, however, that the existence of one of these disabling conditions is not in itself enough to provide an excuse. It is the *effects* of the disability in impairing the person's capacity to understand and control his conduct that are the moral basis for excuse. A person might well be mentally ill or subjected to coercion, but not to a sufficient extent to exculpate. The impairment caused may be too slight to vitiate or even to reduce the person's blameworthiness.

What extent of dysfunction must a disability cause to be sufficient for excuse? There was a time in the United States when some courts thought it was enough that the accused would not have committed the offense *but for* the disability. In a famous 1954 District of Columbia case, *Durham v. United States*, the court held that mental illness would provide an insanity defense if the offense was the "product of" the mental illness. This set a "but for" causal connection between the disability and the offense as adequate for an excuse defense: an offender is excused if he would not have committed the offense "but for" the disabling mental illness.

But this view is now rejected by nearly all courts, and eventually was rejected by the District of Columbia court itself in *United States v. Brawner* in 1972. Many observed that such a test for excuse commonly gives an undeserved defense. One can imagine a situation in which a person is much inclined to commit an offense, where the mildest of intoxicants is enough to push him that last short way. Ninety-nine percent of his motivation may be his own criminal desire and only 1 percent the intoxicant, but it is true that the 1 percent is a necessary cause—the offense would not have occurred *but for* the mild intoxicant. Our shared intuitions of blamelessness typically require something more.

Different people have different predispositions toward conduct that is criminal—and in this sense, some people carry a heavier burden than others to resist a criminal violation—but all persons have an obligation to try to remain law-abiding. Even when one suffers from a disability not of their own making that creates or increases an inclination to break the law, the person has a moral obligation to continue to resist that inclination. A person is blameless for a violation only if the effect of the disability is so strong that we can *no longer reasonably expect the person to remain law-abiding*, that is, if the reasonable person suffering the same predisposition similarly would have been unable to resist committing the offense.

The problem with the *Durham* "product" test is that it fails to inquire into what can be reasonably expected of a person who suffers a disability inclining the person to break the law. The person who could resist the inclination and reasonably could be expected to, but simply does not, may get an undeserved excuse under *Durham*, for such a person can correctly state that he would not have committed the offense if he didn't suffer the predisposition.

The law in most jurisdictions leaves it to the jury to decide whether the extent of the dysfunction caused was such that the person could not reasonably have been expected to remain law-abiding despite the disability. Frequently, for example, the jury is asked whether the defendant "lacked substantial capacity" to remain law-abiding. The juror typically responds to this general standard by reverting to his or her own intuition.

Only New Hampshire continues to give an excuse simply because an offense is a "product of" a disability, such as mental illness.

How would the facts in *Kingston* be analyzed under these standard requirements for an excuse? The proper question to ask about Kingston is not "Would he have done it without the drug?" but rather "Could we reasonably have expected him not to do it even though he was drugged?" Being drugged does not make a person an automaton. There is a continuum of volition, and a person may have his volition impaired, yet retain some capacity to choose actions. The question is, given the degree and effect of the impairment of his volition, "could we reasonably have expected Kingston to have resisted the temptation of the naked boy laid before him?"

If, because of the effects of the involuntary intoxication, we could not have expected him to have resisted, then he is blameless and ought to be exculpated. If, despite the effects of the involuntary intoxication, we could have expected him to resist, then his conduct is blameworthy and a complete defense is inappropriate. Even if his conduct is blameworthy, however, it seems likely that the effect of the involuntary drugging reduces his blameworthiness from what it otherwise would be if he had committed the same offense without having been drugged.

People's Intuitions of Justice

Here is how the people in the survey sentenced Kingston:

no liability	9%	1 year	16%
liability but		3 years	19%
no punishment	5%	7 years	16%
1 day	—	15 years	7%
2 weeks	2%	30 years	1%
2 months	7%	life imprisonment	—
6 months	16%	death	—

Mean = 10.2 months.

Only 14 percent would exculpate with no punishment. Almost two-thirds would impose a sentence of a year or more, even though the facts make clear that Kingston would not have committed the offense but for the involuntary intoxication. This suggests that most people think that Kingston retained sufficient capacity to control his conduct such that he should have refrained from the offense despite the drugging.

On the other hand, only 8 percent give a sentence of fifteen years or more, for what is normally seen as an extremely serious offense, rated only one grade less than murder in most jurisdictions. That suggests that the effects of the involuntary intoxication are taken into account and do provide a mitigation.

The Trial

At trial, the boy testifies that he only remembers falling asleep on the bed and nothing more until he awakes the next morning. The prosecution presents evidence of the types of drugs found at Penn's apartment and medical testimony of the effects of the sedatives. Neither defense nor prosecution witnesses say either drug could cause a person to do something he would not otherwise be inclined to do. The prosecution introduces statements Kingston made on the audiotape that seem to suggest he is aware of and has some control of what he is doing.

Kingston is limited in his ability to detail the blackmail scheme to the jury. Penn declines to give evidence. Fifty-two-year-old Mr. Forman is excused from attending the trial because of a doctor's letter saying the trip from France would be bad for his heart ailment. Mrs. Forman testifies for the prosecution, but on cross-examination by Kingston's counsel, she frequently refuses to answer questions about the blackmail plot, citing her concern that her answers may tend to incriminate her.

At the close of the prosecution's case, Penn pleads guilty to indecent assault. Kingston does not. Although admitting he had tendencies toward boys, Kingston argues in defense that because he was drugged he is not responsible for what he did. He testifies on his own behalf that he would not have done what he did had it not been for the drugs. The prosecution shows the jury some highly explicit homosexual pornography found in Kingston's home and asks Kingston if he enjoyed himself while assaulting the fifteen-year-old boy. "I would not," Kingston tells the prosecutor. "I don't remember it happening and if I had been in command of myself, it would not have happened." The prosecution contends the pornography found at his home proves Kingston wanted to have sex with the boy regardless of the drugs.

The trial judge refuses to allow Kingston's defense of involuntary intoxication. Instead, the judge directs the jurors that if they believe Kingston had the desire to commit the act, the effect of the drugs in actually inducing him to perform the act does not matter. Only if Kingston's desire was wholly a result of the drugs would involuntary intoxication be a defense.

The jury convicts Kingston in March 1992 by a vote of ten to two (which is adequate for conviction under the English system). Kingston is sentenced to five years in prison. He appeals the conviction and sentence to the Court of Appeals. He has been in prison for about a year pending trial, and remains in prison pending the appeal.

On Appeal

In May 1993 the Court of Appeals decides the appeal. It reasons that it is not criminal to have a predilection toward illegal sex, such as pedophilia, that it becomes criminal only when the desire is expressed in an act of forbidden sex. If the only reason Kingston stepped across the boundary from desire to act was the effect of the drugs, which he only involuntarily ingested, then he cannot be found guilty. The court holds that, if through involuntary intoxication, a person loses self-control and because of that forms a criminal intent that he otherwise would not have formed, he cannot be found guilty. Once a defendant introduces some evidence of involuntary intoxication, the court says, the prosecution must prove that the required intent was not caused by the drugs. Thus, the trial judge was wrong to withhold from the jury the defense of involuntary intoxication, which the prosecution should have the burden of disproving. The Court of Appeals reverses Kingston's conviction. Kingston is released from custody, having served two years of the five-year sentence.

The prosecution now appeals to the House of Lords. When the case is heard a year later, the lords conclude that the trial judge, rather than the Court of Appeals, correctly stated the law: there is no general defense of involuntary intoxication. As long as the accused had the intention required for the offense, he is liable, even if he is without moral fault in bringing about that intention. The decision admits that a defense might be available if the effect of the drugging was to cause temporary insanity, such that the defendant did not know the nature of his conduct or that it was wrong. But a loss of control, apparently even a complete loss of the capacity to control one's conduct, would not be a defense. On July 21, 1994, the House of Lords overturns the lower court decision and reinstates the conviction against Kingston.

Kingston's sentence is later reduced to four years, from five. English practice at the time had most offenders serve only half the sentence imposed, so he is not required to return to prison.

The American View

A few American states follow the English lead and deny a defense even for an involuntary loss of control. The states include Connecticut, Nevada, North Dakota, Rhode Island, West Virginia, and Wyoming. Kingston would be convicted in those jurisdictions, just as he was in England.

Most states would allow an excuse where an accused is unable to control his conduct and is not culpable in causing such lack of control, as in involuntary intoxication or insanity. However, at least twenty-seven of these require that the defendant have suffered essentially a complete loss of control. (These states include Alabama, Alaska, Arizona, Arkansas, California, Colorado, Florida, Indiana, Iowa, Louisiana, Maryland, Michigan, Minnesota, Mississippi, Missouri, Montana, Nebraska, New York, North Carolina, Ohio, Oklahoma, South Carolina, Texas, Virginia, Washington, and Wisconsin.) Kingston would get a

Barry Kingston during a recent vacation. (Barry Kingston)

defense in these states only if he could show that the drugs had caused a complete loss of control, which might be difficult on these facts. Other states give a broader defense, allowing an excuse even if the accused's control is not entirely lost but simply substantially impaired. These states include Delaware, Georgia, Hawaii, Illinois, Kansas, Kentucky, Maine, Massachusetts, New Jersey, Oregon, Tennessee, Utah, and Vermont. If Kingston's capacity to control his conduct was sufficiently impaired, he would have a defense in these jurisdictions. But even in these jurisdictions, Kingston would get no defense if the jury concludes, as it might on these facts, that, while Kingston's control was impaired, it was not so impaired that he could not reasonably have been expected to have resisted committing the offense.

Today

Barry Kingston is discharged from his job with the Department of Social Services upon his initial arrest and remains generally unemployed for some time.

On January 13, 1998, Kingston is asked to come to the police station with his solicitor and is there arrested for alleged indecencies with young men that the police say were committed several decades ago. He goes to trial in late 1998 and is convicted despite obvious inconsistencies in the testimony of the young men about events many years before. He is currently in prison on these offenses.

PICKING CLEAN DRUNKS

It is early 1986 and the Reno Police Department is concerned with rising crime in downtown Reno. The department has received a large number of reports of crimes in the area, mainly robbery, grand larceny, and larceny. Many people avoid downtown because of their fear of crime. The casino operators, fearing the loss of tourist trade, are becoming more and more irritated with the police department's ineffectiveness. Some have discussed organizing their own street patrols, a suggestion the police find disturbing.

Reno's small downtown area is predictably dominated by casinos, which have the unfortunate tendency to bring together two groups of people: panhandlers (who often double as petty thieves) and tourists.

The panhandlers gather in the downtown for the cheap casino food and drink and the ample opportunities to collect small change from casino patrons. The tourists, of course, come for the gambling and the drink, the latter making both winners and losers more vulnerable as they walk the streets after their spin at the casino. Tourists present a special problem for effective law enforcement because they often are too embarrassed to notify the police of a robbery or too inconvenienced to return from out of state for court hearings concerning a loss of twenty or a hundred dollars.

The police increase the uniformed squad car and foot patrols, as well as plainclothes officers in the downtown area. Despite these responses, downtown Reno crime continues to increase. Frustrated by the failures, the police and district attorney's office meet several times to discuss ways to control the crime problem, eventually settling on a decoy operation. An earlier operation, while it was functioning, had decreased crime by 50 percent.

Edwin T. Basil, an assistant district attorney, asks the police department to study and report the specific characteristics of the crime problem. The crime statistics analyzed by Lieutenant David Kieckbusch for the last two months show the bulk of the cases to be "crimes of convenience," where the perpetrators do not plan the crimes in advance, but seize an opportunity for an easy score when it presents itself. The ninety-three cases of robbery, larceny, and grand larceny reviewed suggest the perpetrators are typically young men in their late teens or twenties. The victims are generally tourists, most of them female, elderly, or disabled. The analysis also shows the specific downtown areas of greatest risk. Using Kieckbusch's analysis, the police and district attorney tailor a decoy operation that will focus on the high-risk areas and the profiled offenders.

The night of May 27, 1986, a few weeks after the operation begins, is typical of how it works and of the people it snares. Officer Roger Linscott serves as the decoy. He plays the part of a defenseless elderly man, lying in a building alcove near First and Center Streets. The street corner is downtown, but a little off the beaten path. Linscott faces away from pedestrian traffic and is unresponsive to passing pedestrians. Sticking out of his right-rear pants pocket is an IRS tax return envelope inside a blue checkbook. Hanging about a half-inch out from the envelope are the edges of some U.S. currency, a total of $126. The package is not obvious but is visible and will easily slide out of the decoy's pocket if pulled. The police have recorded the serial numbers of the four bills in order to later identify the money.

Linscott is dressed in gray slacks, tennis shoes, a dark multicolored shirt, and a dark brown leisure jacket. His dress and demeanor are intended to give the appearance of a tourist who has had too much to drink and passed out, the type of person commonly the victim in the downtown area. To reduce the chance of having the operation interrupted by "good samaritans" who might intervene to help a drunk old man, the officers do not douse Linscott or leave empty bottles of alcohol near him, yet a passerby might nonetheless come to the conclusion that the prostrate man is passed out from drink.

A number of people pass by as Linscott lies on the sidewalk. Some of the passersby do not fit the profile of the offender at which the operation is aimed. When these people come by, or obvious good samaritans or seriously down-and-out bums who might succumb to the temptation simply because of their own difficult situation, Officer Linda Peters, whose job it is to keep constant visual contact from the third floor of a parking garage across the street, notifies Linscott by radio to cover the money. The bait is exposed only to those who match the general offender profile.

About half an hour after the operation begins, David Kenny Hawkins and a friend pass by on their way to the Brass Moose Saloon. Hawkins, twenty-eight, fits the profile, so Linscott leaves the bait exposed as the pair approach. The two take notice of the "tourist" but do not stop.

About forty-five minutes later, the two leave the saloon and approach Linscott. Hawkins stops and inspects. Hawkins's friend jumps up and down on the ground and yells, to see if the prone man is passed out. Linscott does not move. Hawkins takes a few more moments to look the man over and then bends down and, with his right hand, slowly removes the money from the decoy's right-rear pocket. He moves so carefully that Linscott is unaware the money has been taken. Hawkins walks away, his friend joins him, and they cross the street.

Seeing this, Peters notifies the perimeter officers by radio that the bait has been taken and gives the location of the suspect. Officer David Jenkins approaches Hawkins and observes the bait money protruding from Hawkins's right front pocket. When stopped, Hawkins points to several people on the street and says they told him to do it. Hawkins is arrested and taken to the Reno City Jail. In addition to the bait money,

David Kenny Hawkins, 1991. (Reno Police Department)

he has fifty dollars in his possession, and is wearing designer-label clothes. He works as a dealer at a downtown Reno casino.

Because of past court cases regarding entrapment, the police only charge persons they catch who have a prior criminal record. A check of police records shows that Hawkins has twenty-five to thirty arrests in Nevada and California, mostly small-time property crimes or generally lawless behavior. (Hawkins's friend has no criminal record and is released.) Among Hawkins's highlights are a 1979 arrest for petty larceny, a 1980 arrest for possession of stolen property, a 1981 arrest for petty larceny, a 1982 arrest for receiving stolen property, and a 1984 arrest for theft. Easy crimes of opportunity are not new to him. On one occasion, he took a helmet off an unattended motorcycle and, on another, he picked up a priest's toolbox as he walked by.

Hawkins is charged with grand larceny, the statutory grand larceny threshold being one hundred dollars. Hawkins pleads not guilty and claims police entrapment.

The police continue their decoy operation for several more weeks and arrest other similar offenders.

Would you convict Hawkins? If so, what amount of punishment would you impose?

no liability	☐	1 year	☐
liability but		3 years	☐
no punishment	☐	7 years	☐
1 day	☐	15 years	☐
2 weeks	☐	30 years	☐
2 months	☐	life imprisonment	☐
6 months	☐	death	☐

The Law's Rules

Hawkins can argue that he never would have committed the offense but for the inducement provided by the police, that it was the temptation created by the police that caused the offense. Does the temptation imposed on him by the police excuse Hawkins and render him blameless for the offense?

There are any number of instances where a person may commit an offense but, because of an excusing condition, cannot properly be held blameworthy for it. Mental illness, involuntary intoxication (as claimed in *Kingston*), immaturity, and duress all have been recognized as capable of causing such an excusing condition. But recall that having one of these disabilities is not in itself sufficient for an excuse. The disability must cause sufficient dysfunction to render the offender blameless for the offense conduct. As we saw in *Kingston*, it is not even enough that the offense is a "product of" the dysfunction, that the person would not have committed the offense *but for* the effect of the disability.

It may be true that Hawkins would not have committed the theft but for the police inducement. But under the standard requirements for an excuse defense, an excuse should follow only if the effect of the inducement was sufficiently severe that we could no longer reasonably have expected Hawkins to avoid committing the theft.

Can we say that with regard to Hawkins? Under the circumstances, could we reasonably have expected Hawkins to avoid committing the offense? The answer seems to be clearly yes. The reasonable law-abiding person seeing $126 in a drunk's pocket would hardly feel compelled to steal it. There is no coercion on Hawkins to commit the offense, only a temptation. And unlike Kingston, who was involuntarily drugged, Hawkins has no ground on which to claim he should be excused for giving in to the temptation. In the end, it seems difficult to see how Hawkins can claim to be blameless or deserving of an excuse or mitigation.

People's Intuitions of Justice

This analysis and conclusion are consistent with how the laypersons in the survey sentenced Hawkins:

no liability	3%	1 year	24%
liability but		3 years	25%
no punishment	5%	7 years	6%
1 day	—	15 years	—
2 weeks	5%	30 years	—
2 months	14%	life imprisonment	—
6 months	18%	death	—

Mean = 7.8 months.

Hawkins's offense is a minor one; no violence was used or threatened. Yet 92 percent of the people imposed punishment equivalent to at least a short term of imprisonment.

Legal Conflict over the Reno Decoy Operation

The Nevada courts generally do not favor decoy operations, but with the problems of downtown crime, the police have consistently pushed for their use, and the Reno district attorney agrees.* But the use of such operations has been repeatedly frustrated when the courts reverse the resulting convictions. Because of this uncertainty, and the resulting possibility of a false imprisonment lawsuit, the

---

*The district attorney at the time of the *Hawkins* case was Mills Lane III, one of the most famous referees in professional boxing. He continued his refereeing after he was elevated to the bench and was sitting as a judge of the district court of Washoe County, in which Reno is located, when he refereed the 1997 Holyfield-Tyson rematch. Tyson bit off a piece of Holyfield's ear; then, after being warned by Mills but not disqualified, Tyson bit Holyfield's other ear a few minutes later. Mills disqualified Tyson and awarded the fight to Holyfield. Mills recently stepped down from his Reno judgeship to host *The Judge Mills Lane Show: Let's Get It On!* on the WB cable network.

Previously a judge and well-known boxing referee, now a TV personality, Mills Lane was the Reno district attorney when Hawkins was prosecuted. (Bill Robbins/Rysher)

police release Hawkins on his own recognizance immediately after he is booked.

After each court reversal, the police and district attorney have altered the decoy design as the latest court opinion seems to require, hoping that the new design will pass court approval. Ironically, though the police hope for a court test of the latest procedures, most suspects plead guilty. Only a handful contest the charges. Hawkins does.

The Peculiar Entrapment Defense

Unlike most other defenses in Nevada, the entrapment defense was not created by the legislature. The courts created it themselves; a common move by courts in many American jurisdictions. Why do the courts create such a defense when it seems to have so little intuitive support and seems to let blameworthy persons go free? Few, if any, countries in the world recognize such a defense. Why do U.S. courts?

The key to the puzzle is found in the special nature of the entrapment defense. It is not an excuse—like insanity, duress, immaturity, or involuntary intoxication, at issue in *Kingston*. These latter defenses, excuses, truly exculpate an offender. While the person has committed an offense, the circumstances and personal state of the offender are such that we cannot reasonably blame him for it.

The defense of entrapment is of a different sort. It is of a family of defenses called "nonexculpatory defenses," which include diplomatic immunity and the statute of limitations. The offender is let off—not "excused"—not because he is blameless but because forgoing his conviction advances some other societal interest. The immune diplomat may be fully blameworthy for an offense and may well deserve liability and punishment, but we forgo prosecution because by doing so we help protect our diplomats abroad from interference by legal authorities in host countries.

The analogous reason for giving an entrapment defense, even to blameworthy offenders, is that we benefit from forgoing conviction because it discourages police overreaching and misconduct often inherent in operations of unlawful entrapment. The theory is similar to what is called the "exclusionary rule," which excludes the use of even reliable evidence from use at trial if it was obtained as the result of unlawful police conduct, such as an illegal search. The guilty offender may go free, but police are discouraged from future illegal searches because they know that any evidence obtained cannot be used. This nonexculpatory nature of entrapment is confirmed by the fact that, where the same "entrapping" conduct is performed by a citizen rather than the police, no defense is available even though the temptation to the offender is the same.

People disagree about the competing societal interests in entrapment cases and whether decoy operations, like the one that caught Hawkins, constitute improper police conduct. The Nevada courts apparently thought so.

Some courts have recognized the significant societal cost in letting guilty offenders go free, and have formulated their entrapment defense to reduce that cost. The most common approach is to bar from the entrapment defense offenders who were "predisposed" to commit the offense for which they claim entrapment. The effect of this requirement is to exclude from the defense the habitual criminal and the person open to an opportunity to commit such a crime.

Other courts, however, do not limit the defense; even the career criminal can get the defense if the police conduct is held to be improper because, for example, it creates a temptation that "creates a substantial risk that such an offense will be committed by persons other than those who are ready to commit it." Under the "objective" formulation of the defense, as it is called, if a person not "ready to commit it" might be tempted, then the offender gets off, even if *he* was ready to commit it.

The Outcome

Hawkins is formally indicted for larceny on June 11, 1986. His attorney moves for a writ of habeas corpus, arguing that Hawkins was unlawfully entrapped.

Prosecutors argue that to have unlawful entrapment under existing Nevada court decisions, there must be uncontroverted evidence that (1) the state furnished the opportunity for the crime, and (2) the defendant was not predisposed to commit the offense. (In other words, Nevada follows the "predisposition" formulation, not the "objective" formulation.) Prosecutors contend that Hawkins's predisposition to commit the crime is clearly shown by his criminal record of similar offenses. They also note that because he was employed, had fifty dollars on him when he was arrested, and wore designer clothes, he was not an impoverished and needy person for whom the temptation would have been so overwhelming as to explain his decision to steal.

Hawkins's defense attorney, deputy public defender John Petty, argues that $126 hanging out of a drunk man's pocket presents an extraordinary temptation to any poor, homeless, or down-and-out person. If such a person could not resist the temptation the police presented, then, Petty argues, existing case law supports a finding of entrapment for Hawkins, even though he is not such a person. The point is, he argues, Hawkins should get a defense because the police have acted improperly. To avoid an entrapment claim, he argues, the state must show not simply a predisposition by the accused to commit the offense, but that he approached the victim with larceny in mind.

The police respond that they prosecute only those people, like Hawkins, who have already shown through their prior criminal history a willingness to commit crimes and who meet the police profile of the downtown criminals at which the decoy operation is aimed.

On August 28, 1986, the court grants the writ of habeas corpus, giving Hawkins a defense of improper entrapment. The Nevada Supreme Court later affirms the ruling. The court does not deny that an offender's predisposition would bar an entrapment defense. Nor does it deny that prior arrests and convictions show predisposition. It rules instead that it is not going to allow an offender's prior arrests and convictions to be admitted at trial to show disposition because such evidence might prejudice a jury against a defendant. The court explains, "mere arrests and convictions for misdemeanors may not ordinarily be admitted even for the limited purpose of attacking a witness's credibility," and the court is unwilling to create an exception that would allow their use to prove "predisposition" in entrapment cases.

Legal Disagreements over Entrapment

The Nevada court, more than many, seems intent on insuring a broad entrapment defense. Given the obstacles it places before the prosecutors in proving the "predisposition" of a defendant, one may wonder why the court does not simply adopt a purely "objective" entrapment formulation, as some jurisdictions do, which does away with the "not predisposed" requirement. It might be less confusing for police if the defense formulation ignores the defendant's character altogether and focuses exclusively on the nature of the police conduct.

This more objective formulation of entrapment is avoided by some courts because it reveals more starkly the nonexculpatory nature of the defense. That is, by ignoring the defendant altogether, it becomes clear that even clearly guilty and blameworthy offenders are released by the defense. The subjective formulation, which requires that the defendant not be "predisposed" to commit the offense, gives the entrapment defense the superficial appearance of an excuse, which lets only blameless offenders go free. No matter how it is dressed up, however, the earlier analysis of the entrapment defense makes it clear that even the subjective formulation of entrapment is not an excuse but rather a nonexculpatory defense.

The Aftermath

A month after the court invalidates the charges against Hawkins, a bench warrant is issued for him. He has failed to appear in court on a different larceny case. In 1989 Hawkins is arrested again and pleads guilty to a new offense of grand larceny. He is sentenced to three years in prison. He serves two years, is released on parole, but violates his parole.

The next year he is arrested twice more, once for destruction of property and once for trespassing. His run-ins with the law continue. He is subsequently arrested for shoplifting, trespass again, depositing rubbish or offensive matter, trespass again, disturbing the peace, and trespass again. As of this writing, Hawkins is a fugitive from justice, with outstanding warrants in several states.

Who Will Explain to Kingston Why Hawkins
Gets Off but He Goes to Jail?

The result in *Hawkins*, as in most cases of an entrapment defense, seems somewhat odd in light of the well-established excuse law that denies a defense in *Kingston*. Kingston really is induced to commit an offense he would not otherwise have committed; yet the law denies a complete defense, as it probably should, because he did not struggle hard enough to overcome the disinhibitions of the drugs he had been given.

In contrast, Hawkins has no similar pressure put on him. To the extent that he is tempted to commit the theft, it is as a result of his own

Officer Roger Linscott (right), who served as the decoy, and Officer Tim Naughton of the Reno Police Department, recently standing at the spot where the decoy lay during the operation in which Hawkins was arrested. The area has been redeveloped since the time of the offense. (Alex Paul)

dishonest character. And in resisting that temptation, he has available to him the full power of any moral character he might possess, undiluted by involuntarily administered drugs or anything else. When he gives in to the temptation, then, it is because he simply has chosen to break the law.

To give him a defense because it was the police who presented the temptation may discourage police decoy operations, but it incurs serious costs. One part of the cost is the increased crime rate that will result if such decoy operations are banned. Another part of the cost is the injustice of letting a crook like Hawkins go free. Still another part of the cost, and a less obvious one, is the incremental damage to the criminal law's moral credibility, its reputation for doing justice. Who will explain to Kingston the justice in Hawkins going free while he, Kingston, goes to jail?

5

Martyrs for Our Safety

THE CRIMINAL LAW has done much toward developing a sensible and workable scheme for determining when an offender's wrongful conduct should be excused. As the previous chapter illustrates, there remain some lingering problems. How much should we individualize the reasonable person with the offender's personal characteristics in judging his blameworthiness (*Williams, Leidholm*)? Can we achieve the goal of nonexculpatory defenses, like entrapment, in less costly ways than letting blameworthy people escape justice (*Hawkins*)? But even if we solved all these problems, one troublesome problem would remain, and it is a problem that threatens to override all the good work the law has done in developing a sound theory of excuses.

Put simply, the problem is this: current excuse theory operates by distinguishing, in the case of insanity, for example, the mad from the bad. Where the offender has a special disability, such as mental illness (or coercion, involuntary intoxication, or infancy), and where that disability causes the offense in a way that we think renders the offender blameless, the law gives an excuse defense. In one sense, the law's excuse defenses distinguish those cases in which the disability is responsible for the offense from those in which it is the offender's own bad "self," his own personality, his values and beliefs that are responsible.

But this current approach to excuse defenses presumes that a person in fact is responsible for who he or she is, for having the values and beliefs that he or she has. But as the three following cases illustrate, this is not so clear. In some cases, it seems all too clear that some other force is responsible for who a person is. In other cases, it is clear that a person's "self" has been at the very least highly influenced and shaped by an external force. The danger, of course, is that such talk can end up undermining all of criminal law. If a person is not responsible for who he is, on what moral grounds do we punish the person when that "self"—

for which the person is not responsible—commits an offense? But if a person's blameworthiness cannot be judged until the law determines how the person came to be the person he is, the law will rarely be able to pass moral judgment on anyone.

Can the criminal law save itself by showing that most offenders are responsible for who they are, while at the same time staying true to its justice mission by excusing those offenders whose "self" really is the product of forces beyond the person's control?

A FARM BOY'S TREASON?

It is May 18, 1951. Seventeen-year-old Richard Tenneson is on the line in Korea with the Second Army Division south of the thirty-eighth parallel. The communist Chinese are in the midst of a spring offensive that pushes the Second Division back toward Seoul and cuts it off from the main body of American forces. Communist forces overrun Richard's position and take him prisoner along with hundreds of others.

During the next five months, Richard and the other prisoners are marched north. At first, they move only at night to hide from enemy planes. When out of enemy aircraft range, they are marched all day as well. Prisoners must forage for their own food, often eating insects, raw frogs, and the sides of corn stalks. Dysentery and starvation are common. Prisoners are dying all around Richard. More than half drop before the march ends three hundred miles north at a prison camp on the Yalu River near Chungsong.

It is an experience like nothing before for Richard. He grew up on a small farm in rural Minnesota, some distance from the nearest hamlet of Alden, which is some distance from the nearest town, Albert Lea, population fourteen thousand. He has never before traveled outside rural Minnesota.

His upbringing is neither idyllic nor tragic. His father and mother divorce when he is two, but he is always well cared for. He lives with his stepfather, with whom he does not get along, and his mother, with whom he is close. She is very religious. The family is in the poultry business.

Like most teenagers of the time and place, he knows little of politics or international affairs, but he does know easy patriotism. When the Korean war breaks out, Richard quits high school and persuades his

Richard Tenneson (lower right) in 1955. This photograph was enclosed in a letter he wrote to his mother. (AP/Wide World Photos)

mother to sign his enlistment papers. During his visit home after basic training and before being shipped to Korea, Richard tells his mother, "If I should win the Congressional Medal of Honor, I still wouldn't have done enough for my country."

When the prisoners reach the camp, they are given blue cotton-padded uniforms that look like pajamas. They live in large mud and bamboo huts. Body lice, dysentery, intestinal worms, pneumonia, and other diseases are common. During the winter, temperatures drop below zero.

A few weeks after reaching the camp, Richard is removed from the general population; his captors say he is being hospitalized for pneumonia. When Richard emerges from his "hospital" stay, he has a different view of the world. He is a devoted true believer in the communist Chinese cause.

Richard makes propaganda broadcasts for his captors and works to promote their cause even among the prisoners. A few months later, in February 1952, Richard, now eighteen, formally renounces his United States citizenship and his belief in God, and defects to communist China. If anyone doubts the sincerity of his commitment, the doubts are removed the next year. In December 1953, when the Korean hostilities cease, Richard joins twenty other POWs who refuse repatriation to the United States and elect to stay with their former captors.

His stunned mother travels at her own expense to try to talk him out of his decision. She is not allowed to see him. Instead, she is given a rude and mocking letter, composed by him at a group meeting with his fellow defectors, where each sentence, once composed, is read aloud to be criticized or cheered by the group. At one point in the letter he warns her, "United States authorities . . . have probably told you that I was forced, doped, brainwashed or some other horse manure that they use to slander and defile people like myself who will stand up for his own rights and the rights of man." He tells her he will stay with the communist Chinese because that is how he can best bring peace to mankind.

The Power of Coercive Indoctrination

Why this sudden transformation from patriotic rural Minnesota farm boy to enthusiastic aid to his country's wartime enemy?

In the aftermath of the revolution in China, the communists develop considerable expertise in what is now called "coercive indoctrination." Their methods have been studied by Westerners and their effectiveness proven. In fact, after the experience in Korea, the U.S. military changes its policy to no longer expect POWs to give only name, rank, and serial number, as the Geneva convention provides. The human psyche is too vulnerable, they conclude, to resist indoctrination by an experienced captor. The military services begin giving special training to those in danger of capture to help them resist indoctrination. But early forms of the training, which give trainees a brief taste of the communist Chinese methods, are discontinued when it becomes apparent they are counterproductive, causing trainees to fear the power and inevitability of the indoctrination process.

The communist Chinese coercive indoctrination techniques are derived not from advanced social science theory but from practical trial and error in thousands of hamlets and villages in China, developed as the communists sought to consolidate their control and political reforms after the revolution. Their techniques do not rely on physical beatings or torture. Such were used crudely by the Viet Cong against some POWs in Vietnam, but are judged counterproductive to effective coercive indoctrination because they trigger undesirable resistance by the subject. Nor does effective coercive indoctrination involve drugs or hypnosis, as a popular 1962 movie, *The Manchurian Candidate*, suggests. Torture or drugs may be used to obtain a confession or some other single propaganda performance, but to produce a fully indoctrinated true believer, a more subtle process of several stages is required.

The indoctrinator first establishes isolation and control of the subject—isolation from other persons and information, and control over the prisoner's body and environment. These conditions then allow implementation of the two-stage program: destruction of the previously existing self, and construction of a new self with new beliefs and values.

The destruction stage follows several avenues: (1) systematic physiological debilitation, commonly by means of inadequate diet, insufficient sleep, and poor sanitation; (2) creation of constant background anxiety, including implied threats of injury or death by a seemingly all-powerful captor (often with occasional periods of leniency, which create expectations that can be dashed, thereby reinforcing the subject's helplessness and the captor's power); (3) degradation of the subject's preexisting self, including at late stages the use of peer pressure among indoctrinees, often applied through ritual "struggle" sessions; and (4) required performance of symbolic acts of self-betrayal, betrayal of group norms, and public confession. The severe conditions of the five-month march to the prison camp were a useful prelude to the destruction process, which formally began upon Richard's isolation from the general population for "hospital" treatment.

The construction stage is more prosaic. Once the subject is psychologically broken, he is built up again in the form that the captor desires, through the alleviation of physical stress and deprivation and offerings of emotional support tied to the subject's appreciation of the rightness of the indoctrinator's views. The result is a true believer. While physical or psychological duress may be used during the indoctrination process, once the process is complete, the subject has internalized the captor's values and beliefs. His statements and conduct thereafter are guided by the coercively induced beliefs and values, but are not themselves coerced. Focusing only on the present, one would say that the "brainwashed" subject's beliefs and values are as much his own as our beliefs and values are our own.

In milder form, the techniques of coercive indoctrination are used in cults, which even in their less coercive form have the power to take over lives and even produce mass suicides, as in Jonestown and Heaven's Gate. One may have thought it peculiar for the Jonestown leader to move an entire cult from San Francisco to Guyana. But shifting members to a faraway jungle is an ingenious means for inexpensive and complete isolation and dependency.

The psychological dynamics behind the indoctrination power of the captor are sufficiently strong that a captor can have an effect almost without effort or intention. The Stockholm Syndrome is named for a 1973 episode in which four hostages of bank robbers bonded with their captives during six days in captivity, coming to conclude that the captors actually were protecting them from the police. A 1982 study reports that Stockholm Syndrome develops in half of all victims of hostage cases, even though captors rarely plan such an effect.

Richard's Return

After refusing repatriation, Richard, now twenty, participates in a propaganda campaign of which his defector group is the centerpiece. The group shuttles around China from one event to another, generating a steady stream of newspaper pictures of cheering locals welcoming the group to one or another holiday celebration. Eventually the need for such propaganda passes and the defectors become old news. They are given factory or communal farming jobs and left to themselves. As continued reinforcement of the indoctrination fades, Richard becomes homesick, especially missing his mother. Late in 1955, he arranges through the Red Cross to return to the United States.

During his trip back to the United States, he explains to reporters that he had a falling out with some of his communist colleagues but

Richard Tenneson crosses into British Hong Kong from communist China accompanied by American Red Cross representative Richard Tomlin and British Police Superintendent A. L. Gordon. (AP/Wide World Photos)

does not speak ill of his former captors or of communism. He says he does not regret his earlier decision to refuse repatriation.

After his return to the States, however, his views change quickly. Five days after his return, he is allowed to travel to see his mother in Alden, Minnesota, where he attends church. He becomes increasingly bitter toward his former captors.

It was only four years ago that he left high school and Alden. Much has happened to him since then—his capture, indoctrination, propaganda work, and return. He is now twenty-two years old and still confused by what happened.

Richard is charged with several offenses, including aiding the enemy, and is subject to the death penalty or imprisonment for up to life.

Would you convict Richard? If so, what amount of punishment would you impose?

no liability	☐	1 year	☐
liability but no punishment	☐	3 years	☐
		7 years	☐
1 day	☐	15 years	☐
2 weeks	☐	30 years	☐
2 months	☐	life imprisonment	☐
6 months	☐	death	☐

People's Intuitions of Justice

For many people, their own life experience gives them at least a hint of the natural frailties of the human mind and emotions. We would like to be courageous and heroic in every challenge, as we commonly see in the movies, but reality is different. People struggle, using the talents they have available. It may be that Richard, the unsophisticated

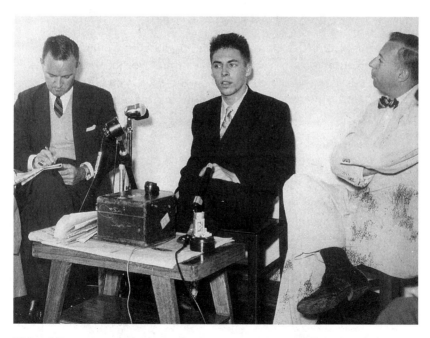

Richard Tenneson at a press conference in a Hong Kong hotel after crossing into British territory. (AP/Wide World Photos)

Minnesota farm boy, could not reasonably have been expected to resist the psychological indoctrination techniques that had proven effective against people stronger than he. Some people will find it difficult to let a traitor go free, no matter what the excuse. But even these people are likely to see Richard as dramatically less blameworthy than one who turns traitor without coercive indoctrination.

This is how the people in the survey sentenced Richard after reading the same facts you read:

no liability	55%	1 year	6%
liability but		3 years	4%
no punishment	24%	7 years	2%
1 day	—	15 years	2%
2 weeks	—	30 years	—
2 months	—	life imprisonment	1%
6 months	3%	death	—

Mean = about three and a half days.

Seventy-nine percent impose either no liability or no punishment. Only 9 percent impose a sentence of over a year. For the serious offenses charged, this suggests that nearly everyone, 91 percent, thinks a significant mitigation appropriate, if not a complete excuse.

The Law's Rules

After return of the POWs at the cessation of hostilities in Korea, the Army court-martials several people who, like Richard, took up the communist line and aided the enemy. But there is strong public reaction against the prosecutions. While the disloyal conduct is condemned, many people feel the conduct clearly was the result of coercive indoctrination that many of the soldiers could not reasonably have been expected to resist. As public dissatisfaction grows, Army prosecutors are forced to carry sidearms to court and to slip out the back door after court sessions.

But no court has ever recognized a defense for coercive indoctrination, "brainwashing." Patty Hearst, when kidnapped by the Symbionese Liberation Army, was held liable for crimes she committed while supposedly transformed into the revolutionary "Tanya." (The law gives a defense to people who are physically coerced to commit an offense, such as a POW tortured into making a propaganda statement. But the coercively indoctrinated POW is not acting under duress in the traditional sense.)

Given the evidence of the power of coercive indoctrination, why such resistance in law to recognizing a defense? If coercive indoctrination renders a Richard blameless for conduct induced by the indoctrination, ought not the criminal law take notice? The criminal law, after all, claims to be in the business of doing "justice." It holds out criminal liability as a signal that moral condemnation and stigmatization are deserved. It claims criminal liability as the justification for imposing "punishment"—that is, suffering thought to be deserved because of a person's blameworthy conduct. To insure a focus on blameworthiness, the criminal law requires proof of a culpable state of mind and provides excuse defenses. It even regularly acquits as blameless, under an insanity defense for example, persons who continue to be dangerous. To do otherwise, the law reasons, would undercut its moral authority, and thereby reduce the law's ability to condemn and stigmatize by criminal conviction those who deserve it. It is this stigmatizing effect of criminal conviction, more than the threat of actual punishment, that for many people gives the law the behavioral influence it has.

If the criminal justice system is to send a moral message, it must be as vigilant to excuse the blameless as to punish the blameworthy. That means that if a person commits an offense entirely because of coercive indoctrination, which he could not reasonably have been expected to resist, his blamelessness ought to bar criminal liability.

In the Army view, however, whatever the extent of the "traitor" POW's blameworthiness or lack thereof, the law is the law. The law does not recognize a defense or mitigation for coercive indoctrination, and therefore neither will the Army. Many former POWs claiming coercive indoctrination are convicted. Prison terms commonly range between eight and twenty years; some get life imprisonment.

But a U.S. Supreme Court decision coming in the midst of the prosecutions changes the ground rules. The Court holds that only the Department of Justice, not the Army, can prosecute soldiers no longer in service, which amounts to about half of the three thousand eligible for prosecution. And the Department of Justice takes a different view of coercive indoctrination than does the Army.

The Department decides not to prosecute. It knows that collaboration was widespread among American prisoners who were coercively indoctrinated. Even many of the prospective witnesses the prosecutors would rely on engaged in some collaboration activities. The Department also concludes that the servicemen had not been adequately prepared for capture and indoctrination. Perhaps most important, the Department fears that any large-scale prosecution would be difficult to win and politically unpopular. The evidence of coercive indoctrination that few could resist would create a "natural sympathy" among jurors, who would be reluctant to convict the defendants on such a serious charge as treason. The law may not recognize a coercive indoctrination defense, but the Justice Department will.

The difference in view between the Department and the Army may stem in part from the fact that the Army, not the Justice Department, suffered the humiliating public relations nightmare of soldiers refusing repatriation. To the Army, the conduct may seem more unforgivable than it does to the Department.

Whatever the reason for the difference in view, the difference creates its own kind of unfairness. Whether a POW gets prosecuted now depends on whether his enlistment term has expired or, for some other reason, he has been discharged from service. It does not depend on the extent of his indoctrination or the nature of his offense.

The disparity in treatment among the former POWs illustrates why we should not leave to prosecutorial discretion such fundamental decisions as the recognition of a defense. Different prosecutors may have different views. Even if they have the same view, the exercise of discretion may have more to do with the prosecutor's situation than the defendant's. Only slightly different circumstances in the Korean POW case might have resulted in a different disposition. Might the Justice Department decision have been different if there had not been so many defendants and therefore less public attention? Might it have been different if the Army prosecutions and public reaction had come only *after* the Department of Justice had made its decision on whether to prosecute? A formally recognized and codified coercive indoctrination defense could give a defense to the blameless and deny it to the blameworthy, no matter what the vagaries of aroused public opinion or the fortuity of individual prosecutorial discretion.

But this only leads back to the original question: Given the evidence of the power of coercive indoctrination, the apparent strength of public opinion in support of it, and the difficulties inherent in leaving the matter to prosecutorial discretion, why does the law so steadfastly refuse to codify a coercive indoctrination defense for even the clearest cases of blamelessness? No criminal code has ever done so.

The reason may be the troublesome inquiry into which the criminal law would be drawn if it had to determine whether a person is responsible for his or her values and beliefs. Creating the potential for defendants to disavow their beliefs and values, it is feared, would render the justice system unworkable, potentially muddying every case where a defendant could claim that his offense was the result of beliefs or values that were induced by others. Instead, the law assumes that all persons are responsible for the beliefs and values they hold, no matter how strong the evidence to the contrary.

But is it clear that the slope is so slippery? Why not recognize a defense in which the burden is on the *defendant* to prove to a jury that (1) his offense conduct would not have occurred but for his coercive indoctrination and (2) he could not reasonably have been expected to resist the indoctrination. This formulation of a defense would parallel the traditional excuse requirements. Richard might be able to prove these two elements and get a defense. Many other cooperating POWs might not. Most POWs were subjected to some form of attempted indoctrination, such as required attendance at "reeducation" classes, but that regime would hardly be likely to persuade a jury that either of the two defense elements above are satisfied.

Finishing the Story

When Richard refuses repatriation after hostilities cease, he is dishonorably discharged by the Army. Under the holding of the subsequent Supreme Court case, then, he falls outside the jurisdiction of the Army and within the jurisdiction of the Justice Department. (Ironically, by dishonorably discharging the soldiers who refused repatriation, the Army gave up its ability to prosecute this most hated group.) Richard is never prosecuted.

But any number of slight variations in the circumstances easily could have left Richard with a long prison term—a different Supreme Court decision on Army jurisdiction, or even an earlier decision,

Mr. and Mrs. Richard Tenneson relaxing in their suburban Minneapolis apartment. Mrs. Tenneson is knitting clothing for a child expected in December. November 6, 1958. (AP/Wide World Photos)

which would have put the Army on notice not to discharge the non-repatriates.

Despite his good luck in escaping liability, Richard becomes increasingly bitter about his treatment by his former captors: "I was just a kid when I was captured. I didn't have the slightest idea [about political theories]. I was the one they picked out to do a real indoctrination job on, maybe because I was immature and weak. When it came time for repatriation I was completely indoctrinated. I was convinced that I could strike a blow against Imperialism by staying with them. If that sounds silly to you now, it sounds just as silly to me. But I really believed it then."

The last report of Richard is a November 1958 local newspaper story, which recounts the projects of the local Junior Chamber of Commerce in which twenty-five-year-old Richard is taking an active role.

OF HIPPIES AND BREAD TRUCKS: THE ABUSED
LEARNS TO ABUSE

Seven years after Richard Tenneson joins the Junior Chamber of Commerce in Minnesota, Alex Cabarga is born in New Jersey. In 1970, when he is five, Alex's parents give up their traditional life in the suburbs, sell their large house, and move to a San Francisco "experimental community" named Project Two. The group at that time includes twenty-five members and lives in an old warehouse. Their common bond, a sign of the times, is their rejection of all traditional social values. All members, including children, are encouraged to live outside the bounds of existing social norms, including participation in open sexuality and smoking marijuana. The dominant message to Alex from his parents and the other adults is that right-thinking people reject the old conventions.

Several weeks after the family's arrival, a thirty-three-year-old man named Luis "Tree Frog" Johnson joins the group. He is a transient who shares the group's goals of throwing off old taboos. He especially favors complete freedom for children. Tree Frog befriends five-year-old Alex and his two older brothers, and the boys begin spending their days with him. The parents do not like Tree Frog but follow their new code to be open to other lifestyles and perspectives.

Two years later, Alex's parents separate. His mother takes legal custody of the boys and moves to a trailer near the warehouse. Tree Frog lives in an old school bus on the same property and continues his relationship with the boys, but now without parental monitoring. Tree Frog courts seven-year-old Alex as he would a girlfriend. As the two other boys grow older, they move out. The parents suspect Tree Frog is having sex with Alex, but do nothing about it. When Alex is nine, his mother hands over parental custody to Tree Frog, and Alex moves in with him. His mother has been a loving parent for many years but, she explains later, she is simply tired of being a parent. After he gains custody, Tree Frog's physical and sexual abuse of Alex becomes regular. He hits Alex and denies him food if Alex resists having sex or otherwise disobeys.

Tree Frog moves away from the warehouse community. He and Alex live a nomadic life in a dilapidated bread van with cardboard on the windows, moving the van from one seedy San Francisco neighborhood to another. For money, Tree Frog sells pornographic movies of Alex.

Alex Cabarga, in court, at age eighteen. February 7, 1983. (*San Francisco Chronicle*)

The bread van in which Tree Frog and Alex lived. (*San Francisco Chronicle*)

Tree Frog believes in a dogmatic and radical approach to child rearing which advocates open sexual relations between adults and children and argues that even a very young girl can conceive a child. Tree Frog decides that they will kidnap a little girl and raise her according to the radical tenets of the book, including having her conceive Tree Frog's child, who then also will be so raised.

On February 6, 1982 (Alex is now seventeen), they kidnap a two-and-a-half-year-old girl named Tara Elizabeth Burke from her parents' van in a Concord, California, auto supply store parking lot, where she had been left with her nine-year-old brother, Jeremy. Tree Frog treats Tara as he treated Alex after gaining custody. She is denied food unless she obeys directions, which include having sex with Tree Frog and Alex. Tree Frog takes pictures and sometimes movies of Alex and Tara having sex. Tara is not allowed to wash and is kept naked from the waist down. Her once blond hair becomes dirty brown. Tree Frog soon cuts it off.

Two months later, an eleven-year-old Vietnamese runaway named Mac Lin Nguyen is befriended by Tree Frog and offered two hundred dollars to babysit Tara. He moves into the van to live with the group. He is treated as Alex was, originally courted, then, once isolated and dependent, increasingly made Tree Frog's subject of abuse. Tree Frog continues his practice of taking pictures and movies as he directs sex between the children.

For eight months, the four live this way in the bread van. Mac sometimes goes on outings with Tree Frog. He explains later that he does not run away because "I didn't know where to run and I was scared." But on one occasion, Mac escapes through the van's roof ventilator while Tree Frog sleeps, and runs to a house and reports the activities at the van. Police return the next day and break down the door of the van. Tree Frog jumps out screaming obscenities. Police find Alex and Tara under blankets, both naked from the waist down. When Tara is reunited with her parents, they do not recognize her. She has an extensive vocabulary, all the most vulgar words imaginable. A therapist later concludes that her ten-month ordeal has scarred her for life.

Several months after the police intervention, Alex says, "I can't believe I did those things." When asked about his sex acts, he says, "I feel dirty about them. I feel stupid. I feel like a dog. I don't like to feel about myself that way."

■

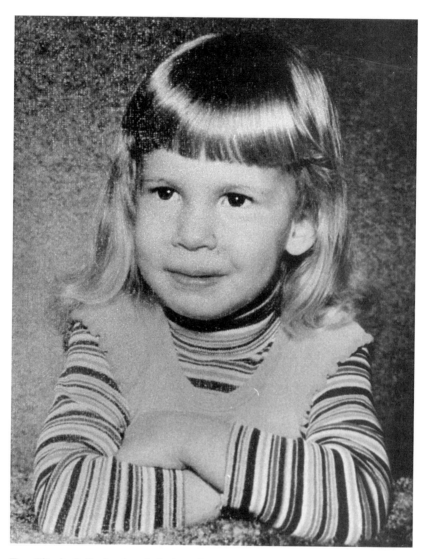

Tara Elizabeth Burke shortly before she was kidnapped from her parents' van. This is the photograph Lieutenant Dick Gordy of the Concord Police Department kept with him during the investigation of the case. (AP/Wide World Photos)

Tara Burke reunited with her mother. December 19, 1982. (AP/Wide World Photos)

Luis "Tree Frog" Johnson in court for sentencing. January 20, 1984. (*San Francisco Chronicle*)

Tree Frog is convicted of 121 counts of kidnapping, false imprisonment, lewd conduct, sodomy, rape, oral copulation, and assault, and imprisoned for life. Should Alex be held criminally liable? If so, what amount of punishment would you impose?

no liability	☐	1 year	☐
liability but		3 years	☐
no punishment	☐	7 years	☐
1 day	☐	15 years	☐
2 weeks	☐	30 years	☐
2 months	☐	life imprisonment	☐
6 months	☐	death	☐

Alex Cabarga and Richard Tenneson

Alex's case has some similarities to Richard Tenneson's, but also some significant differences. Alex was never a prisoner as Richard was. On the other hand, Alex was a psychological captive of sorts of Tree Frog, and perhaps more than that after Tree Frog took parental custody. Indeed, nine-year-old Alex was considerably younger and more vulnerable when given to Tree Frog than was seventeen-year-old Richard when Richard became a POW.

Alex's greater vulnerability was effectively exploited by Tree Frog. Note the similarity between Tree Frog's treatment of Alex and the communist captors' coercive indoctrination of Richard. Tree Frog created isolation and control by living in a bread van from which there was no escape from his constant attention, and a nomadic existence that prevented Alex from developing relationships with other people. In other words, Tree Frog's program followed the standard elements of the destructive phase of coercive indoctrination: (1) physiological debilitation through reduced food, which served in addition as a means of control, and (2) creation of constant background anxiety through the constant fear of abuse and denial of food. (Note Tree Frog's similar controlling and debilitating treatment of Tara, including cutting off her hair, leaving her unwashed, and keeping her undressed from the waist down.)

There was little need for elements (3) and (4)—the degradation of Alex's preexisting self and the required performance of symbolic acts of self-betrayal, betrayal of group norms, and confession. At age nine,

Alex had little preexisting self established, and that which did exist had internalized the counterculture norms of parents and a social group, that the violation of traditional norms was a virtue.

POW Richard, at seventeen, at least had the chance to develop a self, an independent self that had internalized norms he could try to use as an anchor against the current of coercive indoctrination. What was Alex's anchor? The teachings of parents who preached communal and child sex? The moral lessons of parents who turned him over to Tree Frog knowing that Tree Frog was sexually abusing him? Alex's internalized norms from childhood—"right-thinking people reject the old conventions"—were no anchor. They were part of the current. One might conclude that Alex's values and conduct were as induced and manipulated by Tree Frog as were Richard's by his communist captors.

Would Alex qualify for a coercive indoctrination defense under the formulation suggested earlier? (1) It seems clear that Alex would not have engaged in the offense conduct but for Tree Frog's (and his parents') indoctrination. (2) One might conclude that the younger, more vulnerable Alex could not reasonably have been expected to resist Tree Frog's indoctrination any more than POW Richard could have been expected to resist his captors'.

If there is some suspicion on this second point, it is that as Alex grew older, at seventeen or sixteen or earlier, he should have had the strength of character to see the wrongfulness of what he was doing and to break off from Tree Frog. But that assumes Alex had some internal normative conflict over what he was doing, which only brings us back to the lack-of-anchor problem. Certainly most seventeen-year-olds would be repulsed by the conduct. And clearly Alex knew that what he was doing was wrong, at least in the sense that he knew society strongly disapproved of it. After all, he and Tree Frog actively hid what they did. But in Alex's upbringing, societal disapproval meant that it was the "right-thinking" thing to do.

But still, Alex must have known it was wrong in a deeper moral sense. He, better than anyone, knew how it felt to be the object of such manipulation and abuse from Tree Frog. Better than anyone, he could understand what Tara and Mac endured.

On the other hand, Alex *had* chosen to stay with Tree Frog despite the abuse (as did Mac for a time, although he had none of Alex's history of parental collusion and indoctrination).

It is a complex dynamic at work. Abused children often abuse their own children. Fraternity pledges often willingly endure abuse to become a member, and in turn abuse the members of the next year's pledge class. Army recruits, like Richard, volunteer for the abuse of boot camp, and may well aspire to become abusing drill instructors themselves. Knowing the sting of abuse does not always give an understanding of how wrong it is; it sometimes seems only to devalue its wrongfulness, to desensitize the abused to the wrongfulness of abuse.

The misuses of the "abuse excuse" are now well documented. But the unpersuasiveness of some excuse claims does not take away the need for criminal law to make moral judgments. The misuses demonstrate just how important it is for the law to focus, laser-like, on what really matters: the defendant's blameworthiness or lack thereof. Even crime conservatives, of which I am one—and perhaps *especially* crime conservatives—ought to insist on a criminal law with real moral authority. But moral authority requires criminal law to not only condemn the blameworthy, but also to excuse the blameless.

Could we reasonably expect Alex to have resisted Tree Frog's indoctrination? To have spontaneously walked away to start a new life for himself? People will disagree on this. It is not entirely clear in my own mind. But it seems clear that, in judging Alex, the law cannot retain moral credibility if it ignores the indoctrination that brought Alex to the offenses.

People's Intuitions of Justice

Here is how the people in the survey sentenced Alex:

no liability	21%	1 year	9%
liability but		3 years	15%
no punishment	13%	7 years	15%
1 day	1%	15 years	10%
2 weeks	2%	30 years	3%
2 months	2%	life imprisonment	3%
6 months	5%	death	1%

Mean = 7.2 months.

There is wide disagreement among those in our survey. A third impose either no liability or no punishment. But almost half, 47 percent, impose a sentence of three years imprisonment or more. Even among those who impose imprisonment, however, the terms are dramatically less than one might expect for such a collection of serious offenses: only 17 percent suggest prison terms of fifteen years or more. Apparently Alex's history does serve as a substantial mitigation to most people, and as a complete excuse to many.

The Trial and Sentence

Alex is charged by prosecutors with the same range of offenses as Tree Frog. At trial, the prosecution case is based primarily on the pictures and movies taken by Tree Frog. The law has not changed since Richard's time two decades before. Coercive indoctrination is neither a defense nor a mitigation. Alex is convicted of all offenses and sentenced to 208 years in prison. (At the same time, the board of the California Victims of Crime Program concludes that Alex is a victim of Tree Frog's abuse, finds Alex eligible for aid under the program, and agrees to pay ten thousand dollars toward his psychiatric counseling, the same amount that Tara receives.)

Some time later, upon the recommendation of the district attorney, Alex's sentence is reduced to twenty-five years in prison.

The Problem of Discretion

In the end, then, the district attorney and judge see Alex as very different from Tree Frog, who gets no reduction. Alex's ultimate mitigation is not nearly the reduction that the people in our survey would have provided, but nonetheless it is significant. On the other hand, twenty-five years is still a substantial prison term.

Note that even this degree of mitigation depended on the exercise of prosecutorial discretion. The law gives Alex no right to a mitigation or reduction. One easily can imagine slightly different circumstances in which a different result would have occurred. A different person as prosecutor might have had a different view of the case. A prosecutor (or judge) in a tough reelection bid or seeking a different office might have been more afraid of being viewed as soft on a child abuser.

Alex Cabarga's parents, Ted and Diane Cabarga, wait as the jury deliberates. December 22, 1983. (Gary Fong, *San Francisco Chronicle*)

Alex Cabarga after he was sentenced in San Francisco Superior Court to 208 years in prison. (Gary Fong, *San Francisco Chronicle*)

As with the disposition of POWs in Richard's case, we may ask whether Alex's punishment ought to depend in this way on the characteristics and circumstances of the prosecutor rather than on the characteristics and circumstances of the offense and offender? Ought not the legal rules themselves recognize and control a defense or mitigation, according to whether a jury is persuaded that the circumstances warrant it?

Desert versus Dangerousness

Whatever their similarities on the issue of blamelessness resulting from coercive indoctrination, Alex's case is dramatically different from Richard's in an important respect: Richard clearly is no longer dangerous. Even if he did not get himself back on track, he never again will be in the situation where he has the opportunity to repeat his aiding-the-enemy offense. Alex, on the other hand, as a child abuser, is of a class known to commonly reoffend. Further, the arguments used on Alex's behalf to show the inevitability of his indoctrination—his youth and immaturity at the start of the process, the duration and intensity of his indoctrination—are the same facts that suggest his perverted internalized norms will not be so easily straightened as Richard's. Alex won't be welcome at the local Junior Chamber of Commerce any time soon. And even if the prosecutor thinks Alex relatively blameless, he may conclude that a significant prison term is appropriate for Alex simply to protect the community's children.

But note the important shift in the use of the criminal justice system: from doing justice—giving deserved punishment, no more, no less—to protecting the community from future, predicted crimes. It is precisely this shift that is at work in some of the current criminal justice reforms. The "three strikes" laws, which impose automatic life terms on some repeat offenders, are premised on the observation that prior criminal history is one of the best predictors of future criminality. Automatic life terms, then, will protect us from the people most likely to commit crimes in the future. The rise in juvenile crime prompts a similar strategy: starting crime young is one of the best predictors of future criminality. When juvenile offenders are prosecuted as adults, they become eligible for the long adult terms, rather than the limited detentions to which juveniles are subject.

Every society has a right to protect itself and, even if such a right were not formally recognized, a society is likely to find a way to protect itself no matter what obstacles were put in its way. But to use the criminal law for such a protective purpose has serious consequences both for doing justice and for preventing crime in the future.

A sentence that imposes deserved punishment is likely to be different from a sentence designed to incapacitate a dangerous offender. Dangerousness and desert are different. A very minor offense may be committed by someone who is very dangerous. A very serious offense can be committed by someone who is no longer dangerous.

Recall the case of William Rummel in chapter 1, in which the Supreme Court approved the use of life imprisonment for a habitual offender—as in today's "three strikes" laws—where the defendant's life term was imposed for a $129 fraud (taking money to fix an air conditioner he had no intention of fixing). This kind of disconnect between punishment deserved and sentence imposed is not only unjust but also cannot help but incrementally undercut the moral credibility of the criminal law.

The criminal law's moral credibility is essential to effective crime control, as discussed in relation to the *Rummel* case in chapter 1. The threat of punishment may play some role with some people, but the force of norms in influencing conduct plays a substantial role with nearly all people. The real power to enforce compliance with society's rules of prescribed conduct lies not in the threat of official criminal sanction, but in the influence of family and peers in judging each of us and the influence of our own internalized norms by which we judge ourselves. The criminal law can hope to influence these internalized norms and to signal what is truly wrongful, not just prohibited, only if it earns a reputation as a moral authority, as being in the business of doing justice—giving deserved punishment, no more, no less. Using the criminal law for preventive detention may seem an attractive option, but the benefits are short-term and the resulting failures to do justice can only hurt the criminal law's moral credibility in the long run and, thereby, its crime prevention effectiveness.

In contrast, another recent reform—using civil rather than criminal commitment to incarcerate or otherwise control certain sex offenders—offers the protection the community needs, but without damaging the criminal law's moral authority. Ironically, this reform has suffered more criticism than "three strikes," even though it ought to be more attractive to both victims and offenders.

Civil commitment has important differences from criminal commitment. It provides periodic review to determine if the committed person continues to be dangerous. Its protection is more cost-efficient: we pay only for the incarceration needed. At the same time, it is more fair to its subjects, for it requires the minimum restriction of liberty consistent with community safety.

The alternative, the "three strikes" approach, assumes that every repeat offender will be dangerous, and further assumes that each will be dangerous for the rest of his life. Both assumptions are false. Current research suggests that two-thirds of those predicted to commit future offenses are "false positives"; they in fact would not offend again. It also suggests that violent tendencies drop off substantially as offenders move into middle age.

Further, the conditions of civil commitment logically are nonpunitive. The incarceration is not deserved punishment, but rather a sacrifice of individual liberty for community protection. Criminal commitment, in contrast, typically means punitive conditions. The sting is the point of the punishment.

It is puzzling, then, that civil commitment under "sexual predator" laws, as they are called, is opposed by groups like the ACLU. When a state has the power to give life imprisonment under a "three strikes" law, how can it be in a defendant's interest to oppose a system like the "sexual predator" laws that will release the person as soon as he is no longer dangerous, rather than keeping him confined for life? It is an enlightened state (or perhaps a state concerned with cost-efficiency in its protection) that opts for the system that does not commit it so easily to life terms for eighteen-year-olds who may or may not be dangerous when they are fifty. We can obtain greater justice and greater protection by expanding the approach of "sexual predator" laws to cover other dangerous offenders, thereby leaving the criminal justice system to focus solely on investigating blameworthiness and doing justice.

Tara Burke joking with Lieutenant Dick Gordy. October 27, 1997. (*San Francisco Chronicle*)

Today

Tree Frog Johnson remains in prison, serving a 527-year sentence. Alex Cabarga was paroled in 1995, having served eleven years of his twenty-five-year reduced sentence. Tara Burke, kidnapped and abused as a three-year-old, is now attending college (in large part due to the emotional and financial support of the police detective who worked on her abduction case).

Alex Cabarga in an interview room at Soledad Prison. January 1988. (*San Francisco Chronicle*)

GROWING UP GANG: THE SHORT, VIOLENT LIFE
OF ROBERT SANDIFER

While Alex Cabarga is awaiting trial on his offenses, Robert Sandifer is born, the third of eight children, to a Chicago woman who is a drug addict and prostitute. Lorina Sandifer's first child was born when she was fifteen. By the time she is twenty-nine, she has been arrested forty-one times. Robert's father deals drugs and weapons when he is not in prison.

The children frequently are left home alone. When their mother is home, she generally beats the children. (Robert calls his mother "Reen," his grandmother "Mama.") Before age three, Robert has injuries showing regular whippings with an electrical cord and burns from cigarette butts. He and his siblings are placed by Family Services with his grandmother, who is little better. A psychiatric report finds the grandmother to be suffering a "severe borderline personality disorder." At various times, forty children are in her three-bedroom house—ten of her own and thirty grandchildren. Neighbors launch a petition drive to force her to move out of the neighborhood.

Robert's direction of development shows itself early. During a hospital stay when he is not yet three, a social worker says something that angers him. He grabs a toy knife and charges the woman, screaming, "Fuck you, you bitch." He jabs the rubber knife into the woman's arm, saying, "I'm going to cut you."

Robert misses more first grade than he attends, and increasingly lives on the street, where his reputation is bad. "Nobody likes that boy," says thirteen-year-old Morris Anderson, who gets into fistfights with the younger and smaller Robert. A local grocer bars Robert from his store for stealing. "He is a crooked son-of-a-bitch. Always in trouble. He stands out there on the corner and strong-arms other kids." Robert often challenges older, bigger kids to fights, sometimes beating them, and earns a reputation as a street fighter and a bully. "I never played with him 'cause he hung out with the older boys," says Donald Hannah, ten, who attended first grade with Robert. "He would ask you for 50 cents," eleven-year-old Steve Nelson explains, and if he knew you were scared and you gave him the money, he'd ask for another 50 cents." A neighbor says, "You can't really describe how bad he really was. He'd curse you completely out. He broke in school, took money, and burned cars."

One of Robert's first vices is cars. He likes big cars, Lincolns and

Robert Sandifer. (*Chicago Sun-Times*)

Cadillacs, says a seventeen-year-old who knows him. "He can drive real well. It is like a midget driving a luxury car." Robert sometimes hangs out at a garage and shows interest in learning about cars, but mainly he steals them, throws things at them, or burns them. Because he is too young to be locked up, when Robert is arrested, he is usually just taken back to his grandmother's house, then heads back out on the street.

In Robert's world, the strength of the gang speaks loudly. At eight years of age, with his father in prison, his mother absent, and his grandmother disconnected, Robert joins the Black Disciples, one of Chicago's largest street gangs. Young members like Robert are prized because they are immune from detention for more than thirty days.

In the gang Robert finds a family. He picks up the nickname "Yummy" because of his love of cookies and Snickers bars. Although small—four and a half feet tall, eighty-six pounds—Robert is an active and devoted gang member. He has the gang insignia tattooed on his forearm. His first officially recorded offense, at age nine, is an armed robbery. By age eleven, he has compiled a rap sheet of twenty-eight crimes, all but five of which are felonies. His short detentions become less frequent when, because of his violence toward other detained children, Family Services refuses to accept even temporary custody.

On August 28, 1994, Robert is assigned by gang higher-ups to shoot a member of a rival gang, the Gangster Disciples. The attack is part of a larger ongoing conflict between the two groups. At 6:30 P.M.,

One of Robert Sandifer's victims,
Shavon Dean. (Family photo)

eleven-year-old Robert walks up to rival gang member Kianta Britten, sixteen, who is standing on a street corner with other gang members. Robert draws his gun and Kianta turns to run. Robert shoots him twice in the back.

Two hours later, still acting under orders, Robert runs out of a viaduct toward a group of boys playing football and opens fire with his nine-millimeter semiautomatic. He wounds Sammy Saey, seventeen, and hits in the head and kills Shavon Dean, a fourteen-year-old girl.

Robert is now wanted for murder, attempted murder, and aggravated assault.

If Robert, now eleven, is prosecuted as an adult, would you convict? If so, what amount of punishment, if any, would you impose on Robert?

no liability	☐	1 year	☐
liability but		3 years	☐
no punishment	☐	7 years	☐
1 day	☐	15 years	☐
2 weeks	☐	30 years	☐
2 months	☐	life imprisonment	☐
6 months	☐	death	☐

People's Intuitions of Justice

Here is how the people in the survey sentenced Robert:

no liability	2%	1 year	—
liability but		3 years	2%
no punishment	2%	7 years	17%
1 day	—	15 years	22%
2 weeks	—	30 years	16%
2 months	—	life imprisonment	29%
6 months	—	death	8%

Mean = 21 years.

Three-quarters of the people give Robert a substantial prison sentence of fifteen years or more. It is unclear whether such sentences are motivated by a conclusion that Robert is, and is likely to

Lorina Sandifer, the mother of eleven-year-old Robert Sandifer, on her porch with a family friend, Sherman Nelson. (John White, *Chicago Sun-Times*)

remain, dangerous, or by a conclusion that Robert, although only eleven years old, deserves harsh punishment.

Robert Sandifer and Alex Cabarga

Juvenile violence is a serious problem. One-quarter of serious violent crimes are committed by juveniles. Juvenile violence is escalating. Killings by juveniles have more than doubled in the last two decades. The number of juveniles killed also has more than doubled. A society sensitive to the safety of its members will do what is necessary to protect them, especially when the victims of the violence frequently are children. It is common for people to look to the criminal justice system for protection from crime, thus it should be no surprise that many states have revised their criminal law to allow the prosecution of juveniles as adults. Twenty-seven states would now allow the prosecution of Robert as an adult, despite his being eleven years old: Alaska, Arizona, Delaware, Florida, Georgia, Indiana, Maine, Maryland, Massachusetts, Michigan, Mississippi, Montana, Nebraska, Nevada, New Hampshire, New York, Ohio, Oklahoma, Oregon, Pennsylvania, Rhode Island, South Carolina, South Dakota, Vermont, Washington, West Virginia, and Wyoming.

Does Robert deserve the life imprisonment or long prison term that an adult prosecution for multiple murders would bring?

Robert's case is very different from that of Richard and Alex. Robert is not a prisoner of anyone, even in the sense that Alex is a prisoner of Tree Frog. Indeed, Robert's life is one of complete freedom, to do anything, any time, without restriction.

But in another sense, in looking at the cause of the offenses, one might argue that even Alex had a better chance to internalize society's norms than Robert had. As misguided as his parents were, Alex did have caring, loving parents until he was nine. He would not have been "stabbing" social workers at age three. From its beginning Robert's life has been one of violence. The little adult influence he had taught him the norms of self-indulgence, irresponsibility, and disregard for others. At the age that Alex came under Tree Frog's control, Robert already had the Black Disciples tattooed on his body and adopted as his family.

On the other hand, Robert's life was not one of isolation, as Alex's was in the nomadic bread van. But one might argue that it is precisely the artificiality of Alex's existence that makes Robert's situation more compelling in its effect. It was clear to Alex that there was a world outside the van that did not share the norms Tree Frog taught. Things are less clear for Robert. His bread van is the community around him.

Certainly many people in his community steadfastly oppose norms of violence. After all, they more than anyone else are the innocent victims of the violence. But it is equally clear that for a young boy growing up on the streets, the dominant values will be those of the streets and the gangs. Robert's indoctrinator is not a perverted Tree Frog, but the forces of the world in which he lives. Anyone who doubts the power of such larger forces, compared to those of a single manipulator, need only look at the many cultures dramatically different from our own. Why is it that Japanese culture, for example, produces a level of crime and violence so much lower than our own? When the bread truck is an entire island country, there is no escape; there are no significant alternative norms. Robert's street culture is something less than the near consensus found in Japan's homogeneous island society, but in judging his blameworthiness, we cannot ignore the pervasiveness of the norms of violence in Robert's world.

Would Robert qualify for the coercive indoctrination defense outlined above? (1) Is it true that Robert would not have shot the teenagers but for the norms internalized from his life on the street and in the gang? That seems a safe "yes"; he would not otherwise have committed the offenses. But showing such a "but for" causal connection is not, in itself, adequate to show blamelessness. (2) Could we reasonably have expected Robert to avoid internalizing the norms he did? As in Alex's case, people will disagree. As the comparison above suggests, one can argue that Robert was as vulnerable to corruption as was Alex, but the picture is a complicated one.

Many if not most of the children in Robert's community have difficult lives and messy family situations, but few, I suspect, could satisfy a jury that they ought not to be responsible for the values they have chosen. Most have some kind of positive adult connection, a mother, a grandmother, or an aunt, some alternative source of values that would lead many jurors to say, "Here is an adult who by her deeds offered the boy a different set of values, and the boy can be faulted for choosing instead the more exciting life of the street." But Robert's case is extreme in how little chance he had to learn a different set of norms. Given his life, some people will conclude that we "could not reasonably have expected him to have resisted the indoctrination" of violence and disregard for others.

Many will see a similarity between Robert's situation and Alex's. They may conclude that Robert and Alex could not reasonably have been expected to resist internalizing deviant values, and that neither ought to be accountable for conduct inspired by those deviant values. But the two cases are different in important ways.

First, Alex seems to have figured out that what he was doing is truly wrong. If we do not yet trust him, at least he seems to be moving in the right direction. But juveniles like Robert often have a different attitude, one of continued contempt and hostility for the system and its norms. Displays of hostility and the flashing of gang signs are not uncommon during trials of juveniles. This difference between Robert and Alex might be predicted from their different backgrounds: the earlier and longer the indoctrination, the deeper and longer-lasting its effect.

Even more significant is the differing frequencies of the two kinds of cases. It is one thing to say we will excuse an offender in a bizarre case like Alex's, who has attended pedophile school in a bread truck. But it is something else altogether to give a defense to a dangerous juvenile like Robert, who is different only in degree from many other juveniles making up a noticeable portion of the population. In some inner cities, as many as half the black males have juvenile or adult arrest records. As a political matter, the large number of cases similar in nature if not degree to Robert's means that the fear of abuse of a defense may overwhelm the desire for a just result.

Thus, the difference of greatest practical importance between the two cases is that Alex's indoctrination as a pedophile puts him in a class recognized by both mental health and legal authorities as one of "mental abnormality." This is important because it allows the use of civil commitment, the availability of which can relieve the natural pressure to use long *criminal* commitment terms for societal protection. Under the new "sexual predator" statutes, for example, Alex could be given little or no prison time, but rather civilly committed until he no longer poses a danger.

While mental health professionals might consider Robert psychologically abnormal—what might be termed a "sociopath"—the law has not recognized such a condition as a "mental abnormality" for legal purposes. Until it does, or until traditional limitations on civil commitment are relaxed, the more humane and more fair civil commitment option will not be available, and a society seeking protection will have only the criminal justice system to which to turn. Thus, even if one were

Cragg Hardaway, sixteen, a fellow gang member. He and his fourteen-year-old brother killed Robert Sandifer to keep him quiet. (*Chicago Sun-Times*)

persuaded that Robert's circumstances deserve a mitigation or excuse from punishment, his dangerousness is likely to get him a criminal term in prison for much or most of his life.

The Aftermath

After the shootings, Robert spends three days running from the police, hidden by the gang and moved from house to house. When gang leaders learn that he is thinking of turning himself in, they order him killed. Two brothers, fourteen-year-old Derrick Hardaway and sixteen-year-old Cragg Hardaway, called C.R., are assigned the task.

That night Robert appears on a neighbor's porch, visibly frightened, asking that she call his grandmother so he can turn himself in. He asks if they can pray together.

When the neighbor goes to his grandmother, Derrick Hardaway appears and calls to Robert, telling him to come with him, explaining that the gang is going to take care of him and get him out of town. Robert

The South Side Chicago viaduct under which Robert "Yummy" Sandifer was shot to death. (John White, *Chicago Sun-Times*)

follows him down the alley to a waiting car, a late-model Oldsmobile Delta 88. C.R. is behind the wheel. Robert is told to get in the back seat, face down, which he does.

The three drive several blocks to a viaduct at 108th Street and Dauphin Avenue. C.R. explains they are to meet a gang higher-up. C.R. and Robert get out of the car and head for the viaduct. C.R. tells Derrick to stay with the car and to keep it running. Without Robert hearing, he instructs Derrick to keep the passenger door open and, when he hears shots, to be ready to drive.

C.R. and Robert walk into the viaduct. C.R. lags a bit behind, pulls a gun, and shoots Robert twice in the back of the head.

About a half hour later, two pedestrians flag down a police squad car to report seeing a child's body crumpled in a pool of blood in the viaduct.

At the time of Robert's death, his father is serving a prison sentence in Wisconsin for drug and weapons offenses. One of Robert's siblings is in juvenile detention; another is in a program for neglected children; two others have been recently arrested. Lorina, his mother, blames the government, the media, society, and welfare workers for Robert's death. At Robert's autopsy, forty-nine scars are found on his eleven-year-old body. The only picture of him for display at his funeral is his mug shot.

Desert versus Dangerousness, Again

Many people think Robert's death is justice of a sort: live by the gun, die by the gun. But I am less sure. I am a crime conservative, a former federal prosecutor, but I cannot see eleven-year-old Robert as a criminal, deserving of moral condemnation. I understand the law's fear of looking beyond people's present character to ask how they became who they are. But a narrow coercive indoctrination defense, for which a defendant has the burden of proof, would not open the floodgates.

Janice Field, grandmother of Sandifer, Sherman Nelson, a family friend, and Thenesia McGee, Sandifer's great-aunt, grieve for Robert at his funeral. (John White, *Chicago Sun-Times*)

Perhaps it would give a defense in a case like Robert's, perhaps only a mitigation. But to ignore the corrupting forces at work and the lack of opportunity to internalize society's norms is to ignore the moral and practical importance of doing justice.

People can disagree about this. People have every reason to fear violence and to want to protect themselves. Using the criminal justice system, rather than civil law measures, may be the easiest and surest course of protection. But I would argue that we ought to take the risk of trying other protective measures, other than the criminal justice system, not just for the Richards, Alexes, and Roberts, but for ourselves. To deny a deserved defense or mitigation is to undercut the moral authority of our criminal law, an authority that stands as the root of the criminal law's greatest power to influence conduct. Only a criminal law with moral credibility can hope to transform a criminal prohibition into a moral wrong. Certainly a law that regularly punishes those who do not deserve it, or punishes more than is deserved, increasingly will be seen as in some business other than doing justice.

If we refuse a just sentence for defendants like Alex and Robert, and punish them for our protection, at the very least we ought to recognize them for what they are: martyrs for our safety.

Epilogue

This book has examined a variety of basic questions about criminal liability and punishment: Does law punish having a guilty mind, causing harm, or being dangerous? Do we know what the criminal law commands of us? Does the criminal law care if we don't? Can committing a crime be doing the right thing? Is unjustified wrongdoing ever excused? Are we responsible for who we are?

That examination has provided some answers (all, no, no, yes, yes, and it depends) but, more important, it reveals some inconsistencies and contradictions in the way the law assigns criminal liability and punishment. Those inconsistencies often reflect conflicting, or simply confused, views of lawmakers, views that more often than not exist because of conflicts or confusion in public views and, therefore, in public demands to legislatures.

My hope is that this book will contribute to a clearer public view of the challenge of criminal law and, through that, to a law better suited to meet that challenge.

Appendix

Governing Law, Then and Now

I. THE CASE OF LARRY EUGENE PHILLIPS (CALIFORNIA, 1993)

A. Existing Law at the Time of the Case

California Penal Code (1988)

§ 21(a)—Attempt to Commit Crime; Specific Intent and Ineffectual Act

An attempt to commit a crime consists of two elements: a specific intent to commit the crime, and a direct but ineffectual act done toward its commission.

§ 664—Attempts; Punishment

Every person who attempts to commit any crime, but fails, or is prevented or intercepted in the perpetration thereof, is punishable, where no provision is made by law for the punishment of such attempts, as follows:

(a) If the offense so attempted is punishable by imprisonment in the state prison, the person guilty of that attempt is punishable by imprisonment in the state prison for one-half the term of imprisonment prescribed upon a conviction of the offense so attempted; provided, however, that if the crime attempted is willful, deliberate, and premeditated murder, as defined in Section 189, the person guilty of that attempt shall be punishable by imprisonment in the state prison for life with the possibility of parole; provided, further, that if the crime attempted is any other one in which the maximum sentence is life imprisonment or death the person guilty of the attempt shall be punishable by imprisonment in the state prison for a term of five, seven, or nine years. . . .

(b) If the offense so attempted is punishable by imprisonment in a county jail, the person guilty of such attempt is punishable by imprisonment in a county jail for a term not exceeding one-half the term of imprisonment prescribed upon a conviction of the offense so attempted.

(c) If the offense so attempted is punishable by a fine, the offender convicted of that attempt is punishable by a fine not exceeding one-half the largest fine which may be imposed upon a conviction of the offense so attempted.

. . .

§ 211—Robbery (Definition)

Robbery is the felonious taking of personal property in the possession of another, from his person or immediate presence, and against his will, accomplished by means of force or fear.

§ 212—Fear (Definition)

The fear mentioned in Section 211 may be either:

(1) The fear of an unlawful injury to the person or property of the person robbed, or of any relative of his or member of his family; or,

(2) The fear of an immediate and unlawful injury to the person or property of anyone in the company of the person robbed at the time of the robbery.

§ 212.5—Robbery; Degrees

(a) Every robbery of any person who is performing his or her duties as an operator of any bus, taxicab, cable car, streetcar, trackless trolley, or other vehicle, including a vehicle operated on stationary rails or on a track or rail suspended in the air, and used for the transportation of persons for hire, every robbery of any passenger which is perpetrated on any of these vehicles, and every robbery which is perpetrated in an inhabited dwelling house, a vessel as defined in Section 21 of the Harbors and Navigation Code which is inhabited and designed for habitation, an inhabited floating home as defined in subdivision (d) of Section 18075.55 of the Health and Safety Code, a trailer coach as defined in the Vehicle Code which is inhabited, or the inhabited portion of any other building is robbery of the first degree.

(b) All kinds of robbery other than those listed in subdivisions (a) are of the second degree.

§ 213—Robbery; Punishment

(a) Robbery is punishable as follows:

(1) Robbery of the first degree: by imprisonment in the state prison for three, four, or six years.

(2) Robbery of the second degree: by imprisonment in the state prison for two, three, or five years.

(b) Notwithstanding Section 664, attempted robbery is punishable by imprisonment in the state prison.

§ 182—Conspiracy (Definition); Punishment; Venue; Evidence
Necessary to Support Conviction

(a) If two or more persons conspire:

(1) To commit any crime.

(2) Falsely and maliciously to indict another for any crime, or to procure another to be charged or arrested for any crime.

(3) Falsely to move or maintain any suit, action or proceeding.

(4) To cheat and defraud any person of any property, by any means which are in themselves criminal, or to obtain money or property by false pretenses or by false promises with fraudulent intent not to perform such promises.

(5) To commit any act injurious to the public health, to public morals, or to pervert or obstruct justice, or the due administration of the laws.

(6) To commit any crime against the person of the President or Vice President of the United States, the governor of any state or territory, any United States justice or judge, or the secretary of any of the executive departments of the United States.

They are punishable as follows:

When they conspire to commit any crime against the person of any official, . . . they are guilty of a felony and are punishable by imprisonment in the state prison for five, seven, or nine years.

When they conspire to commit any other felony, they shall be punishable in the same manner and to the same extent as is provided for the punishment of that felony. If the felony is one for which different punishments are prescribed for different degrees, the jury or court which finds the defendant guilty thereof shall determine the degree of the felony defendant conspired to commit. If the degree is not so determined, the punishment for conspiracy to commit the felony shall be that prescribed for the lesser degree, except in the case of conspiracy to commit murder, in which case the punishment shall be that prescribed for murder in the first degree.

If the felony is conspiracy to commit two or more felonies which have different punishments and the commission of those felonies constitute but one offense of conspiracy, the penalty shall be that prescribed for the felony which has the greater maximum term. . . .

§ 183—Non-criminal Conspiracies; No Criminal Punishment

No conspiracies, other than those enumerated in the preceding section, are punishable criminally.

§ 184—Overt Act; Venue

No agreement amounts to a conspiracy, unless some act, beside such agreement, be done within this state to effect the object thereof, by one or more of the parties to such agreement and the trial of cases of conspiracy may be had in any county in which any such act be done.

§ 12285—Registration; Contents; Fee; . . . Possession of Weapons;
Conditions; Restrictions; Forgiveness Period

(a) Any person who lawfully possesses an assault weapon, as defined in Section 12276, prior to June 1, 1989, shall register the firearm by January 1, 1991, and any person who lawfully possessed an assault weapon prior to the date it was specified as an assault weapon pursuant to Section 12276.5 shall register the firearm within 90 days, with the Department of Justice pursuant to those procedures that the department may establish. The registration shall contain a description of the firearm that identifies it uniquely, including all identification marks, the full name, address, date of birth, and thumbprint of the owner, and any other information that the department may deem appropriate. The department may charge a fee for registration of up to twenty dollars ($20) per person but not to exceed the actual processing costs of the department. After the department establishes fees sufficient to reimburse the department for processing costs, fees charged shall increase at a rate not to exceed the legislatively approved annual cost-of-living adjustment for the department's budget or as otherwise increased through the Budget Act.

. . .

(c) A person who has registered an assault weapon under this section may possess it only under any of the following conditions unless a permit allowing additional uses is first obtained under Section 12286:

(1) At that person's residence, place of business, or other property owned by that person, or on property owned by another with the owner's express permission.

(2) While on the premises of a target range of a public or private club or organization organized for the purpose of practicing shooting at targets.

(3) While on a target range that holds a regulatory or business license for the purpose of practicing shooting at that target range.

(4) While on the premises of a shooting club which is licensed pursuant to the Fish and Game Code.

(5) While attending any exhibition, display, or educational project which is about firearms and which is sponsored by, conducted under the auspices of, or approved by a law enforcement agency or a nationally or state recognized entity that fosters proficiency in, or promotes education about, firearms.

(6) While on publicly owned land if the possession and use of a firearm described in Section 12276 is specifically permitted by the managing agency of the land.

(7) While transporting the assault weapon between any of the places mentioned in this subdivision, or to any licensed gun dealer, as defined in subdivision (c) of Section 12290, for servicing or repair pursuant to subdivision (b) of Section 12290, if the assault weapon is transported as required by Section 12026.1.

California Penal Code (1988)

§ 30—*Classification*
The parties to crimes are classified as:
(1) Principals; and,
(2) Accessories.

§ 31—*Principals Defined*
All persons concerned in the commission of a crime, whether it be felony or misdemeanor, and whether they directly commit the act constituting the offense, or aid and abet in its commission, or, not being present, have advised and encouraged its commission, and all persons counseling, advising, or encouraging children under the age of fourteen years, lunatics or idiots, to commit any crime, or who, by fraud, contrivance, or force, occasion the drunkenness of another for the purpose of causing him to commit any crime, or who, by threats, menaces, command, or coercion, compel another to commit any crime, are principals in any crime so committed.

§ 32—Accessories Defined
Every person who, after a felony has been committed, harbors, conceals or aids a principal in such felony, with the intent that said principal may avoid or escape from arrest, trial, conviction or punishment, having knowledge that said principal has committed such felony or has been charged with such felony or convicted thereof, is an accessory to such felony.

People v. Manson, 132 Cal. Rptr. 265, 61 Cal. App.3d 102, certiorari denied 97 S.Ct. 1686, 430 U.S. 986, 52 L.Ed.2d. 382 (App. 2 Dist. 1976) (each member of conspiracy is liable for all acts of his coconspirators, intended, unintended, or even actually forbidden provided only that such acts be in furtherance of common purpose of conspiracy).

People v. Johnson, 108 Cal. Rptr. 671, 33 Cal. App.3d 9 (App. 2 Dist. 1973) (once it was conceded that defendant and codefendant were engaged in a conspiracy to rob victim, it was immaterial whether homicide, which allegedly was committed only by codefendant, was part of common plan).

People v. Sconce, 279 Cal. Rptr. 59, 228 Cal. App.3d 693 (App. 2 Dist. 1991) (withdrawal from conspiracy requires affirmative and bona fide rejection or repudiation of conspiracy, communicated to coconspirators).

People v. Dillon, 34 Cal.3d 441, 453 (1983) (an attempt to commit a crime consists of two elements, namely, a specific intent to commit the crime, and a direct but ineffectual act done toward its commission. In determining whether such an act was done, it is necessary to distinguish between mere preparation, on the one hand, and the actual commencement of the doing of the criminal deed, on the other. Mere preparation, which may consist of planning the offense or of devising, obtaining, or arranging the means for its commission, is not sufficient to constitute an attempt. However, acts of a person who intends to commit a crime will constitute an attempt where those acts clearly indicate a certain, unambiguous intent to commit that specific crime. These acts must be an immediate step in the present execution of the criminal design, the progress of which would be completed unless interrupted by some circumstance not intended in the original design).

People v. Lopez, 24 Cal. Rptr.2d 649, 20 Cal. App.4th 897 (1993) (in order to sustain conviction for conspiracy, prosecution must show conspirators agreed that one of them would commit offense which was object of conspiracy, and also that one or more of parties to agreement committed some overt act, besides agreement itself, in furtherance of conspiracy).

B. Current Law That Would Be Applied If the Case Were Prosecuted Today

[The relevant statutes are unchanged.]

2. THE CASE OF JOSEPH B. WOOD (VERMONT, 1879)

A. Existing Law at the Time of the Case

Vermont Statutes, Chapter 189 (1870)

§ 4086—*Murder; Degrees Defined*

Murder committed by means of poison, or by lying in wait, or by wilful, deliberate and premeditated killing, or committed in perpetrating or attempting to perpetrate arson, rape, robbery or burglary, shall be murder of the first degree. All other kinds of murder shall be murder of the second degree.

§ 4088—*Punishment of Murder*

The punishment of murder in the first degree shall be death, and the punishment of murder in the second degree shall be imprisonment in the state prison for life.

§ 4089—*Manslaughter*

A person who commits manslaughter shall be imprisoned in the state prison for life or for not less than seven years, or be fined not more than one thousand dollars.

§ 4119—*With Intent to Kill or Murder, by One Armed*

A person who, armed with a dangerous weapon, assaults another with intent to kill or murder, shall be imprisoned in the state prison for life or for not less than five years.

Acts and Resolves of Vermont (1878)

No. 23—An Act for the Punishment of Attempts to Commit Offenses
   Sec. 1. Every person who shall attempt to commit an offense prohibited by law, punishable by death or imprisonment in the state
prison, and in such attempt shall do any act toward the commission of
such offense, but shall fail in the perpetration by reason of being interrupted or prevented in the execution of the same,—in case no express
provision is made by law for the punishment of such attempt,—shall be
punished, where the offense attempted to be committed is punishable
with death or by imprisonment in the state prison for life, by imprisonment in the state prison for not more than ten years; and where any
other of such offenses is so attempted to be committed, he shall be punished by imprisonment in the state prison, or in the county jail, or in the
state workhouse, or by fine, respectively, as the offense so attempted to
be committed is by law punishable; but in no case shall the punishment
of such last mentioned attempt exceed one half the greatest punishment
which might have been inflicted if the offense so attempted had been
committed.
   Sec. 2. Under an indictment or information charging any principal
offense, the jury may, according as the proof may be, return a verdict
that the respondent is not guilty of the principal offense of the character named in the preceding section charged, but is guilty of an attempt
to commit the same, in the manner provided in the first section of this
act.

Vermont Statutes, Chapter 111 (1851)

§ 13—Accessory Before the Fact in Cases of Murder, etc., How Punished
   Every person, who shall be aiding in the commission of any offense,
punishable with death, or by imprisonment in the state prison, or who
shall be accessory thereto before the fact, by counseling hiring or otherwise procuring such offense to be committed, shall be punished in the
same manner as is now, or which may be hereafter, provided for the
punishment of the principal offender.

State v. Tatro, 50 Vt. 483, 492-93 (1878) (to constitute murder of the first
degree, the act must be done with malice aforethought, and that malice
must be actual, not constructive; where the act is committed deliber-

ately, with a deadly weapon, and is likely to be attended with dangerous consequences, the malice requisite to murder will be presumed; intent for an instant before the blow, is sufficient to constitute malice).

State v. George Scates, 5 Jones Law (N.C.) 425 (1858) (man who inflicted
lethal blow to boy's head cannot be convicted of murder if boy is
burned to death before he can die from blow, as long as man is not acting in concert with arsonist).

B. Current Law That Would Be Applied If the Case Were Prosecuted Today

*Vermont Statutes Annotated, Title 13—Crimes & Criminal Procedure
(1974 & Supp. 1998)*

§ 2301—Murder; Degrees Defined

Murder committed by means of poison, or by lying in wait, or by
wilful, deliberate and premeditated killing, or committed in perpetrating or attempting to perpetrate arson, sexual assault, aggravated sexual
assault, robbery or burglary, shall be murder in the first degree. All
other kinds of murder shall be murder in the second degree.

§ 2302—Determination of Degree

The jury by whom a person is tried for murder, if it finds such person guilty thereof, shall state in its verdict whether it is murder in the
first or in the second degree. If such person is convicted on confession
in open court, the court, by examination of witnesses, shall determine
the degree of the crime and give sentence accordingly.

§ 2303—Penalties for First and Second Degree Murder

(a) The punishment for murder in the first degree shall be imprisonment for life and for a minimum term of 35 years unless the
court finds that there are aggravating or mitigating factors which justify a different minimum term. If the court finds that the aggravating
factors outweigh any mitigating factors, the minimum term may be
longer than 35 years, up to and including life without parole. If the
court finds that the mitigating factors outweigh any aggravating factors the minimum term may be set at less than 35 years but not less
than 15 years.

(b) The punishment for murder in the second degree shall be imprisonment for life and for a minimum term of 20 years unless the court finds that there are aggravating or mitigating factors which justify a different minimum term. If the court finds that the aggravating outweigh any mitigating factors, the minimum term may be longer than 20 years, up to and including life without parole. If the court finds that the mitigating factors outweigh any aggravating factors, the minimum term may be set at less than 20 years but not less than 10 years.

(c) Before sentencing a defendant for first degree murder, the court shall allow the parties to present arguments concerning aggravating and mitigating factors and sentence recommendations. The court shall enter written findings of fact, summarizing the offense and the defendant's participation in it. The court shall also enter specific written findings concerning aggravating and mitigating factors. These findings shall be based on the evidence taken at trial and at the sentence hearing, and on information from the presentence investigation report.

(d) Aggravating factors shall include the following:

(1) The murder was committed while the defendant was in custody under sentence of imprisonment.

(2) The defendant was previously convicted of a felony involving the use of violence to a person.

(3) The murder was committed while the defendant was engaged in the commission of, or in an attempt to commit, or in immediate flight after committing a felony.

(4) The victim of the murder was particularly weak, vulnerable or helpless.

(5) The murder was particularly severe, brutal or cruel.

(6) The murder involved multiple victims.

(7) The murder was random, predatory or arbitrary in nature.

(8) Any other factor that the state offers in support of a greater minimum sentence.

(e) Mitigating factors shall include the following:

(1) The defendant had no significant history of prior criminal activity before sentencing.

(2) The defendant was suffering from a mental or physical disability or condition that significantly reduced his or her culpability for the murder.

(3) The defendant was an accomplice in the murder committed by another person and his or her participation was relatively minor.

(4) The defendant, because of youth or old age, lacked substantial judgement in committing the murder.

(5) The defendant acted under duress, coercion, threat or compulsion insufficient to constitute a defense but which sufficiently affected his or her conduct.

(6) The victim was a participant in the defendant's conduct or consented to it.

(7) Any other factor that the defendant offers in support of a lesser minimum sentence.

§ 9—Attempts

(a) A person who attempts to commit an offense and does an act toward the commission thereof, but by reason of being interrupted or prevented fails in the execution of the same, shall be punished as herein provided unless other express provision is made by law for the punishment of the attempt. If the offense attempted to be committed is murder, aggravated murder, Kidnapping, arson causing death, aggravated sexual assault or sexual assault, a person shall be punished as the offense attempted to be committed is by law punishable.

(b) If the offense attempted to be committed is a felony other than those set forth in subsection (a) of this section, a person shall be punished by the less severe of the following punishments:

(1) imprisonment for not more than ten years and fined not more than $10,000.00 or both; or

(2) as the offense attempted to be committed is by law punishable.

(c) If the offense attempted to be committed is a misdemeanor, a person shall be imprisoned or fined, or both, in an amount not to exceed one-half the maximum penalty for which the offense so attempted to be committed is by law punishable.

Vermont Statutes, Title 13—Crimes & Criminal Procedure (1974 & Supp. 1998)

§ 3—Accessory Aiding Commission of Felony

A person who aids in the commission of a felony shall be punished as a principal.

State v. Barr, 126 Vt. 112, 223 A.2d 462 (1966) (where several persons combine under a common understanding and with a common purpose to do an illegal act, each one is criminally responsible for the act of each and all who participate with him in the execution of the unlawful design).

3. THE CASE OF WILLIAM JAMES RUMMEL (TEXAS, 1973)

A. Existing Law Applied in the Case

Vernon's Texas Penal Code Annotated (1953)

§ 1555b—Intent to Defraud; Credit Card Fraud; Punishment
Section 1. It shall be unlawful for any person to present a credit card or alleged credit card, with the intent to defraud, to obtain or attempt to obtain any item of value or service of any type; or to present such credit card or alleged credit card, with the intent to defraud, to pay for items of value or services rendered.

. . .

Section (4)(d). For a violation of this Act, in the event the amount of the credit obtained or the value of the items or services is Fifty Dollars ($ 50) or more, punishment shall be confinement in the penitentiary for not less than two (2) nor more than ten (10) years.

§ 996—Forgery; Punishment
If any person shall knowingly pass as true, or attempt to pass as true, any such forged instrument in writing as is mentioned and defined in the preceding articles of this chapter, he shall be confined in the penitentiary not less than two nor more than five years.

§ 1410—Theft (Defined)
Theft is the fraudulent taking of corporeal personal property belonging to another from his possession, or from the possession of some person holding the same for him, without his consent, with intent to deprive the owner of the value of the same, and to appropriate it to the use or benefit of the person taking.

§ 1421—Punishment for Felony Theft

Theft of property of the value of fifty dollars or over shall be punished by confinement in the penitentiary not less than two nor more than ten years.

§ 1422—Punishment for Misdemeanor Theft

Theft of property under the value of fifty dollars and over the value of five dollars shall be punished by imprisonment in jail not exceeding two years, and by fine not exceeding five hundred dollars, or by such imprisonment without fine; theft of property of the value of five dollars or under shall be punished by a fine not exceeding two hundred dollars.

§ 63—Third Conviction for Felony

Whoever shall have been three times convicted of a felony less than capital shall on such third conviction be imprisoned for life in the penitentiary.

B. Current Law That Would Be Applied If the Case Were Prosecuted Today

Vernon's Texas Penal Code Annotated (1994 & Supp. 1998)

[The offense definitions of credit card abuse (§ 32.31), forgery (§ 32.21), and theft (§ 31.03) are now considerably more detailed than in 1973. Credit card abuse and forgery are generally "state jail felonies." Theft is a "state jail felony" only if the value of the property is $1,500 or more; otherwise it is only a misdemeanor. If the amount is $500 or more but less than $1,500, the offense is a class A misdemeanor. If the amount is $50 or more, or $20 or more if theft by check (§ 31.06), the offense is a class B misdemeanor. Otherwise the offense is a class C misdemeanor.]

§ 12.03—Classification of Misdemeanors

(a) Misdemeanors are classified according to the relative seriousness of the offense into three categories:

(1) Class A misdemeanors;

(2) Class B misdemeanors;

(3) Class C misdemeanors;

(b) An offense designated a misdemeanor in this code without specification as to punishment or category is a Class C misdemeanor.

(c) Conviction of a Class C misdemeanor does not impose any legal disability or disadvantage.

§ 12.04—Classification of Felonies
(a) Felonies are classified according to the relative seriousness of the offense into five categories:
    (1) capital felonies;
    (2) felonies of the first degree;
    (3) felonies of the second degree;
    (4) felonies of the third degree;
    (5) state jail felonies.

(b) An offense designated a felony in this code without specification as to category is a state jail felony.

§ 12.21—Class A Misdemeanor
An individual adjudged guilty of a Class A misdemeanor shall be punished by:
    (1) a fine not to exceed $4,000;
    (2) confinement in jail for a term not to exceed one year; or
    (3) both such fine and confinement.

§ 12.22—Class B Misdemeanor
An individual adjudged guilty of a Class B misdemeanor shall be punished by:
    (1) a fine not to exceed $2,000;
    (2) confinement in jail for a term not to exceed 180 days; or
    (3) both such fine and confinement.

§ 12.23—Class C Misdemeanor
An individual adjudged guilty of a Class C misdemeanor shall be punishable by a fine not to exceed $500.

§ 12.31—Capital Felony
(a) An individual adjudged guilty of a capital felony in a case in which the state seeks the death penalty shall be punished by imprisonment in the institutional division for life or by death. An individual adjudged guilty of a capital felony in a case in which the state does not seek the death penalty shall be punished by imprisonment in the institutional division for life.

(b) In a capital felony trial in which the state seeks the death penalty, prospective jurors shall be informed that a sentence of life imprisonment or death is mandatory on conviction of a capital felony. In a capital felony trial in which the state does not seek the death penalty, prospective jurors shall be informed that the state is not seeking the death penalty and that a sentence of life imprisonment is mandatory on conviction of the capital felony.

§ 12.32—First Degree Felony Punishment
(a) An individual adjudged guilty of a felony of the first degree shall be punished by imprisonment in the institutional division for life or for any term of not more than 99 years or less than 5 years.

(b) In addition to imprisonment, an individual adjudged guilty of a felony of the first degree may be punished by a fine not to exceed $10,000.

§ 12.33—Second Degree Felony Punishment
(a) An individual adjudged guilty of a felony of the second degree shall be punished by imprisonment in the institutional division for any term of not more than 20 years or less than 2 years.

(b) In addition to imprisonment, an individual adjudged guilty of a felony of the second degree may be punished by a fine not to exceed $10,000.

§ 12.34—Third Degree Felony Punishment
(a) An individual adjudged guilty of a felony of the third degree shall be punished by imprisonment in the institutional division for any term of not more than 10 years or less than 2 years.

(b) In addition to imprisonment, an individual adjudged guilty of a felony of the third degree may be punished by a fine not to exceed $10,000.

§ 12.35—State Jail Felony Punishment
(a) Except as provided by Subsection (c), an individual adjudged guilty of a state jail felony shall be punished by confinement in a state jail for any term of not more than two years or less than 180 days.

(b) In addition to confinement, an individual adjudged guilty of a state jail felony may be punished by a fine not to exceed $10,000.

(c) An individual adjudged guilty of a state jail felony shall be punished for a third degree felony if it is shown on the trial of the offense that:

    (1) a deadly weapon as defined by Section 1.07 was used or exhibited during the commission of the offense or during immediate flight following the commission of the offense, and that the individual used or exhibited the deadly weapon or was a party to the offense and knew that a deadly weapon would be used or exhibited; or

    (2) the individual has previously been finally convicted of any felony:

        (A) listed in Section 3g(a)(1), Article 42.12, Code of Criminal Procedure; or

        (B) for which the judgement contains an affirmative finding under Section 3g(a)(2), Article 42.12, Code of Criminal Procedure.

§ 12.41—Classification of Offenses outside This Code

For purposes of this subchapter, any conviction not obtained from a prosecution under this code shall be classified as follows:

    (1) "Felony of the third degree" if imprisonment in a penitentiary is affixed to the offense as a possible punishment;

    (2) "Class B misdemeanor" if the offense is not a felony and confinement in a jail is affixed to the offense as a possible punishment;

    (3) "Class C misdemeanor" if the offense is punishable by fine only.

§ 12.42—Penalties for Repeat and Habitual Felony Offenders

    (a)

        (1) If it is shown on the trial of a state jail felony . . . that the defendant has previously been finally convicted of two state jail felonies, on conviction the defendant shall be punished for a third-degree felony.

        (2) If it is shown on the trial of a state jail felony . . . that the defendant has previously been finally convicted of two felonies, and the second previous felony conviction is for an offense that occurred subsequent to the first previous conviction having become final, on conviction the defendant shall be punished for a second-degree felony.

        (3) If it is shown on the trial of . . . a third-degree felony that the defendant has been once before convicted of a felony, on conviction he shall be punished for a second-degree felony.

(b) If it is shown on the trial of a second-degree felony that the defendant has been once before convicted of a felony, on conviction he shall be punished for a first-degree felony.

(c) If it is shown on the trial of a first-degree felony that the defendant has been once before convicted of a felony, on conviction he shall be punished by imprisonment in the institutional division of the Texas Department of Criminal Justice for life, or for any term of not more than 99 years or less than 15 years. In addition to imprisonment, an individual may be punished by a fine not to exceed $10,000.

(d)

(1) If it is shown on the trial of a felony offense other than a state jail felony . . . that the defendant has previously been finally convicted of two felony offenses, and the second previous felony conviction is for an offense that occurred subsequent to the first previous conviction having become final, on conviction he shall be punished by imprisonment in the institutional division of the Texas Department of Criminal Justice for life, or for any term of not more than 99 years or less than 25 years.

(2) A defendant shall be punished by imprisonment in the institutional division for life if:

(A) the defendant is convicted of an offense:

(i) under Section 22.021, Penal Code;

(ii) under Section 20.04(a)(4), Penal Code, if the defendant committed the offense with the intent to violate or abuse the victim sexually; or

(iii) under Section 30.02, Penal Code, punishable under Subsection (d) of that section, if the defendant committed the offense with the intent to commit a felony described by Subparagraph (i) or (ii) or a felony under Section 21.11 or 22.011, Penal Code; and

(B) the defendant has been previously convicted of two felony offenses, at least one of which is an offense:

(i) under Section 43.25 or 43.26, Penal Code;

(ii) under Section 21.11, 22.011, 22.021, or 25.02, Penal Code;

(iii) under Section 20.04(a)(4), Penal Code, if the defendant committed the offense with the intent to violate or abuse the victim sexually; or

(iv) under Section 30.02, Penal Code, punishable

under Subsection (d) of that section, if the defendant committed the offense with the intent to commit a felony described by Subparagraph (ii) or (iii).

(e) A previous conviction for a state jail felony punished under Section 12.35(a) may not be used for enhancement purposes under Subsection (b), (c), or (d).

(f) For the purposes of Subsections (a)-(c) and (e), an adjudication by a juvenile court under Section 54.03, Family Code, that a child engaged in delinquent conduct constituting a felony offense for which the child is committed to the Texas Youth Commission under Section 54.04(d)(2), (d)(3), or (m), Family Code, or Section 54.05(f), Family Code, is a final felony conviction.

§ 12.43—Penalties for Repeat and Habitual Misdemeanor Offenders

(a) If it is shown on the trial of a Class A misdemeanor that the defendant has been before convicted of a Class A misdemeanor or any degree of felony, on conviction he shall be punished by:

(1) a fine not to exceed $4,000;

(2) confinement in jail for any term of not more than one year or less than 90 days; or

(3) both such fine and confinement.

(b) If it is shown on the trial of a Class B misdemeanor that the defendant has been before convicted of a Class A or Class B misdemeanor or any degree of felony, on conviction he shall be punished by:

(1) a fine not to exceed $2,000;

(2) confinement in jail for any term of not more than 180 days or less than 30 days; or

(3) both such fine and confinement.

(c) If the punishment scheme for an offense contains a specific enhancement provision increasing punishment for a defendant who has previously been convicted of the offense, the specific enhancement provision controls over this section.

4. THE CASE OF CANNA BAKER (ARKANSAS, 1948)

A. Existing Law Applied in the Case

Arkansas Statutes (1947)

§ 1-101—*Common and Statute Law of England Adopted*

The common law of England, so far as the same is applicable and of a general nature, and all statutes of the British Parliament in aid of or to supply the defects of the common law made prior to the fourth year of James the First [1606] (that are applicable to our own form of government), of a general nature and not local to that kingdom, and not inconsistent with the Constitution and laws of the United States or the Constitution and laws of this State, shall be the rule of decision in this State unless altered or repealed by the General Assembly of this State.

§ 41-107—*Common Law Crimes and Misdemeanors; Jurisdiction; Penalty*

In cases of crimes and misdemeanors committed in this State, the punishment of which has not been provided for by statute, the court having the jurisdiction thereof shall proceed to punish the offender under the provisions of the common or statute law of England put in force in this State by this act [§§ 1-101, 41-107]; but the punishment in such cases shall only be fine and imprisonment, and in such cases the fine shall not exceed one hundred dollars [$100.00] and the imprisonment shall not exceed three [3] months.

Corpus Juris, vol. 17, p. 1148. At common law it was an offense to treat the dead human body indecently, and various specific offenses were recognized. Ordinarily it is a misdemeanor for one upon whom the duty is imposed of having a dead body buried to refuse or neglect to perform such duty.

Wharton's Criminal Law, 12th ed., vol. 2, p. 1704. Indecency in treatment of a dead human body is an offense at common law, as an insult to public decency. Hence it is indictable to expose such a body without proper burial.

Kanavan's Case, 1 Me. 226 (1821) (to cast dead body of bastard child into river, without rites of christian sepulture, is indictable under common law, as offense against common decency).

State v. Bradbury, 136 Me. 347, 9 Atl. 2d 657 (1939) (where man cremates sister, who died of natural causes, in the furnace of their home, man is guilty of common law offense of abuse of corpse).

Thompson v. State, 105 Tenn. 177, 58 S. W. 213 (1900) (undertaker entrusted with body of pauper, who ships body away instead of burying it, is guilty of common law offense of abuse of corpse).

B. Current Law That Would Be Applied If the Case Were Prosecuted Today

Arkansas Statutes (1987 & Supp. 1998)

[§ 1-101, recodified as § 1-2-119, has not changed in substance. § 41-107 has been repealed and replaced with § 5-1-105.]

§ 1-2-202—Liberal Construction

All general provisions, terms, phrases, and expressions used in any statute shall be liberally construed in order that the true intent and meaning of the General Assembly may be fully carried out.

§ 1-2-201—Applicability of §§ 1-2-202 and 1-2-203

The rules prescribed in §§ 1-2-202 . . . shall apply in all cases, both civil and criminal, unless it is otherwise specially provided or unless there is something in the context or subject matter repugnant to that construction.

§ 5-1-105—Offenses; Court Authority Not Limited

(a) An offense is conduct for which a sentence to a term of imprisonment or fine or both is authorized by statute.

(b) Offenses are classified as follows:

(1) Felonies;

(2) Misdemeanors;

(3) Violations.

(c) Nothing in this code shall be construed to limit the power of a court to punish for contempt or to employ any sanction authorized by law for the enforcement of an order, judgement, or decree.

§ 5-4-401—Sentence

(a) A defendant convicted of a felony shall receive a determinate sentence according to the following limitations:

(1) For a Class Y felony, the sentence shall be not less than ten (10) years and not more than forty (40) years, or life;

(2) For a Class A felony, the sentence shall be not less than six (6) years nor more than thirty (30) years;

(3) For a Class B felony, the sentence shall be not less than five (5) years nor more than twenty (20) years;

(4) For a Class C felony, the sentence shall be not less than three (3) years nor more than ten (10) years;

(5) For a Class D felony, the sentence shall not exceed six (6) years;

(6) For an unclassified felony, the sentence shall be in accordance with the limitations of the statute defining the felony.

(b) A defendant convicted of a misdemeanor may be sentenced according to the following limitations:

(1) For a Class A misdemeanor, the sentence shall not exceed one (1) year;

(2) For a Class B misdemeanor, the sentence shall not exceed ninety (90) days;

(3) For a Class C misdemeanor, the sentence shall not exceed thirty (30) days;

(4) For an unclassified misdemeanor, the sentence shall be in accordance with the limitations of the statute defining the misdemeanor.

§ 5-60-101—Abuse of a Corpse

(a) A person commits abuse of a corpse if, except as authorized by law, he knowingly:

(1) Disinters, removes, dissects, or mutilates a corpse; or

(2) Physically mistreats a corpse in a manner offensive to a person of reasonable sensibilities.

(b) Abuse of a corpse is a Class D felony.

5. THE CASE OF JULIO MARRERO (NEW YORK, 1977)

A. Existing Law Applied in the Case

McKinney's Consolidated Laws of New York—Penal Law (1970)

§ 265.01—Criminal Possession of a Weapon in the Fourth Degree

A person is guilty of criminal possession of a weapon in the fourth degree when:

(1) He possesses any firearm, electronic dart gun, gravity knife, switchblade knife, cane sword, billy, blackjack, bludgeon, metal knuckles, chuka stick, sand bag, sandclub, or slingshot, or

(2) He possesses any dagger, dangerous knife, dirk, razor, stiletto, imitation pistol, or any other dangerous or deadly instrument or weapon with intent to use the same unlawfully against another; or

(3) He knowingly has in his possession a rifle, shotgun or firearm in or upon a building or grounds, used for educational purposes, of any school, college or university, except the forestry lands, wherever located, owned and maintained by the State University of New York college of environmental science and forestry, without the written authorization of such educational institution; or

(4) He possesses a rifle or shotgun and has been convicted of a felony or serious offense; or

(5) He possesses any dangerous or deadly weapon and is not a citizen of the United States; or

(6) He is a person who has been certified not suitable to possess a rifle or shotgun, as defined in subsection sixteen of section 265.00, and refuses to yield possession of such rifle or shotgun upon the demand of a police officer. Whenever a person is certified not suitable to possess a rifle or shotgun, a member of the police department to which such certification is made, or of the state police, shall forthwith seize any rifle or shotgun possessed by such person. A rifle or shotgun seized as herein provided shall not be destroyed, but shall be delivered to the headquarters of such police department, or state police, and there retained until the aforesaid certificate has been rescinded by the director or physician in charge, or other disposition of such rifle or shotgun has been ordered or authorized by a court of competent jurisdiction.

§ 265.02—Criminal Possession of a Weapon in the Third Degree
A person is guilty of criminal possession of a weapon in the third degree when:

(1) He commits the crime of criminal possession of a weapon in the fourth degree as defined in subdivision one, two, three or five of section 265.01, and has been previously convicted of any crime; or

(2) He possesses any explosive or incendiary bomb, bombshell, firearm silencer, machine-gun or any other firearm or weapon simulating a machine-gun and which is adaptable for such use; or

(3) He knowingly has in his possession a machine-gun or firearm which has been defaced for the purpose of concealment or prevention of the detection of a crime or misrepresenting the identity of such machine-gun or firearm; or

(4) He possesses any loaded firearm. Such possession shall not, except as provided in subdivision one, constitute a violation of this section if such possession takes place in such person's home or place of business.

(5) (i) He possesses twenty or more firearms; or (ii) he possesses a firearm and has been previously convicted of a felony or a class A misdemeanor defined in this chapter within the five years immediately preceding the commission of the offense and such possession did not take place in the person's home or place of business.

Criminal possession of a weapon in the third degree is a class D felony.

§ 265.20—Exemptions

(A) Sections 265.01, 265.02, 265.03, 265.04, 265.05, 265.10, 265.15 and 270.05 shall not apply to:

(1) Possession of any of the weapons, instruments, appliances or substances specified in sections 265.01, 265.02, 265.03, 265.04, 265.05 and 270.05 by the following:

(a) Persons in the military service of the state of New York when duly authorized by regulations issued by the chief of staff to the governor to possess the same, members of the division of state police, and peace officers as defined in subdivision thirty-three of section 1.20 of the criminal procedure law and persons appointed as railroad policemen pursuant to section eighty-eight of the railroad law.

(b) Persons in the military or other service of the United States, in pursuit of official duty or when duly authorized by federal law, regulation or order to possess the same.

(c) Persons employed in fulfilling defense contracts with the government of the United States or agencies thereof when possession of the same is necessary for manufacture, transport, installation and testing under the requirements of such contract.

(d) A person voluntarily surrendering such weapon, instrument, appliance or substance, provided that such surrender shall be made to the sheriff of the county in which such person resides and in the county of Nassau to the commissioner of police or a member of the police department thereof designated by him, or if such person resides in a city having a population of seventy-five thousand or more to the police commissioner or head of the police force or department, or to a member of the force or department designated by such commissioner or head; and provided, further, that the same shall be surrendered by such person only after he gives notice in writing to the appropriate authority, stating his name, address, the nature of the weapon to be surrendered, and the approximate time of day and the place where such surrender shall take place. Such notice shall be acknowledged immediately upon receipt thereof by such authority. Nothing in this paragraph shall be construed as granting immunity from prosecution for any crime or offense except that of unlawful possession of such weapons, instruments, appliances or substances surrendered as herein provided. A person who possesses any such weapon, instrument, appliance or substance as an executor or administrator or any other lawful possessor of such property of a decedent may continue to possess such property for a period not over fifteen days. If such property is not lawfully disposed of within such period the possessor shall deliver it to an appropriate official described in this paragraph or such property may be delivered to the superintendent of state police. Such officer shall hold it and shall thereafter deliver it on the written request of such executor, administrator or other lawful possessor of such property to a named person, provided such named person is licensed to or is otherwise lawfully permitted to possess the same. If no request to deliver the property is received within two years of the delivery of such property to such official he shall dispose of it in accordance with the provisions of section 400.05 of the penal law.

(2) Possession of a machine-gun, firearm, switchblade knife, gravity knife, billy or blackjack by a warden, superintendent, headkeeper or deputy of a state prison, penitentiary, workhouse, county jail or other institution for the detention of persons convicted or accused of crime or detained as witnesses in criminal cases, in pursuit

of official duty or when duly authorized by regulation or order to possess the same.

(3) Possession of a pistol or revolver by a person to whom a license therefor has been issued as provided under section 400.00; provided, that such a license shall not preclude a conviction for the offense defined in subdivision three of section 265.01.

(4) Possession of a rifle, shotgun or longbow for use while hunting, trapping or fishing, by a person, not a citizen of the United States, carrying a valid license issued pursuant to section 11-0713 of the environmental conservation law.

(5) Possession of a rifle or shotgun by a person who has been convicted as specified in subdivision four of section 265.01 to whom a certificate of good conduct has been issued pursuant to section two hundred forty-two, subdivision three of the executive law.

(6) Possession of a switchblade or gravity knife for use while hunting, trapping or fishing by a person carrying a valid license issued to him pursuant to section 11-0713 of the environmental conservation law.

(7) Possession, at an indoor or outdoor rifle range for the purpose of loading and firing the same, of a rifle of not more than twenty-two caliber rim fire, the propelling force of which may be either gunpowder, air or springs, by a person under sixteen years of age but not under twelve, who is a duly enrolled member of any club, team or society organized for educational purposes and maintaining as a part of its facilities, or having written permission to use, such rifle range under the supervision, guidance and instruction of (a) a duly commissioned officer of the United States army, navy, marine corps or coast guard, or of the national guard of the state of New York; or (b) a duly qualified adult citizen of the United States who has been granted a certificate as an instructor in small arms practice issued by the United States army, navy or marine corps, or by the adjutant general of this state, or by the National Rifle Association of America, a not-for-profit corporation duly organized under the laws of this state.

(8) The manufacture of machine-guns, pilum ballistic knives, switchblade or gravity knives, billies or blackjacks as merchandise and the disposal and shipment thereof direct to a regularly consti-

tuted or appointed state or municipal police department, sheriff, policeman or other peace officer, or to a state prison, penitentiary, workhouse, county jail or other institution for the detention of persons convicted or accused of crime or held as witnesses in criminal cases, or to the military service of this state or of the United States.

(9)

(a) The regular and ordinary transport of firearms as merchandise, provided that the person transporting such firearms, where he knows or has reasonable means of ascertaining what he is transporting, notifies in writing the police commissioner, police chief or other law enforcement officer performing such functions at the place of delivery, of the name and address of the consignee and the place of delivery, and withholds delivery to the consignee for such reasonable period of time designated in writing by such police commissioner, police chief or other law enforcement officer as such official may deem necessary for investigation as to whether the consignee may lawfully receive and possess such firearms.

(b) The transportation of such pistols or revolvers into, out of or within the city of New York may be done only with the consent of the police commissioner of the city of New York. To obtain such consent, the manufacturer must notify the police commissioner in writing of the name and address of the transporting manufacturer, or agent or employee of the manufacturer who is authorized in writing by such manufacturer to transport pistols or revolvers, the number, make and model number of the firearms to be transported and the place where the manufacturer regularly conducts business within the city of New York and such other information as the commissioner may deem necessary. The manufacturer must not transport such pistols and revolvers between the designated places of business for such reasonable period of time designated in writing by the police commissioner as such official may deem necessary for investigation and to give consent. The police commissioner may not unreasonably withhold his consent.

(10) Engaging in the business of gunsmith or dealer in firearms by a person to whom a valid license therefor has been issued pursuant to section 400.00.

(11) Possession of a pistol or revolver by a police officer or sworn peace officer of another state while conducting official business within the state of New York.

(B) At any time, any person who voluntarily delivers to a peace officer any weapon, instrument, appliance or substance specified in section 265.01, 265.02, 265.03, 265.04, or 265.05, under circumstances not suspicious, peculiar or involving the commission of any crime, shall not be arrested. Instead, the officer who might make the arrest shall issue or cause to be issued in a proper case a summons or other legal process to the person for investigation of the source of the weapon, instrument, appliance or substance.

(C) Section 265.01 shall not apply to possession of that type of billy commonly known as a "police baton" which is twenty-four to twenty-six inches in length and no more than one and one-quarter inches in thickness by members of an auxiliary police force of a city with a population in excess of one million persons when duly authorized by regulation or order issued by the police commissioner of such city. Such regulations shall require training in the use of the baton and instruction in the legal use of deadly physical force pursuant to article thirty-five of this chapter. Notwithstanding the provisions of this section or any other provision of law, possession of such baton shall not be authorized when used intentionally to strike another person except in those situations when the use of deadly physical force is authorized by such article thirty-five.

§ 5.00—Penal Law Not Strictly Construed

The general rule that a penal statute is to be strictly construed does not apply to this chapter, but the provisions herein must be construed according to the fair import of their terms to promote justice and effect the objects of the law.

§ 15.00—Culpability; Definitions of Terms

The following definitions are applicable to this chapter:

(1) "Act" means a bodily movement.

(2) "Voluntary act" means a bodily movement performed consciously as a result of effort or determination, and includes the possession of property if the actor was aware of his physical possession or control thereof for a sufficient period to have been able to terminate it.

(3) "Omission" means a failure to perform an act as to which a duty of performance is imposed by law.

(4) "Conduct" means an act or omission and its accompanying mental state.

(5) "To act" means either to perform an act or to omit to perform an act.

(6) "Culpable mental state" means "intentionally"or "knowingly" or "recklessly" or with "criminal negligence," as these terms are defined in section 15.05.

§ 15.05—Culpability; Definitions of Culpable Mental States

The following definitions are applicable to this chapter:

(1) "Intentionally." A person acts intentionally with respect to a result or to conduct described by a statute defining an offense when his conscious objective is to cause such result or to engage in such conduct.

(2) "Knowingly." A person acts knowingly with respect to conduct or to a circumstance described by a statute defining an offense when he is aware that his conduct is of such nature or that such circumstance exists.

(3) "Recklessly." A person acts recklessly with respect to a result or to a circumstance described by a statute defining an offense when he is aware of and consciously disregards a substantial and unjustifiable risk that such result will occur or that such circumstance exists. The risk must be of such nature and degree that disregard thereof constitutes a gross deviation from the standard of conduct that a reasonable person would observe in the situation. A person who creates such a risk but is unaware thereof solely by reason of voluntary intoxication also acts recklessly with respect thereto.

(4) "Criminal negligence." A person acts with criminal negligence with respect to a result or to a circumstance described by a statute defining an offense when he fails to perceive a substantial and unjustifiable risk that such result will occur or that such circumstance exists. The risk must be of such nature and degree that the failure to perceive it constitutes a gross deviation from the standard of care that a reasonable person would observe in the situation.

§ 15.10—Requirements for Criminal Liability in General and
for Offenses of Strict Liability and Mental Culpability

The minimal requirement for criminal liability is the performance by a person of conduct which includes a voluntary act or the omission to perform an act which he is physically capable of performing. If such conduct is all that is required for commission of a particular offense, or if an offense or some material element thereof does not require a culpable mental state on the part of the actor, such offense is one of "strict liability." If a culpable mental state on the part of the actor is required with respect to every material element of an offense, such offense is one of "mental culpability."

§ 15.15—Construction of Statutes with Respect to
Culpability Requirements

(1) When the commission of an offense defined in this chapter, or some element of an offense, requires a particular culpable mental state, such mental state is ordinarily designated in the statute defining the offense by use of the terms "intentionally," "knowingly," "recklessly" or "criminal negligence," or by use of terms, such as "with intent to defraud" and "knowing it to be false," describing a specific kind of intent or knowledge. When one and only one of such terms appears in a statute defining an offense, it is presumed to apply to every element of the offense unless an intent to limit its application clearly appears.

(2) Although no culpable mental state is expressly designated in a statute defining an offense, a culpable mental state may nevertheless be required for the commission of such offense, or with respect to some or all of the material elements thereof, if the proscribed conduct necessarily involves such culpable mental state. A statute defining a crime, unless clearly indicating a legislative intent to impose strict liability, should be construed as defining a crime of mental culpability. This subdivision applies to offenses defined both in and outside this chapter.

§ 15.20—Effect of Ignorance or Mistake upon Liability

(1) A person is not relieved of criminal liability for conduct because he engages in such conduct under a mistaken belief of fact, unless:

(a) Such factual mistake negatives the culpable mental state required for the commission of an offense; or

(b) The statute defining the offense or a statute related thereto expressly provides that such factual mistake constitutes a defense or exemption; or

(c) Such factual mistake is of a kind that supports a defense of justification as defined in article thirty-five of this chapter.

(2) A person is not relieved of criminal liability for conduct because he engages in such conduct under a mistaken belief that it does not, as a matter of law, constitute an offense, unless such mistaken belief is founded upon an official statement of the law contained in:

(a) a statute or other enactment; or

(b) an administrative order or grant of permission; or

(c) a judicial decision of a state or federal court; or

(d) an interpretation of the statute or law relating to the offense, officially made or issued by a public servant, agency or body legally charged or empowered with the responsibility or privilege of administering, enforcing or interpreting such statute or law.

(3) Notwithstanding the use of the term "knowingly" in any provision of this chapter defining an offense in which the age of a child is an element thereof, knowledge by the defendant of the age of such child is not an element of any such offense and it is not, unless expressly so provided, a defense to a prosecution therefor that the defendant did not know the age of the child or believed such age to be the same as or greater than that specified in the statute.

McKinney's Consolidated Laws of New York Annotated—Criminal Procedure Law (1970)

§ 1.20—Definitions of Terms of General Use in this Chapter

Except where different meanings are expressly specified in subsequent provisions of this chapter, the term definitions contained in section 10.00 of the penal law are applicable to this chapter, and, in addition, the following terms have the following meanings:

(1) "Accusatory instrument" means an indictment, an information, a simplified information, a prosecutor's information, a superior court information, a misdemeanor complaint or a felony complaint. Every accusatory instrument, regardless of the person designated therein as accuser, constitutes an accusation on behalf of the state as plaintiff and must be entitled "the people of the state of New York" against a designated person, known as the defendant.

(2) "Local criminal court accusatory instrument" means any accusatory instrument other than an indictment or a superior court information.

(3) "Indictment" means a written accusation by a grand jury, more fully defined and described in article two hundred, filed with a superior court, which charges one or more defendants with the commission of one or more offenses, at least one of which is a crime, and which serves as a basis for prosecution thereof.

(3)-a. "Superior court information" means a written accusation by a district attorney more fully defined and described in articles one hundred ninety-five and two hundred, filed with a superior court pursuant to article one hundred ninety-five, which charges one or more defendants with the commission of one or more offenses, at least one of which is a crime, and which serves as a basis for prosecution thereof.

(4) "Information" means a verified written accusation by a person, more fully defined and described in article one hundred, filed with a local criminal court, which charges one or more defendants with the commission of one or more offenses, none of which is a felony, and which may serve both to commence a criminal action and as a basis for prosecution thereof.

(5) [See, also, subd. 5 below.] "Simplified traffic information" means a written accusation, more fully defined and described in article one hundred, by a police officer or other public servant authorized by law to issue same, filed with a local criminal court, which, being in a brief or simplified form prescribed by the commissioner of motor vehicles, charges a person with one or more traffic infractions or misdemeanors relating to traffic, and which may serve both to commence a criminal action for such offense and as a basis for prosecution thereof.

(5) [See, also, subd. 5 above.]

(a) "Simplified information" means a simplified traffic information, a simplified parks information, or a simplified environmental conservation information.

(b) "Simplified traffic information" means a written accusation by a police officer, or other public servant authorized by law to issue same, more fully defined and described in article one hundred, filed with a local criminal court, which, being in a brief or simplified form prescribed by the commissioner of motor vehicles, charges a person with one or more traffic infractions or misdemeanors relating to traffic, and which may serve both to commence a criminal action for such offense and as a basis for prosecution thereof.

(c) "Simplified parks information" means a written accusation by a police officer, or other public servant authorized by law to issue same, filed with a local criminal court, which, being in a brief or simplified form prescribed by the commissioner of parks and recreation, charges a person with one or more offenses, other than a felony, for which a uniform simplified parks information may be issued pursuant to the parks and recreation law and the navigation law, and which may serve both to commence a criminal action for such offense and as a basis for prosecution thereof.

(d) "Simplified environmental conservation information" means a written accusation by a police officer, or other public servant authorized by law to issue same, filed with a local criminal court, which being in a brief or simplified form prescribed by the commissioner of environmental conservation, charges a person with one or more offenses, other than a felony, for which a uniform simplified environmental conservation simplified information may be issued pursuant to the environmental conservation law, and which may serve both to commence a criminal action for such offense and as a basis for prosecution thereof.

(6) "Prosecutor's information" means a written accusation by a district attorney, more fully defined and described in article one hundred, filed with a local criminal court, which charges one or more defendants with the commission of one or more offenses, none of which is a felony, and which serves as a basis for prosecution thereof.

(7) "Misdemeanor complaint" means a verified written accusation by a person, more fully defined and described in article one hundred, filed with a local criminal court, which charges one or more defendants with the commission of one or more offenses, at least one of which is a misdemeanor and none of which is a felony, and which serves to commence a criminal action but which may not, except upon the defendant's consent, serve as a basis for prosecution of the offenses charged therein.

(8) "Felony complaint" means a verified written accusation by a person, more fully defined and described in article one hundred, filed with a local criminal court, which charges one or more defendants with the commission of one or more felonies and which serves to commence a criminal action but not as a basis for prosecution thereof.

(9) "Arraignment" means the occasion upon which a defendant against whom an accusatory instrument has been filed appears before the court in which the criminal action is pending for the purpose of having such court acquire and exercise control over his person with respect to such accusatory instrument and of setting the course of further proceedings in the action.

(10) "Plea," in addition to its ordinary meaning as prescribed in sections 220.10 and 340.20, means, where appropriate, the occasion upon which a defendant enters such a plea to an accusatory instrument.

(11) "Trial." A jury trial commences with the selection of the jury and includes all further proceedings through the rendition of a verdict. A non-jury trial commences with the first opening address, if there be any, and, if not, when the first witness is sworn, and includes all further proceedings through the rendition of a verdict.

(12) "Verdict" means the announcement by a jury in the case of a jury trial, or by the court in the case of a non-jury trial, of its decision upon the defendant's guilt or innocence of the charges submitted to or considered by it.

(13) "Conviction" means the entry of a plea of guilty to, or a verdict of guilty upon, an accusatory instrument other than a felony complaint, or to one or more counts of such instrument.

(14) "Sentence" means the imposition and entry of sentence upon a conviction.

(15) "Judgment." A judgment is comprised of a conviction and the sentence imposed thereon and is completed by imposition and entry of the sentence.

(16) "Criminal action." A criminal action (a) commences with the filing of an accusatory instrument against a defendant in a criminal court, as specified in subdivision seventeen; (b) includes the filing of all further accusatory instruments directly derived from the initial one, and all proceedings, orders and motions conducted or made by a criminal court in the course of disposing of any such accusatory instrument, or which, regardless of the court in which they occurred or were made, could properly be considered as a part of the record of the case by an appellate court upon an appeal from a judgment of conviction; and (c) terminates with the imposition of sentence or some other final disposition in a criminal court of the last accusatory instrument filed in the case.

(17) "Commencement of criminal action." A criminal action is commenced by the filing of an accusatory instrument against a defen-

dant in a criminal court, and, if more than one accusatory instrument is filed in the course of the action, it commences when the first of such instruments is filed.

(18) "Criminal proceeding" means any proceeding which (a) constitutes a part of a criminal action or (b) occurs in a criminal court and is related to a prospective, pending or completed criminal action, either of this state or of any other jurisdiction, or involves a criminal investigation.

(19) "Criminal court" means any court defined as such by section 10.10.

(20) "Superior court" means any court defined as such by subdivision two of section 10.10.

(21) "Local criminal court" means any court defined as such by subdivision three of section 10.10.

(22) "Intermediate appellate court" means any court possessing appellate jurisdiction, other than the court of appeals.

(23) "Judge" means any judicial officer who is a member of or constitutes a court, whether referred to in another provision of law as a justice or by any other title.

(24) "Trial jurisdiction." A criminal court has "trial jurisdiction" of an offense when an indictment or an information charging such offense may properly be filed with such court, and when such court has authority to accept a plea to, try or otherwise finally dispose of such accusatory instrument.

(25) "Preliminary jurisdiction." A criminal court has "preliminary jurisdiction" of an offense when, regardless of whether it has trial jurisdiction thereof, a criminal action for such offense may be commenced therein, and when such court may conduct proceedings with respect thereto which lead or may lead to prosecution and final disposition of the action in a court having trial jurisdiction thereof.

(26) "Appearance ticket" means a written notice issued by a public servant, more fully defined in section 150.10, requiring a person to appear before a local criminal court in connection with an accusatory instrument to be filed against him therein.

(27) "Summons" means a process of a local criminal court, more fully defined in section 130.10, requiring a defendant to appear before such court for the purpose of arraignment upon an accusatory instrument filed therewith by which a criminal action against him has been commenced.

(28) "Warrant of arrest" means a process of a local criminal court, more fully defined in section 120.10, directing a police officer to arrest a defendant and to bring him before such court for the purpose of arraignment upon an accusatory instrument filed therewith by which a criminal action against him has been commenced.

(29) "Superior court warrant of arrest" means a process of a superior court directing a police officer to arrest a defendant and to bring him before such court for the purpose of arraignment upon an indictment filed therewith by which a criminal action against him has been commenced.

(30) "Bench warrant" means a process of a criminal court in which a criminal action is pending, directing a police officer, or a uniformed court officer, pursuant to paragraph b of subdivision two of section 530.70 of this chapter, to take into custody a defendant in such action who has previously been arraigned upon the accusatory instrument by which the action was commenced, and to bring him before such court. The function of a bench warrant is to achieve the court appearance of a defendant in a pending criminal action for some purpose other than his initial arraignment in the action.

(31) "Prosecutor" means a district attorney or any other public servant who represents the people in a criminal action.

(32) "District attorney" means a district attorney, an assistant district attorney or a special district attorney, and, where appropriate, the attorney general, an assistant attorney general, a deputy attorney general or a special deputy attorney general.

(33) "Peace officer." The following persons are peace officers:

(a) A police officer;

(b) An attendant, uniformed court officer or an official of the supreme court in the first and second departments;

(c) An attendant, uniformed court officer or other official attached to the county courts of Nassau and Suffolk counties;

(d) A marshal, clerk or attendant of a district court;

(e) A clerk, uniformed court officer or other official of the criminal court of the city of New York;

(f) A uniformed court officer or an official of the civil court of the city of New York;

(g) An attendant, clerk or uniformed court officer of the family court;

(h) An attendant, or an official, or guard of any state prison or of any penal correctional institution.

(i) A parole officer in the department of correctional services;

(j) A harbor master appointed by a county, city, town or village;

(k) An investigator of the office of the state commission of investigation;

(l) Onondaga county park rangers;

(m) An officer or agent of a duly incorporated society for the prevention of cruelty to animals and children;

(n) An inspector or investigator of the department of agriculture and markets;

(o) An employee of the department of taxation and finance assigned to enforcement of the tax on cigarettes imposed by article twenty of the tax law by the commissioner of taxation and finance;

(p) An employee of the New York City finance administration assigned to enforcement of the tax on cigarettes imposed by section D46-2.0 of the administrative code of the city of New York by the finance administrator;

(q) A constable or police constable of a city, county, town or village; or a bay constable of the town of Hempstead;

(r) Suffolk county park rangers;

(s) A probation officer;

(t) The sheriff, under-sheriff and deputy sheriffs of New York City;

(u) Long Island railroad police.

(34) "Police officer." The following persons are police officers:

(a) A sworn officer of the division of state police;

(b) Sheriffs, under-sheriffs and deputy sheriffs of counties outside of New York City;

(c) A sworn officer of an authorized county or county parkway police department;

(d) A sworn officer of an authorized police department or force of a city, town, village or police district;

(e) A sworn officer of an authorized police department of an authority or a sworn officer of the state regional park police in the office of parks and recreation;

(f) A sworn officer of the capital police force of the office of general services;

(g) An investigator employed in the office of a district attorney;

(h) An investigator employed by a commission created by an interstate compact who is, to a substantial extent, engaged in the enforcement of the criminal laws of this state;

(i) The chief and deputy fire marshals, the supervising fire marshals and the fire marshals of the bureau of fire investigation of the New York City fire department;

(j) A sworn officer of the division of law enforcement in the department of environmental conservation;

(k) A sworn officer of a police force of a public authority created by an interstate compact;

(l) [See, also, par. (l) below] Long Island railroad police.

(l) [See, also, par. (l) above] An employee of the department of taxation and finance assigned to enforcement of the tax on cigarettes imposed by article twenty of the tax law by the commissioner of taxation and finance for the purpose of applying for and executing search warrants under article six hundred ninety of this chapter in connection with the enforcement of such tax on cigarettes.

(34)-a. "Geographical area of employment." The "geographical area of employment" of certain police officers is as follows:

(a) New York state constitutes the "geographical area of employment" of any police officer employed as such by an agency of the state or by an authority which functions throughout the state;

(b) A county, city, town or village, as the case may be, constitutes the "geographical area of employment" of any police officer employed as such by an agency of such political subdivision or by an authority which functions only in such political subdivision; and

(c) Where an authority functions in more than one county, the "geographical area of employment" of a police officer employed thereby extends through all of such counties.

(35) "Commitment to the custody of the sheriff," when referring to an order of a court located in a county or city which has established a department of correction, means commitment to the commissioner of correction of such county or city.

(36) "County" ordinarily means (a) any county outside of New York City or (b) New York City in its entirety. Unless the context re-

quires a different construction, New York City, despite its five counties, is deemed a single county within the meaning of the provisions of this chapter in which that term appears.

(37) "Lesser included offense." When it is impossible to commit a particular crime without concomitantly committing, by the same conduct, another offense of lesser grade or degree, the latter is, with respect to the former, a "lesser included offense." In any case in which it is legally possible to attempt to commit a crime, an attempt to commit such crime constitutes a lesser included offense with respect thereto.

(38) "Oath" includes an affirmation and every other mode authorized by law of attesting to the truth of that which is stated.

(39) "Petty offense" means a violation or a traffic infraction.

(40) "Evidence in chief" means evidence, received at a trial or other criminal proceeding in which a defendant's guilt or innocence of an offense is in issue, which may be considered as a part of the quantum of substantive proof establishing or tending to establish the commission of such offense or an element thereof or the defendant's connection therewith.

B. Current Law That Would Be Applied If the Case Were Prosecuted Today

McKinney's Consolidated Laws of New York—Criminal Procedure Law (1987 & Supp. 1998)
[The relevant statutes are unchanged, except for the following.]

§ 1.20—Definitions

Except where different meanings are expressly specified in subsequent provisions of this chapter, the term definitions contained in section 10.00 of the penal law are applicable to this chapter, and, in addition, the following terms have the following meanings:

. . .

33. "Peace officer" means *a person listed in section 2.10 of this chapter.*

34. "Police officer." The following persons are police officers: [nine additional categories are added to the definitions of persons who are "police officers."]

. . .

§ 2.10—*Persons Designated as Peace Officers*

Notwithstanding the provisions of any general, special or local law or charter to the contrary, only the following persons shall have the powers of, and shall be peace officers:

(1) Constables or police constables of a town or village, provided such designation is not inconsistent with local law.

(2) The sheriff, undersheriff and deputy sheriffs of New York city and sworn officers of the Westchester county department of public safety services appointed after January thirty-first, nineteen hundred eighty-three to the title of public safety officer and who perform the functions previously performed by a Westchester county deputy sheriff on or prior to such date.

(3) Investigators of the office of the state commission of investigation.

(4) Employees of the department of taxation and finance designated by the commissioner of taxation and finance as peace officers and assigned by the commissioner of taxation and finance (a) [Eff. until Oct. 31, 1997, as amended by L.1995, c. 2, § 70. See, also, par. (a) below.] to the enforcement of any of the criminal or seizure and forfeiture provisions of the tax law relating to (i) taxes imposed under or pursuant to the authority of article twelve-A of the tax law and administered by the commissioner, (ii) taxes imposed under or pursuant to the authority of article eighteen of the tax law and administered by the commissioner, (iii) taxes imposed under article twenty of the tax law, or (iv) sales or compensating use taxes relating to automotive fuel or cigarettes imposed under article twenty-eight or pursuant to the authority of article twenty-nine of the tax law and administered by the commissioner or

(a) [Eff. Oct. 31, 1997, as amended by L.1995, c. 2, § 71. See, also, par. (a) above.] to the enforcement of any of the criminal or seizure and forfeiture provisions of the tax law relating to (i) taxes imposed under or pursuant to the authority of article twelve-A of the tax law and administered by the commissioner of taxation and finance, (ii) taxes imposed under article twenty of the tax law, or (iii) sales or compensating use taxes relating to automotive fuel or cigarettes imposed under article twenty-eight or pursuant to the authority of article twenty-nine of the tax law and administered by the commissioner of taxation and finance or

(b) to the enforcement of any provision of the penal law relating to any of the taxes described in paragraph (a) of this subdivision or (c) [Eff. until Oct. 31, 1997, as amended by L.1993, c. 508. See, also, par. (c) below.] as revenue crimes specialist and assigned to the enforcement of any of the criminal provisions of the tax law or any provision of the penal law relating to taxes imposed under article twenty-eight or pursuant to the authority of article twenty-nine of the tax law and administered by the commissioner or

(c) [Eff. Oct. 31, 1997. See, also, par. (c) above.] as revenue crimes specialist and assigned to the enforcement of any of the criminal provisions of the tax law or any provision of the penal law relating to taxes imposed under article twenty-eight or pursuant to the authority of article twenty-nine of the tax law and administered by the state tax commission or

(d) to the enforcement of any provision of law which is subject to enforcement by criminal penalties and which relates to the performance by persons employed by the department of taxation and finance of the duties of their employment.

Provided, however, that nothing in this subdivision shall be deemed to authorize any such employee designated as a peace officer after November first, nineteen hundred eighty-five to carry, possess, repair or dispose of a firearm unless the appropriate license therefor has been issued pursuant to section 400.00 of the penal law, and further provided that, prior to such designation by the commissioner each such employee shall have successfully completed the training requirements specified in section 2.30 of this chapter.

(5) Employees of the New York city department of finance assigned to enforcement of the tax on cigarettes imposed by title D of chapter forty-six of the administrative code of the city of New York by the commissioner of finance.

(6) Confidential investigators and inspectors, as designated by the commissioner, of the department of agriculture and markets, pursuant to rules of the department.

(7) Officers or agents of a duly incorporated society for the prevention of cruelty to animals.

(7)(a) Officers or agents of a duly incorporated society for the prevention of cruelty to children; provided, however, that nothing in this subdivision shall be deemed to authorize such officer or agent to carry, possess, repair, or dispose of a firearm unless the appropriate license therefor has been issued pursuant to section 400.00 of the penal law; and provided further that such officer or agent shall exercise the powers of a peace officer only when he is acting pursuant to his special duties.

(8) Inspectors and officers of the New York city department of health when acting pursuant to their special duties as set forth in section 564-11.0 of the administrative code of the city of New York; provided, however, that nothing in this subdivision shall be deemed to authorize such officer to carry, possess, repair or dispose of a firearm unless the appropriate license therefor has been issued pursuant to section 400.00 of the penal law.

(9) Park rangers in Suffolk county, who shall be authorized to issue appearance tickets, simplified traffic informations, simplified parks informations and simplified environmental conservation informations.

(10) Broome county park rangers who shall be authorized to issue appearance tickets, simplified traffic informations, simplified parks informations, and simplified environmental conservation informations; provided, however, that nothing in this subdivision shall be deemed to authorize such officer to carry, possess, repair or dispose of a firearm unless the appropriate license therefor has been issued pursuant to section 400.00 of the penal law.

(11) Park rangers in Onondaga and Cayuga counties, who shall be authorized to issue appearance tickets, simplified traffic informations, simplified parks informations and simplified environmental conservation informations, within the respective counties of Onondaga and Cayuga.

(12) Special policemen designated by the commissioner and the directors of in- patient facilities in the office of mental health pursuant to section 7.25 of the mental hygiene law, and special policemen designated by the commissioner and the directors of facilities under his jurisdiction in the office of mental retardation and developmental disabilities pursuant to section 13.25 of the mental hygiene law; provided, however, that nothing in this subdivision shall be deemed to authorize such officers to carry, possess, repair or dispose of a firearm unless the appropriate license therefor has been issued pursuant to section 400.00 of the penal law.

(13) Persons designated as special policemen by the director of a hospital in the department of health pursuant to section four hundred fifty-five of the public health law; provided, however, that nothing in this subdivision shall be deemed to authorize such officer to carry, pos-

sess, repair or dispose of a firearm unless the appropriate license therefor has been issued pursuant to section 400.00 of the penal law.

(14) Peace officers appointed by the state university pursuant to paragraph l of subdivision two of section three hundred fifty-five of the education law; provided, however, that nothing in this subdivision shall be deemed to authorize such officer to carry, possess, repair or dispose of a firearm unless the appropriate license therefor has been issued pursuant to section 400.00 of the penal law.

(15) Uniformed enforcement forces of the New York state thruway authority, when acting pursuant to subdivision two of section three hundred sixty-one of the public authorities law; provided, however, that nothing in this subdivision shall be deemed to authorize such officer to carry, possess, repair or dispose of a firearm unless the appropriate license therefor has been issued pursuant to section 400.00 of the penal law.

(16) Employees of the department of health designated pursuant to section thirty-three hundred eighty-five of the public health law; provided, however, that nothing in this subdivision shall be deemed to authorize such officer to carry, possess, repair or dispose of a firearm unless the appropriate license therefor has been issued pursuant to section 400.00 of the penal law.

(17) Uniformed housing guards of the Buffalo municipal housing authority.

(18) Bay constables of the city of Rye, the villages of Mamaroneck, South Nyack and bay constables of the towns of East Hampton, Hempstead, Oyster Bay, Riverhead, Southampton, Southold, Islip, Shelter Island, Brookhaven, Babylon, Smithtown, Huntington and North Hempstead; provided, however, that nothing in this subdivision shall be deemed to authorize the bay constables in the city of Rye, the village of South Nyack or the towns of Brookhaven, Babylon, Southold, East Hampton, Riverhead, Islip, Smithtown, Huntington and Shelter Island to carry, possess, repair or dispose of a firearm unless the appropriate license therefor has been issued pursuant to section 400.00 of the penal law.

(19) Harbor masters appointed by a county, city, town or village.

(20) Bridge and tunnel officers, sergeants and lieutenants of the Triborough bridge and tunnel authority.

(21)
> (a) Uniformed court officers of the unified court system.

(b) Court clerks of the unified court system in the first and second departments.

(c) Marshall, deputy marshall, clerk or uniformed court officer of a district court.

(d) Marshalls or deputy marshalls of a city court, provided, however, that nothing in this subdivision shall be deemed to authorize such officer to carry, possess, repair or dispose of a firearm unless the appropriate license therefor has been issued pursuant to section 400.00 of the penal law.

(e) Uniformed court officers of the city of Mount Vernon.

(f) Uniformed court officers of the city of Jamestown.

(22) Patrolmen appointed by the Lake George park commission; provided however that nothing in this subdivision shall be deemed to authorize such officer to carry, possess, repair or dispose of a firearm unless the appropriate license therefor has been issued pursuant to section 400.00 of the penal law.

(23) Parole officers or warrant officers in the division of parole.

(24) Probation officers.

(25) Officials, as designated by the commissioner of the department of correctional services pursuant to rules of the department, and correction officers of any state correctional facility or of any penal correctional institution.

(26) Peace officers designated pursuant to the provisions of the New York state defense emergency act, as set forth in chapter seven hundred eighty-four of the laws of nineteen hundred fifty-one, as amended, when acting pursuant to their special duties during a period of attack or imminent attack by enemy forces, or during official drills called to combat natural or man-made disasters, or during official drills in preparation for an attack by enemy forces or in preparation for a natural or man-made disaster; provided, however, that nothing in this subdivision shall be deemed to authorize such officer to carry, possess, repair or dispose of a firearm unless the appropriate license therefor has been issued pursuant to section 400.00 of the penal law; and provided further, that such officer shall have the powers set forth in section 2.20 of this article only during a period of imminent or actual attack by enemy forces and during drills authorized under section twenty-nine-b of article two-B of the executive law, providing for the use of civil defense forces in disasters. Notwithstanding any other provision of law, such officers shall have the power to direct and control traffic during of-

ficial drills in preparation for an attack by enemy forces or in preparation for combating natural or man-made disasters; however, this grant does not include any of the other powers set forth in section 2.20 of this article.

(27) New York city special patrolmen appointed by the police commissioner pursuant to subdivision c or e of section 434a-7.0 or subdivision c or e of section 14-106 of the administrative code of the city of New York; provided, however, that nothing in this subdivision shall be deemed to authorize such officer to carry, possess, repair or dispose of a firearm unless the appropriate license therefor has been issued pursuant to section 400.00 of the penal law and the employer has authorized such officer to possess a firearm during any phase of the officer's on-duty employment. Special patrolmen shall have the powers set forth in section 2.20 of this article only when they are acting pursuant to their special duties; provided, however, that the following categories of New York city special patrolmen shall have such powers whether or not they are acting pursuant to their special duties: campus peace officers-level I, level II and level III and campus public safety officers employed by the city university of New York; school safety officers employed by the board of education of the city of New York; parking control specialists, taxi and limousine inspectors, urban park rangers and evidence and property control specialists employed by the city of New York; and further provided that, with respect to the aforementioned categories of New York city special patrolmen, where such a special patrolman has been appointed by the police commissioner and, upon the expiration of such appointment the police commissioner has neither renewed such appointment nor explicitly determined that such appointment shall not be renewed, such appointment shall remain in full force and effect indefinitely, until such time as the police commissioner expressly determines to either renew or terminate such appointment.

(28) All officers and members of the uniformed force of the New York city fire department as set forth and subject to the limitations contained in section 487a-15.0 of the administrative code of the city of New York; provided, however, that nothing in this subdivision shall be deemed to authorize such officer to carry, possess, repair or dispose of a firearm unless the appropriate license therefor has been issued pursuant to section 400.00 of the penal law.

(29) Special policemen for horse racing, appointed pursuant to the provisions of the pari-mutuel revenue law as set forth in chapter two

hundred fifty-four of the laws of nineteen hundred forty, as amended; provided, however, that nothing in this subdivision shall be deemed to authorize such officer to carry, possess, repair or dispose of a firearm unless the appropriate license therefor has been issued pursuant to section 400.00 of the penal law.

(30) Supervising fire inspectors, fire inspectors, the fire marshal and assistant fire marshals, all of whom are full-time employees of the county of Nassau fire marshal's office, when acting pursuant to their special duties.

(31) A district ranger, assistant district ranger or a forest ranger employed by the state department of environmental conservation.

(32) Investigators of the department of motor vehicles, pursuant to section three hundred ninety-two-b of the vehicle and traffic law; provided, however, that nothing in this subdivision shall be deemed to authorize such officer to carry, possess, repair or dispose of a firearm unless the appropriate license therefor has been issued pursuant to section 400.00 of the penal law.

(33) A city marshall of the city of New York who has received training in firearms handling from the federal bureau of investigation or in the New York city police academy, or in the absence of the available training programs from the federal bureau of investigation and the New York city police academy, from another law enforcement agency located in the state of New York, and who has received a firearms permit from the license division of the New York city police department.

(34) Waterfront and airport investigators, pursuant to subdivision four of section ninety-nine hundred six of the unconsolidated laws; provided, however, that nothing in this subdivision shall be deemed to authorize such officer to carry, possess, repair or dispose of a firearm unless the appropriate license therefor has been issued pursuant to section 400.00 of the penal law.

(35) Special investigators appointed by the state board of elections, pursuant to section 3-107 of the election law.

(36) Investigators appointed by the state liquor authority, pursuant to section fifteen of the alcoholic beverage control law; provided, however, that nothing in this subdivision shall be deemed to authorize such officer to carry, possess, repair or dispose of a firearm unless the appropriate license therefor has been issued pursuant to section 400.00 of the penal law.

(37) Special patrolmen of a political subdivision, appointed pursuant to section two hundred nine-v of the general municipal law; provided, however, that nothing in this subdivision shall be deemed to authorize such officer to carry, possess, repair or dispose of a firearm unless the appropriate license therefor has been issued pursuant to section 400.00 of the penal law.

(38) A special investigator of the New York city department of investigation who has received training in firearms handling in the New York police academy and has received a firearms permit from the license division of the New York city police department.

(39) Broome county special patrolman, appointed by the Broome county attorney; provided, however, that nothing in this subdivision shall be deemed to authorize such officer to carry, possess, repair or dispose of a firearm unless the appropriate license therefor has been issued pursuant to section 400.00 of the penal law.

(40) Special officers employed by the city of New York or by the New York city health and hospitals corporation; provided, however, that nothing in this subdivision shall be deemed to authorize such officer to carry, possess, repair or dispose of a firearm unless the appropriate license therefor has been issued pursuant to section 400.00 of the penal law.

(41) Fire police squads organized pursuant to section two hundred nine-c of the general municipal law, at such times as the fire department, fire company or an emergency rescue and first aid squad of the fire department or fire company are on duty, or when, on orders of the chief of the fire department or fire company of which they are members, they are separately engaged in response to a call for assistance pursuant to the provisions of section two hundred nine of the general municipal law; provided, however, that nothing in this subdivision shall be deemed to authorize such officer to carry, possess, repair or dispose of a firearm unless the appropriate license therefor has been issued pursuant to section 400.00 of the penal law.

(42) Special deputy sheriffs appointed by the sheriff of a county within which any part of the grounds of Cornell university or the grounds of any state institution constituting a part of the educational and research plants owned or under the supervision, administration or control of said university are located pursuant to section fifty-seven hundred nine of the education law; provided, however, that nothing in this subdivision shall be deemed to authorize such officer to carry, pos-

sess, repair or dispose of a firearm unless the appropriate license therefor has been issued pursuant to section 400.00 of the penal law.

(43) Housing patrolmen of the Mount Vernon housing authority, acting pursuant to rules of the Mount Vernon housing authority; provided, however, that nothing in this subdivision shall be deemed to authorize such officer to carry, possess, repair or dispose of a firearm unless the appropriate license therefor has been issued pursuant to section 400.00 of the penal law.

(44) The officers, employees and members of the New York city division of fire prevention, in the bureau of fire, as set forth and subject to the limitations contained in subdivision one of section 487a-1.0 of the administrative code of the city of New York; provided, however, that nothing in this subdivision shall be deemed to authorize such officer to carry, possess, repair or dispose of a firearm unless the appropriate license therefor has been issued pursuant to section 400.00 of the penal law.

(45) Persons appointed and designated as peace officers by the Niagara frontier transportation authority, pursuant to subdivision thirteen of section twelve hundred ninety-nine-e of the public authorities law.

(46) Persons appointed as peace officers by the Sea Gate Association pursuant to the provisions of chapter three hundred ninety-one of the laws of nineteen hundred forty, provided, however, that nothing in this subdivision shall be deemed to authorize such officer to carry, possess, repair or dispose of a firearm unless the appropriate license therefor has been issued pursuant to section 400.00 of the penal law.

(47) Employees of the insurance frauds bureau of the state department of insurance when designated as peace officers by the superintendent of insurance and acting pursuant to their special duties; provided, however, that nothing in this subdivision shall be deemed to authorize such officer to carry, possess, repair or dispose of a firearm unless the appropriate license therefor has been issued pursuant to section 400.00 of the penal law.

(48) New York state air base security guards when they are designated as peace officers under military regulations promulgated by the chief of staff to the governor and when performing their duties as air base security guards pursuant to orders issued by appropriate military authority; provided, however, that nothing in this subdivision shall be deemed to authorize such guards to carry, possess, repair or dispose of

a firearm unless the appropriate license therefor has been issued pursuant to section 400.00 of the penal law.

(49) Members of the army national guard military police and air national guard security personnel belonging to the organized militia of the state of New York when they are designated as peace officers under military regulations promulgated by the adjutant general and when performing their duties as military policemen or air security personnel pursuant to orders issued by appropriate military authority; provided, however, that nothing in this subdivision shall be deemed to authorize such military police or air security personnel to carry, possess, repair or dispose of a firearm unless the appropriate license therefor has been issued pursuant to section 400.00 of the penal law.

(50) Transportation supervisors in the city of White Plains appointed by the commissioner of public safety in the city of White Plains; provided, however, that nothing in this subdivision shall be deemed to authorize such officer to carry, possess, repair or dispose of a firearm unless the appropriate license therefor has been issued pursuant to section 400.00 of the penal law.

(51) Officers and members of the fire investigation division of the fire department of the city of Rochester, the city of Binghamton and the city of Utica, when acting pursuant to their special duties in matters arising under the laws relating to fires, the extinguishment thereof and fire perils; provided, however, that nothing in this subdivision shall be deemed to authorize such officer to carry, possess, repair or dispose of a firearm unless the appropriate license therefor has been issued pursuant to section 400.00 of the penal law.

(52) Security hospital treatment assistants, as so designated by the commissioner of the office of mental health while transporting persons convicted of a crime to court, to other facilities within the jurisdiction of the office of mental health, or to any state or local correctional facility; provided, however, that nothing in this subdivision shall be deemed to authorize such employee to carry, possess, repair or dispose of a firearm unless the appropriate license therefor has been issued pursuant to section 400.00 of the penal law.

(53) Authorized agents of the municipal directors of weights and measures in the counties of Suffolk, Nassau and Westchester when acting pursuant to their special duties as set forth in section one hundred eighty-one of the agriculture and markets law; provided, however, that nothing in this subdivision shall be deemed to authorize such officer to

carry, possess, repair or dispose of a firearm unless the appropriate license therefor has been issued pursuant to section 400.00 of the penal law.

(54) Special policemen appointed pursuant to section one hundred fifty-eight of the town law; provided, however, that nothing in this subdivision shall be deemed to authorize such officer to carry, possess, repair or dispose of a firearm unless the appropriate license therefor has been issued pursuant to section 400.00 of the penal law.

[55. Expired.]

(56) Dog control officers of the town of Brookhaven, who at the discretion of the town board may be designated as constables for the purpose of enforcing article twenty-six of the agriculture and markets law and for the purpose of issuing appearance tickets permitted under article seven of such law; provided, however, that nothing in this subdivision shall be deemed to authorize such officer to carry, possess, repair or dispose of a firearm unless the appropriate license therefor has been issued pursuant to section 400.00 of the penal law.

(57) Harbor Park rangers employed by the Snug Harbor cultural center in Richmond county and appointed as New York city special patrolmen by the police commissioner pursuant to subdivision c of section 14-106 of the administrative code of the city of New York. Notwithstanding any provision of law, rule or regulation, such officers shall be authorized to issue appearance tickets pursuant to section 150.20 of this chapter, and shall have such other powers as are specified in section 2.20 of this article only when acting pursuant to their special duties. Nothing in this subdivision shall be deemed to authorize such officers to carry, possess, repair or dispose of a firearm unless the appropriate license therefor has been issued pursuant to section 400.00 of the penal law and the employer has authorized such officer to possess a firearm during any phase of the officer's on-duty employment.

(57)(a) [See, also, subd. 57-a below.] Seasonal park rangers of the Westchester county department of public safety while employed as authorized by the commissioner of public safety/sheriff of the county of Westchester; provided, however, that nothing in this subdivision shall be deemed to authorize such officer to carry, possess, repair or dispose of a firearm unless the appropriate license therefor has been issued pursuant to section 400.00 of the penal law.

(57)(a) [See, also, subd. 57-a above.] Officers of the Westchester county public safety emergency force, when activated by the commissioner of public safety/sheriff of the county of Westchester; provided, however that nothing in this subdivision shall be deemed to authorize such officer to carry, possess, repair or dispose of a firearm unless the appropriate license therefor has been issued pursuant to section 400.00 of the penal law.

(58) Uniformed members of the security force of the Troy housing authority provided, however, that nothing in this subdivision shall be deemed to authorize such officer to carry, possess, repair or dispose of a firearm unless the appropriate license therefor has been issued pursuant to section 400.00 of the penal law.

(59) Officers and members of the sanitation police of the department of sanitation of the city of New York, duly appointed and designated as peace officers by such department; provided, however, that nothing in this subdivision shall be deemed to authorize such officer to carry, possess, repair or dispose of a firearm unless the appropriate license therefor has been issued pursuant to section 400.00 of the penal law. Provided, further, that nothing in this subdivision shall be deemed to apply to officers and members of the sanitation police regularly and exclusively assigned to enforcement of such city's residential recycling laws.

[60. Expired.]

(61) [As added by L.1992, c. 257. See, also, subd. 61 below.] Chief fire marshall, assistant chief fire marshall, fire marshall II and fire marshall I, all of whom are full-time employees of the Suffolk county department of fire, rescue and emergency services, when acting pursuant to their special duties in matters arising under the laws relating to fires, the extinguishment thereof and fire perils; provided, however, that nothing in this subdivision shall be deemed to authorize such officer to carry, possess, repair or dispose of a firearm unless the appropriate license therefor has been issued pursuant to section 400.00 of the penal law.

(61) [As added by L.1992, c. 321. See, also, subd. 61 above.] Investigators employed by the criminal investigations bureau when assigned to such bureau by the superintendent of banks and acting pursuant to their special duties as set forth in article two-B of the banking law; provided, however, that nothing in this subdivision shall be deemed to authorize such officer to carry, possess, repair or dispose of a firearm unless the appropriate license therefor has been issued pursuant to section 400.00 of the penal law.

(62) [As amended by L.1993, c. 204. See, also, subd. 62 below.] Chief fire marshall, assistant chief fire marshall, fire marshall II and fire marshall I, all of whom are full-time employees of the town of Babylon, when acting pursuant to their special duties in matters arising under the laws relating to fires, the extinguishment thereof and fire perils; provided, however, that nothing in this subdivision shall be deemed to authorize such officer to carry, possess, repair or dispose of a firearm unless the appropriate license therefor has been issued pursuant to section 400.00 of the penal law.

(62) [As added by L.1993, c. 687. See, also, subd. 62 above.] Employees of the division for youth assigned to transport and warrants units who are specifically designated by the director in accordance with section five hundred four-b of the executive law, provided, however, that nothing in this subdivision shall be deemed to authorize such employees to carry, possess, repair or dispose of a firearm unless the appropriate license therefor has been issued pursuant to section 400.00 of the penal law.

(63) [As added by L.1994, c. 519. See, also, subd. 63 below.] Uniformed members of the fire marshal's office in the town of Southhampton, when acting pursuant to their special duties in matters arising under the laws relating to fires, the extinguishment thereof and fire perils; provided, however that nothing in this subdivision shall be deemed to authorize such officer to carry, possess, repair or dispose of a firearm unless the appropriate license therefor has been issued pursuant to section 400.00 of the penal law.

(63) [As added by L.1994, c. 620. See, also, subd. 63 above.] Employees of the town court of the town of Greenburgh serving as a security officer; provided, however, that nothing in this subdivision will be deemed to authorize such officer to carry, possess, repair or dispose of a firearm unless the appropriate license therefor has been issued pursuant to section 400.00 of the penal law or to authorize such officer to carry or possess a firearm except while on duty.

(64) [As added by L.1995, c. 206. See, also, subds. 64 below.] Cell block attendants employed by the city of Buffalo police department; provided, however, that nothing in this subdivision shall be deemed to authorize such officer to carry, possess, repair or dispose of a firearm unless the appropriate license therefor has been issued pursuant to section 400.00 of the penal law.

(64) [As added by L.1995, c. 462. See, also, subds. 64 above and below.] Chief fire marshall, assistant chief fire marshall, fire marshall II and fire marshall I, all of whom are full-time employees of the town of Brookhaven, when acting pursuant to their special duties in matters arising under the laws relating to fires, the extinguishment thereof and fire perils; provided, however, that nothing in this subdivision shall be deemed to authorize such officer to carry, possess, repair or dispose of a firearm unless the appropriate license thereof has been issued pursuant to section 400.00 of the penal law.

(64) [As added by L.1995, c. 521. See, also, subds. 64 above and below.] Employees of the village court of the village of Spring Valley serving as security officers at such village court; provided, however, that nothing in this subdivision shall be deemed to authorize such officer to carry, possess, repair or dispose of a firearm unless the appropriate license therefor has been issued pursuant to section 400.00 of the penal law.

(64) [As added by L.1996, c. 314. See, also, subds. 64 above.] Employees of the town court of the town of Putnam Valley serving as a security officer; provided, however, that nothing in this subdivision will be deemed to authorize such officer to carry, possess, repair or dispose of a firearm unless the appropriate license therefor has been issued pursuant to section 400.00 of the penal law or to authorize such officer to carry or possess a firearm except while on duty.

(65) Employees of the town court of the town of Southampton serving as uniformed court officers at such town court; provided, however, that nothing in this subdivision shall be deemed to authorize such officer to carry, possess, repair or dispose of a firearm unless the appropriate license therefor has been issued pursuant to section 400.00 of the penal law.

6. THE CASE OF RAY EDWIN BILLINGSLEA (TEXAS, 1984)

A. Existing Law Applied in the Case

Vernon's Texas Penal Code Annotated (1974)

§ *1.07—Definitions*
   (a) In this code:

(1) "Act" means a bodily movement, whether voluntary or involuntary, and includes speech.

. . .

(7) "Bodily injury" means physical pain, illness, or any impairment of physical condition.

. . .

(8) "Conduct" means an act or omission and its accompanying mental state.

. . .

(23) "Omission" means failure to act.

. . .

(34) "Serious bodily injury" means bodily injury that creates a substantial risk of death or that causes death, serious permanent disfigurement, or protracted loss or impairment of the function of any bodily member or organ.

. . .

§ 22.04—*Injury to a Child or an Elderly Individual*

(a) A person commits an offense if he intentionally, knowingly, recklessly, or with criminal negligence, by act or omission, engages in conduct that causes to a child who is 14 years of age or younger or to an individual who is 65 years of age or older:

    (1) serious bodily injury;

    (2) serious physical or mental deficiency or impairment;

    (3) disfigurement or deformity; or

    (4) bodily injury.

(b) An offense under Subsection (a)(1), (2), or (3) of this section is a felony of the first degree when the conduct is committed intentionally or knowingly. When the conduct is engaged in recklessly it shall be a felony of the third degree.

(c) An offense under Subsection (a)(4) of this section is a felony of the third degree when the conduct is committed intentionally or knowingly. When the conduct is engaged in recklessly it shall be a Class A misdemeanor.

(d) An offense under Subsection (a) of this section when the person acts with criminal negligence shall be a Class A misdemeanor.

. . .

§ 6.01—Requirement of Voluntary Act or Omission

(a) A person commits an offense only if he voluntarily engages in conduct, including an act, an omission, or possession.

(b) Possession is a voluntary act if the possessor knowingly obtains or receives the thing possessed or is aware of his control of the thing for a sufficient time to permit him to terminate his control.

(c) A person who omits to perform an act does not commit an offense unless a statute provides that the omission is an offense or otherwise provides that he has a duty to perform the act.

B. Other Existing Law at the Time of the Case

Vernon's Texas Penal Code—Annotated (1974)

§ 12.04—Rights, Privileges, Duties, and Powers of Parent

Except as otherwise provided by judicial order or by an affidavit of relinquishment of parental rights executed under Section 15.03 of this code, the parent of a child has the following rights, privileges, duties, and powers:

(1) the right to have physical possession of the child and to establish its legal domicile;

(2) the duty of care, control, protection, moral and religious training, and reasonable discipline of the child;

(3) the duty to support the child, including providing the child with clothing, food, shelter, medical care, and education;

(4) the duty, except when a guardian of the child's estate has been appointed, to manage the estate of the child, including a power as an agent of the child to act in relation to the child's estate if the child's action is required by a state, the United States, or a foreign government;

(5) the right to the services and earnings of the child;

(6) the power to consent to marriage, to enlistment in the armed forces of the United States, and to medical, psychiatric, and surgical treatment;

(7) the power to represent the child in legal action and to make other decisions of substantial legal significance concerning the child;

(8) the power to receive and give receipt for payments for the support of the child and to hold or disburse any funds for the benefit of the child;

(9) the right to inherit from and through the child; and

(10) any other right, privilege, duty, or power existing between a parent and child by virtue of law.

§ 6.02—*Requirement of Culpability*

(a) Except as provided in subsection (b) of this section, a person does not commit an offense unless he intentionally, knowingly, recklessly, or with criminal negligence engages in conduct as the definition of the offense requires.

(b) If the definition of an offense does not prescribe a culpable mental state, a culpable mental state is nevertheless required unless the definition plainly dispenses with any mental element.

(c) If the definition of an offense does not prescribe a culpable mental state, but one is nevertheless required under subsection (b) of this section, intent, knowledge, or recklessness suffices to establish criminal responsibility.

(d) Culpable mental states are classified according to relative degrees, from highest to lowest, as follows:

(1) intentional;

(2) knowing;

(3) reckless;

(4) criminal negligence.

(e) Proof of a higher degree of culpability than that charged constitutes proof of the culpability charged.

§ 6.03—*Definitions of Culpable Mental States*

(a) A person acts intentionally, or with intent, with respect to the nature of his conduct or to a result of his conduct when it is his conscious objective or desire to engage in the conduct or cause the result.

(b) A person acts knowingly, or with knowledge, with respect to the nature of his conduct or to circumstances surrounding his conduct when he is aware of the nature of his conduct or that the circumstances exist. A person acts knowingly, or with knowledge, with respect to a result of his conduct when he is aware that his conduct is reasonably certain to cause the result.

(c) A person acts recklessly, or is reckless, with respect to circumstances surrounding his conduct or the result of his conduct when he is aware of but consciously disregards a substantial and unjustifiable risk that the circumstances exist or the result will occur. The risk must be of such a nature and degree that its disregard constitutes a gross deviation from the standard of care that an ordinary person would exercise under all the circumstances as viewed from the actor's standpoint.

(d) A person acts with criminal negligence, or is criminally negligent, with respect to circumstance surrounding his conduct or the result of his conduct when he ought to be aware of a substantial and unjustifiable risk that the circumstance exists or the result will occur. The risk must be of such a nature and degree that the failure to perceive it constitutes a gross deviation from the standard of care that an ordinary person would exercise under all the circumstances as viewed from the actor's standpoint.

§ 19.01—Types of Criminal Homicide

(a) A person commits criminal homicide if he intentionally, knowingly, recklessly, or with criminal negligence causes the death of an individual.

(b) Criminal homicide is murder, capital murder, voluntary manslaughter, involuntary manslaughter, or criminally negligent homicide.

§ 19.04—Manslaughter

(a) A person commits an offense if he recklessly causes the death of an individual.

(b) An offense under this section is a felony of the second degree.

§ 19.05—Criminally Negligent Homicide

(a) A person commits an offense if he causes the death of an individual by criminal negligence.

(b) An offense under this section is a state jail felony.

C. Current Law That Would Be Applied If the Case Were Prosecuted Today

Vernon's Texas Penal Code Annotated (1994 & Supp. 1998)

§ 1.07—Definitions

[The only relevant subsection that has changed is the following.]

(30) "Law" means the constitution or a statute of this state or of the United States, a written opinion of a court of record, a municipal

ordinance, an order of a county commissioners court, or a rule authorized by and lawfully adopted under a statute.

§ 6.01—*Requirement of Voluntary Act or Omission*

(a) A person commits an offense only if he voluntarily engages in conduct, including an act, an omission, or possession.

(b) Possession is a voluntary act if the possessor knowingly obtains or receives the thing possessed or is aware of his control of the thing for a sufficient time to permit him to terminate his control.

(c) A person who omits to perform an act does not commit an offense unless a [statute] *law as defined by Section 1.07* provides that the omission is an offense or otherwise provides that he has a duty to perform the act.

§ 22.04—*Injury to a Child, Elderly Individual, or Disabled Individual*

(a) A person commits an offense if he intentionally, knowingly, recklessly, or with criminal negligence, by act or intentionally, knowingly, or recklessly by omission, causes to a child, elderly individual, or *disabled individual*:

　　(1) serious bodily injury;

　　(2) serious mental deficiency, impairment, *or injury*; or

　　(3) bodily injury.

　　[(3) disfigurement or deformity]

(b) An omission that causes a condition described by Subsections (a)(1) through (a)(3) is conduct constituting an offense under this section if:

　　(1) the actor has a legal or statutory duty to act; or

　　(2) the actor has assumed care, custody, or control of a child, elderly individual, or disabled individual.

(c) In this section:

　　(1) "Child" means a person 14 years of age or younger.

　　(2) "Elderly individual" means a person 65 years of age or older.

　　(3) "Disabled individual" means a person older than 14 years of age who by reason of age or physical or mental disease, defect, or injury is substantially unable to protect himself from harm or to provide food, shelter, or medical care for himself.

(d) The actor has assumed care, custody, or control if he has by act, words, or course of conduct acted so as to cause a reasonable person to conclude that

*he has accepted responsibility for protection, food, shelter, and medical care for
a child, elderly individual, or disabled individual.*

    (e) An offense under Subsection (a)(1) or (2) is a felony of the first
degree when the conduct is committed intentionally or knowingly.
When the conduct is engaged in recklessly it shall be a felony of the
[~~third~~] *second* degree.

    (f) An offense under Subsection (a)(3) is a felony of the third degree
when the conduct is committed intentionally or knowingly. When the
conduct is engaged in recklessly it shall be a *state jail felony*. [~~class A mis-
demeanor~~]

    (g) An offense under Subsection (a) when the person acts with
criminal negligence shall be a *state jail felony*. [~~class A misdemeanor~~]

    . . .

    [Other relevant code sections are unchanged.]

7. THE CASE OF LINDA RUSCHIONI (MASSACHUSETTS, 1993)

A. Existing Law at the Time of the Case

*Annotated Laws of Massachusetts, Chapter 266—Crimes
against Property (1992)*

§ 30—Larceny; General Provisions and Penalties

    (1) Whoever steals, or with intent to defraud obtains by a false
pretense, or whoever unlawfully, and with intent to steal or embez-
zle, converts, or secretes with intent to convert, the property of another as defined in this section, whether such property is or is not
in his possession at the time of such conversion or secreting, shall
be guilty of larceny, and shall . . . if the value of the property stolen
exceeds two hundred and fifty dollars, be punished by imprisonment in the state prison for not more than five years, or by a fine
of not more than twenty-five thousand dollars and imprisonment in
jail for not more than two years; or, if the value of the property
stolen, other than a firearm as so defined, does not exceed two hundred and fifty dollars, shall be punished by imprisonment in jail for
not more than one year or by a fine of not more than three hundred
dollars; . . .

Annotated Laws of Massachusetts, Chapter 134—Lost Goods and Stray Beasts (1989)

§ 1—*Report of Lost Money or Goods by Finder*

Any person who finds lost money or goods of the value of three dollars or more, the owner of which is unknown, shall within two days report the finding thereof to the officer in charge at a police station in the town where said property was found, or, if there is no police station, post notice thereof in two public places therein, or, instead of such report or posting, cause notice thereof to be advertised in a newspaper published therein.

§ 3—*Restitution of Property*

If, within three months after the finding of stray beasts, or within one year after the finding of lost money or goods, the owner appears and, except as otherwise provided in section two, pays all reasonable expenses incurred by the finder in keeping such goods or beasts and in complying with this chapter, he shall have restitution of the money, goods or beasts.

Commonwealth v. Lucian, 116 Mass. 42 (1874) (finder of lost traveling bags who at the time of taking has reasonable means of knowing or ascertaining who is owner, is guilty of larceny when he does not return the bags and intends to deprive the owner of them).

Commonwealth v. Everson, 140 Mass. 292 (1885) (ignorance of law no defense for man and woman selling liquor with an innkeeper's liquor license and not a liquor license for a public bar, as was required).

Commonwealth v. O'Brien, 172 Mass. 248 (1898) (ignorance of law no defense for man obtaining money by false pretenses).

B. Current Law That Would Be Applied If the Case Were Prosecuted Today

[The relevant statutes are unchanged.]

8. THE CASE OF JOHN CHARLES GREEN (MISSOURI, 1967)

A. Existing Law Applied in the Case

Missouri Statutes Annotated (1953)

§ 557.351—*Escapes or Attempts to Escape from State Institutions or Custody, Penalty*

Any person sentenced to the state division of corrections upon conviction of escaping or attempting to escape from any state institution in which he was lawfully confined or from the lawful custody of any person or willfully failing to remain within the extended limits of confinement or to return to an institution or facility designated by the director of the division of corrections when permitted to go at large shall be sentenced to the division of corrections for a term of not less than two and not exceeding five years.

People v. Richards, 269 Cal. App.2d 768, 75 Cal. Rptr. 597, 604 (1969) (principle of justification by necessity, if applicable, involves a determination that "the harm or evil sought to be avoided by such conduct is greater than that sought to be prevented by the law defining the offense charged." . . . The compulsion from the harm or evil which actor seeks to avoid must be present and impending). [This is an out-of-state opinion cited by the Missouri court in deciding the *Green* case.]

State v. King, 372 S.W.2d 857 (Mo. 1963) (conditions of confinement do not justify escape and are not a defense).

State v. St. Clair, 262 S.W.2d 25, 27-8 (Mo. 1953) (to constitute a defense to a criminal charge, the coercion must be present, imminent, and impending and of such a nature as to induce a well grounded apprehension of death or serious bodily injury if the act is not done. Threat of future injury is not enough. Nor can one who has a reasonable opportunity to avoid doing the act without undue exposure to death or serious bodily injury invoke the doctrine as an excuse).

B. Current Law That Would Be Applied If the Case Were Prosecuted Today

Missouri Statutes Annotated (1997 & Supp. 1998)

§ 575.210—Escape or Attempted Escape from Confinement

1. A person commits the crime of escape or attempted escape from confinement if, while being held in confinement after arrest for any crime, while serving a sentence after conviction for any crime, or while at an institutional treatment center operated by the department of corrections as a condition of probation or parole, he escapes or attempts to escape from confinement.

2. Escape or attempted escape from confinement in the department of corrections is a class B felony.

3. Escape or attempted escape from confinement in a county or city correctional facility is a class D felony except that it is:

(1) A class A felony if it is effected or attempted by means of a deadly weapon or dangerous instrument or by holding any person as hostage;

(2) A class C felony if escape or attempted escape is facilitated by striking or beating any person.

§ 558.011—Sentence of Imprisonment, Terms; Conditional Release

1. The authorized terms of imprisonment, including both prison and conditional release terms, are:

(1) For a class A felony, a term of years not less than ten years and not to exceed thirty years, or life imprisonment;

(2) For a class B felony, a term of years not less than five years and not to exceed fifteen years;

(3) For a class C felony, a term of years not to exceed seven years;

(4) For a class D felony, a term of years not to exceed five years;

(5) For a class A misdemeanor, a term not to exceed one year;

(6) For a class B misdemeanor, a term not to exceed six months;

(7) For a class C misdemeanor, a term not to exceed fifteen days.

. . .

§ 562.071—Duress

1. It is an affirmative defense that the defendant engaged in the conduct charged to constitute an offense because he was coerced to do

so, by the use of, or threatened imminent use of, unlawful physical force upon him or a third person, which force or threatened force a person of reasonable firmness in his situation would have been unable to resist.

2. The defense of "duress" as defined in subsection 1 is not available:

(1) As to the crime of murder;

(2) As to any offense when the defendant recklessly places himself in a situation in which it is probable that he will be subjected to the force or threatened force described in subsection 1.

§ 563.026 Justification Generally

1. Unless inconsistent with other provisions of this chapter defining justifiable use of physical force, or with some other provision of law, conduct which would otherwise constitute any crime other than a class A felony or murder is justifiable and not criminal when it is necessary as an emergency measure to avoid an imminent public or private injury which is about to occur by reason of a situation occasioned or developed through no fault of the actor, and which is of such gravity that, according to ordinary standards of intelligence and morality, the desirability of avoiding the injury outweighs the desirability of avoiding the injury sought to be prevented by the statute defining the crime charged.

2. The necessity and justifiability of conduct under subsection 1 may not rest upon considerations pertaining only to the morality and advisability of the statute, either in its general application or with respect to its application to a particular class of cases arising thereunder. Whenever evidence relating to the defense of justification under this section is offered, the court shall rule as a matter of law whether the claimed facts and circumstances would, if established, constitute a justification.

3. The defense of justification under this section is an affirmative defense.

St. Louis v. Klocker, 637 S.W.2d 174 (Mo. 1982) (necessity is often expressed in terms of choice of evils: when the pressure of circumstances presents one with a choice of evils, the law prefers that the actor avoid the greater evil by bringing about the lesser evil).

9. THE CASE OF JOHANN SCHLICHT (GERMANY, 1919)

A. Law at the Time of the Case

[There was no applicable statute at the time; this was a case of first impression.]

B. Current Law That Would Be Applied If the Case Were Prosecuted Today

Federal Republic of Germany—Penal Code (1997)

§ 211—Murder

(1) The murderer shall be punished by imprisonment for life.

(2) A murderer is anyone who kills a human being: from a lust to kill, to satisfy his sex drive, from covetousness or other base motives; treacherously or cruelly or by means endangering the community or for the purpose of making possible or concealing the commission of another crime.

§ 212—Manslaughter

(1) Whoever kills a human being under circumstances not constituting murder shall be punished for manslaughter by not less than five years' imprisonment.

(2) Life imprisonment shall be imposed in especially serious cases.

§ 213—Less Serious Case of Manslaughter

If the person committing manslaughter, through no fault of his own, had been aroused to anger by the abuse of his own person or of a relative of his or by the grossly insulting behavior of the victim, and committed the homicide while in a state of passion, or the circumstances otherwise indicate the existence of a less serious case, imprisonment from six months to five years shall be imposed.

§ 223—Bodily Harm

(1) Whoever physically abuses another, or causes impairment to his health, shall be punished by up to three years' imprisonment or by fine.

(2) If the offense is committed against a lineal ancestor, up to five years' imprisonment or a fine shall be imposed.

§ 223a—Dangerous Bodily Harm

(1) If bodily harm has been committed by means of a weapon, in particular a knife or other dangerous instrument, or by means of a sneak attack, or by several people acting in concert, or by a life endangering act, imprisonment from three months to five years shall be imposed.

(2) The attempt is punishable.

§ 224—Aggravated Bodily Harm

(1) If the bodily harm committed on the victim results in the loss of an important part of his body, sight in one or both eyes, hearing, speech or his procreative capacity, or in a serious permanent deformity, or deteriorates into invalidity, paralysis or mental illness, imprisonment from one to five years shall be imposed.

(2) In less serious cases imprisonment from three months to five years shall be imposed.

§ 225—Intentional Aggravated Bodily Harm

(1) If any of the results described in (224) take place, and if the offender intended that they should occur, imprisonment from two to ten years shall be imposed.

(2) Imprisonment from six months to five years shall be imposed in less serious cases.

§ 230—Negligent Bodily Harm

Whoever causes bodily harm to another through negligence shall be punished by up to three years' imprisonment or by fine.

§ 242—Theft

(1) Whoever takes moveable property not his own from another with the intention of unlawfully appropriating it to himself shall be punished by up to five years' imprisonment or by fine.

(2) The attempt is punishable.

§ 32—The Emergency Defense

(1) Whoever commits an act necessitated by an emergency defense does not act unlawfully.

(2) The emergency defense is that defense which is necessary to avert a present unlawful attack upon oneself or another.

§ 33—Exceeding the Emergency Defense

If the actor exceeds the bounds of the emergency defense due to confusion, fear or fright, then he is not punished.

§ 34—State of Emergency as Justification

Whoever commits an act in order to avert a present and otherwise unavertable danger to life, body, liberty, honor, property or another legal interest to himself or another, does not act unlawfully if, in weighing the conflicting interests, particularly the affected legal interests and the degree of the danger threatening them, the interest protected substantially outweighs the interest injured. However, this is applicable only insofar as the act is an appropriate means to avert the danger.

§ 35—State of Emergency as Excuse

(1) Whoever commits an unlawful act in a present and otherwise unavertable danger to life, body or liberty to avert the danger from himself, a relative or another person close to him, acts without guilt. This is not applicable insofar as the actor can be expected to accept the danger, particularly because he himself caused the danger or because he held a special legal relationship; however, the punishment can be mitigated according to § 49(1) if the actor did not have to accept the danger in consideration of a special legal relationship.

(2) If the actor in committing the act mistakenly assumes circumstances that would excuse him according to subsection (1), then he is punished only if he could have avoided the mistake. The punishment is to be mitigated according to § 49(1).

§ 49—Special Statutory Mitigating Circumstances

(1) If under this provision reduction of punishment is prescribed or permitted, the following shall apply:

1. Imprisonment for not less than three years shall be substituted for life imprisonment.

2. For other imprisonment, a maximum of three quarters of the prescribed maximum may be imposed. For fines, the same shall apply to the maximum number of daily rated units.

3. The increased minimum term of imprisonment shall be reduced:

In cases where the minimum term is ten or five years, to two years;
In cases where the minimum term is three or two years, to six months;
In cases where the minimum term is one year, to three months;
In all other cases, to the statutorily prescribed minimum term.

. . .

10. THE CASE OF MOTTI ASHKENAZI (ISRAEL, 1997)

A. Existing Law at the Time of the Case

Israeli Penal Law (5737-1977, as Amended in 5754-1994)

§ 383—*Definition of Theft*
    (a) A person commits theft—
      1) if he takes and carries away—without the owner's consent, fraudulently, and without claiming a right in good faith—a thing capable of being stolen, with the intention— when he takes it—of permanently depriving its owner;
      2) if he—while having lawful possession of a thing capable of being stolen, being its bailee or part owner—fraudulently converts it to his own use or to the use of another person who is not the owner.
    (b) In respect of theft under subsection (a), it is immaterial that the person who takes or converts the object in question is a director or officer of a body corporate which is its owner, provided that the aggregate of other circumstances amounts to stealing—
    (c) For the matter of stealing—
      1) "taking" includes obtaining possession—
        a) by a trick;
        b) by intimidation;
        c) by a mistake on the owner's part, the person who takes the object knowing that the possession has been so obtained;
        d) by finding, if the finder at that time believes that the owner can be discovered by reasonable means;

2) "carrying away" includes the removal of a thing from the place which it occupies, but in the case of an attached object, only if it has been completely detached;

3) "ownership" includes part ownership, possession, a right to possession and control;

4) "thing capable of being stolen"—a thing which has value and is the property of a person, but if the thing is attached to an immovable object, only if it has been detached from it.

§ 384—Punishment for Theft

If a person commits theft, he is liable to three years imprisonment, unless some other punishment is provided in view of the circumstances of the theft or of the nature of the stolen object.

§ 34J—Self-Defense

No person shall bear criminal responsibility for an act that was immediately necessary in order to repel an unlawful attack, which posed real danger to his own or another person's life, freedom, bodily welfare or property; however, a person is not acting in self defense when his own wrongful conduct caused the attack, the possibility of such a development having been foreseen by himself.

§ 34K—Necessity

No person shall bear criminal responsibility for an act that was immediately necessary in order to save his own or another person's life, freedom, bodily welfare or property from a real danger of severe injury, due to the conditions prevalent at the time the act was committed, there being no alternative but to commit the act.

§ 34M—Justification

No person shall bear criminal responsibility for an act, which he committed under any of the following circumstances:

(1) he was lawfully obligated or authorized to commit it;

(2) he committed it under the order of a competent authority, which he lawfully was obligated to obey, unless the order is obviously unlawful;

(3) in respect of an act which lawfully requires consent, when the

act was immediately necessary in order to save a person's life or his bodily welfare, or to prevent severe injury to his health, if, under the circumstances, he was not able to obtain the consent;

(4) he committed it on a person with lawful consent, in the course of a medical procedure or treatment, the objective of which was that person's or another person's benefit.

(5) he committed it in the course of a sports activity or of a sports game, such as are not prohibited by law and do not conflict with public order, in accordance with rules customary for them.

§ 34P—Unreasonableness

The provisions of sections 34J, 34K, and 34L shall not apply, if, under the circumstance, the act was not a reasonable one for the prevention of the injury.

§ 34R—Misinterpretation of Situation

(a) If a person commits an act, while imagining a situation that does not exist, he shall not bear criminal responsibility, except to the extent that he would have had to bear it, had the situation really been as he imagined it.

(b) Subsection (a) shall also apply to an offense of negligence, on condition that the mistake was reasonable, and to an offense of strict liability, . . .

§ 25—What Constitutes an Attempt

A person attempts to commit an offense if he, with intent to commit the offense, does an act that constitutes more than mere preparation and the offense is not completed.

§ 26—Commission of the Offense Is Impossible

For the purpose of attempt, it shall be immaterial if the commission of the offense was impossible because of circumstances of which the person attempting the offense was not aware and of which the person was mistaken.

§ 27—Special Penalty for Attempt

If a provision sets a mandatory or minimum penalty for offense, it shall not apply to an attempt to commit the offense.

§ 28—Exemption Because of Remorse

If a person attempts to commit an offense, he shall not bear criminal responsibility for it if he proves that, of his own free will and out of
remorse, he stopped its commission or substantially contributed to the
prevention of results upon which completion of the offense depends;
however, this shall not derogate from his criminal liability for another
completed offense connected to the same act.

B. Current Law That Would Be Applied If the Case Were Prosecuted Today

[The relevant statutes are unchanged.]

II. THE CASE OF BERNICE J. AND WALTER L. WILLIAMS (WASHINGTON, 1968)

A. Existing Law Applied in the Case

Revised Code of Washington—Annotated, 1961

§ 9.48.010—Homicide; Defined and Classified

Homicide is the killing of a human being by the act, procurement or
omission of another and is either (1) murder, (2) manslaughter, (3) excusable homicide or (4) justifiable homicide.

§ 9.48.040—Murder in the Second Degree

The killing of a human being, unless it is excusable or justifiable, is
murder in the second degree when:

(1) Committed with a design to effect the death of the person killed
or of another, but without premeditation; or

(2) When perpetrated by a person engaged in the commission of,
or in attempt to commit, or in withdrawing from the scene of, a felony
other than those enumerated in RCW 9.48.030.

Murder in the second degree shall be punished by imprisonment in
the state penitentiary for not less than ten years.

§ 9.48.060—Manslaughter

In any case other than those specified in RCW 9.48.030 [murder—
first degree—death penalty up to jury], 9.48.040 [murder in the second

degree], 9.48.050 [killing in duel], homicide, not being excusable or justifiable, is manslaughter.

Manslaughter is punishable by imprisonment in the state penitentiary for not more than twenty years, or by imprisonment in the county jail for not more than one year, or by a fine of not more than one thousand dollars, or by both fine and imprisonment.

§ 9.48.150—Homicide; When Excusable

Homicide is excusable when committed by accident or misfortune in doing any lawful act by lawful means, with ordinary caution and without any unlawful intent.

State v. Sowders, 190 Wash.10, 186 P. 260 (1919) (accident is event happening without occurrence of the will, which takes place without one's expectation).

State v. Hedges, 8 Wash.2d 652, 113 P.2d 530 (1941) ("by lawful means with ordinary caution and without any unlawful intent," does not require a finding by jury that accused was guilty of gross negligence before conviction for manslaughter may be had. Only ordinary negligence is required).

State v. Stentz, 33 Wash. 444, 74 P. 588 (1903) (that defendant tried to avoid accident after it was too late is no excuse, where death was result of his negligent driving).

B. Other Existing Law at the Time of the Case

Revised Code of Washington—Annotated, 1961

§ 26.20.030—Desertion or Nonsupport; Penalty

(1) Every person who:

(a) Has a child dependent upon him or her for care, education or support and deserts such child in any manner whatever with intent to abandon it; or

(b) Wilfully omits, without lawful excuse, to furnish necessary food, clothing, shelter, or medical attendance for his or her child or children or ward or wards; or

(c) Has sufficient ability to provide for his wife's support or is able to earn the means for his wife's support and wilfully abandons and leaves her in a destitute condition or who refuses or neglects to provide his wife with necessary food, clothing, shelter, or medical attendance, unless by her misconduct he is justified in abandoning her, shall be guilty of the crime of family desertion or nonsupport.

(2) When children are involved under the age of sixteen years, such act shall be a felony and punished by imprisonment in the state penitentiary for not more than twenty years or by imprisonment in the county jail for not more than one year or by fine of not more than one thousand dollars or by both fine and imprisonment.

(3) When there is no child under sixteen years, such act shall be a gross misdemeanor and shall be punished by imprisonment in the county jail for not more than one year or by fine of not more than one thousand dollars, or by both fine and imprisonment.

C. Current Law That Would Be Applied If the Case Were Prosecuted Today

Revised Code of Washington—Annotated (1988 & Supp. 1998)

§ 9A.32.010—Homicide Defined
   Homicide is the killing of a human being by the act, procurement or omission of another, *death occurring within three years and a day*, and is either (1) murder, *(2) homicide by abuse*, (3) manslaughter, (4) excusable homicide, or (5) justifiable homicide.

§ 9A.32.060—Manslaughter in the First Degree
   (1) A person is guilty of manslaughter in the first degree when:
      (a) He recklessly causes the death of another person; or
      (b) He intentionally and unlawfully kills an unborn quick child by inflicting any injury upon the mother of such child.
   (2) Manslaughter in the first degree is a class B felony.

§ 9A.32.070—Manslaughter in the Second Degree
   (1) A person is guilty of manslaughter in the second degree when, with criminal negligence, he causes the death of another person.
   (2) Manslaughter in the second degree is a class C felony.

§ 9A.16.030—Homicide; When Excusable

Homicide is excusable when committed by accident or misfortune in doing any lawful act by lawful means, without criminal negligence, or without any unlawful intent.

§ 9A.08.010—General Requirements of Culpability

(1) Kinds of Culpability Defined

(a) Intent. A person acts with intent or intentionally when he acts with the objective or purpose to accomplish a result which constitutes a crime.

(b) Knowledge. A person knows or acts knowingly or with knowledge when:

(i) he is aware of a fact, facts, or circumstances or result described by a statute defining an offense; or

(ii) he has information which would lead a reasonable man in the same situation to believe that facts exist which facts are described by a statute defining an offense.

(c) Recklessness. A person is reckless or acts recklessly when he knows of and disregards a substantial risk that a wrongful act may occur and his disregard of such substantial risk is a gross deviation from conduct that a reasonable man would exercise in the same situation.

(d) Criminal negligence. A person is criminally negligent or acts with criminal negligence when he fails to be aware of a substantial risk that a wrongful act may occur and his failure to be aware of such substantial risk constitutes a gross deviation from the standard of care that a reasonable man would exercise in the same situation.

(2) Substitutes for Criminal Negligence, Recklessness, and Knowledge. When a statute provides that criminal negligence suffices to establish an element of an offense, such element also is established if a person acts intentionally, knowingly or recklessly. When recklessness suffices to establish an element, such element also is established if a person acts intentionally or knowingly. When acting knowingly suffices to establish an element, such element also is established if a person acts intentionally.

. . .

§ 26.20.030—Family Abandonment; Penalty

(1) Any person who has a child dependent upon him or her for care, education or support and deserts such child in any manner whatever with intent to abandon it is guilty of the crime of family [~~desertion or nonsupport~~] abandonment.

(2) *The crime of family abandonment is a class C felony under chapter 9A.20 RCW.*

[Prior subsections (1)(b), (1)(c), (2) and (3) are deleted.]

12. THE CASE OF JANICE LEIDHOLM (NORTH DAKOTA, 1981)

A. Existing Law Applied in the Case

North Dakota Century Code, 1976

§ 12.1-16-01—Murder

A person is guilty of murder, a class AA felony, if he:

(1) Intentionally or knowingly causes the death of another human being;

(2) Causes the death of another human being under circumstances manifesting extreme indifference to the value of human life; or

(3) Acting either alone or with one or more other persons, commits or attempts to commit treason, robbery, burglary, Kidnaping, felonious restraint, arson, gross sexual imposition, or escape and, in the course of and in furtherance of such crime or of immediate flight therefrom, he, or another participant, if there be any, causes the death of any person; except that in any prosecution under this subsection in which the defendant was not the only participant in the underlying crime, it is an affirmative defense that the defendant:

(a) Did not commit the homicidal act or in any way solicit, command, induce, procure, counsel, or aid the commission thereof; and

(b) Was not armed with a firearm, destructive device, dangerous weapon, or other weapon which under the circumstances indicated a readiness to inflict serious bodily injury; and

(c) Reasonably believed that no other participant was armed with such a weapon; and

(d) Reasonably believed that no other participant intended to engage in conduct likely to result in death or serious bodily injury. Subsections (1) and (2) shall be inapplicable in the circumstances covered by subsection 2 of section 12.1-16-02.

§ 12.1-16-02—Manslaughter

A person is guilty of manslaughter, a class B felony, if he

(1) recklessly causes the death of another human being; or

(2) causes the death of another human being under circumstances which would be class AA felony murder, except that the person causes the death under the influence of extreme emotional disturbance for which there is reasonable excuse. The reasonableness of the excuse must be determined from the viewpoint of a person in his situation under the circumstances as he believes them to be. An extreme emotional disturbance is excusable, within the meaning of this subsection only, if it is occasioned by substantial provocation, or a serious event, or situation for which the offender was not culpably responsible.

§ 12.1-16-03—Negligent Homicide

A person is guilty of a class C felony if he negligently causes the death of another human being.

§ 12.1-32.01—Classifications of Offenses; Penalties

Offenses are divided into seven classes, which are denominated and subject to maximum penalties, as follows:

(1) Class AA felony, for which a maximum penalty of life imprisonment may be imposed. Notwithstanding the provisions of section 12-59-05, a person found guilty of a class AA felony shall not be eligible to have his sentence considered by the parole board for thirty years, less sentence reduction earned for good conduct, after his admission to the penitentiary.

(2) Class A felony, for which a maximum penalty of twenty years' imprisonment, a fine of ten thousand dollars, or both, may be imposed.

(3) Class B felony, for which a maximum penalty of ten years' imprisonment, a fine of ten thousand dollars, or both, may be imposed.

(4) Class C felony, for which a maximum penalty of five years imprisonment, a fine of five thousand dollars, or both, may be imposed.

. . .

§ 12.1-02-02—Requirements of Culpability

(1) For the purposes of this title, a person engages in conduct:

(a) "Intentionally" if, when he engages in the conduct, it is his purpose to do so.

(b) "Knowingly" if, when he engages in the conduct, he knows or has a firm belief, unaccompanied by substantial doubt, that he is doing so, whether or not it is his purpose to do so.

(c) "Recklessly" if he engages in the conduct in conscious and clearly unjustifiable disregard of a substantial likelihood of the existence of the relevant facts or risks, such disregard involving a gross deviation from acceptable standards of conduct, except that, as provided in section 12.1-04-02, awareness of the risk is not required where its absence is due to self-induced intoxication.

(d) "Negligently" if he engages in the conduct in unreasonable disregard of a substantial likelihood of the existence of the relevant facts or risks, such disregard involving a gross deviation from acceptable standards of conduct.

(e) "Willfully" if he engages in the conduct intentionally, knowingly, or recklessly.

(2) If a statute or regulation thereunder defining a crime does not specify any culpability and does not provide explicitly that a person may be guilty without culpability, the culpability that is required is willfully.

(3)

(a) Except as otherwise expressly provided, where culpability is required, that kind of culpability is required with respect to every element of the conduct and to those attendant circumstances specified in the definition of the offense, except that where the required culpability is "intentionally", the culpability required as to an attendant circumstance is "knowingly".

(b) Except as otherwise expressly provided, if conduct is an offense if it causes a particular result, the required degree of culpability is required with respect to the result.

(c) Except as otherwise expressly provided, culpability is not required with respect to any fact which is solely a basis for grading.

(d) Except as otherwise expressly provided, culpability is not required with respect to facts which establish that a defense does not exist, if the defense is defined in chapters 12.1-01 through 12.1-

06; otherwise the least kind of culpability required for the offense is required with respect to such facts.

(e) A factor as to which it is expressly stated that it must "in fact" exist is a factor for which culpability is not required.

(4) Any lesser degree of required culpability is satisfied if the proven degree of culpability is higher.

(5) Culpability is not required as to the fact that conduct is an offense, except as otherwise expressly provided in a provision outside this title.

§ 12.1-05-03—Self-Defense

A person is justified in using force upon another person to defend himself against danger of imminent unlawful bodily injury, sexual assault, or detention by such other person, except that:

(1) A person is not justified in using force for the purpose of resisting arrest, execution of process, or other performance of duty by a public servant under color of law, but excessive force may be resisted.

(2) A person is not justified in using force if:

(a) He intentionally provokes unlawful action by another person to cause bodily injury or death to such other person; or

(b) He has entered into a mutual combat with another person or is the initial aggressor unless he is resisting force which is clearly excessive in the circumstances. A person's use of defensive force after he withdraws from an encounter and indicates to the other person that he has done so is justified if the latter nevertheless continues or menaces unlawful action.

§ 12.1-05-07—Limits on the Use of Force; Excessive Force; Deadly Force

(1) A person is not justified in using more force than is necessary and appropriate under the circumstances.

(2) Deadly force is justified in the following instances:

(a) When it is expressly authorized by law or occurs in the lawful conduct of war.

(b) When used in lawful self-defense, or in lawful defense of others, if such force is necessary to protect the actor or anyone else against death, serious bodily injury, or the commission of a felony involving violence. The use of deadly force is not justified if it can be avoided, with safety to the actor and others, by retreat or other conduct involving minimal interference with the freedom of the person menaced. A person seeking to protect someone else must, before using deadly force, try to cause that person to retreat, or otherwise comply with the requirements of this provision, if safety can be obtained thereby. But, (1) a public servant justified in using force in the performance of his duties or a person justified in using force in his assistance need not desist from his efforts because of resistance or threatened resistance by or on behalf of the person against whom his action is directed; and (2) no person is required to retreat from his dwelling, or place of work, unless he was the original aggressor or is assailed by a person who he knows also dwells or works there.

(c) When used by a person in possession or control of a dwelling or place of work, or a person who is licensed or privileged to be there, if such force is necessary to prevent commission of arson, burglary, robbery, or a felony involving violence upon or in the dwelling or place of work, and the use of force other than deadly force for such purposes would expose anyone to substantial danger of serious bodily injury.

. . .

§ 12.1-05-08—Excuse

A person's conduct is excused if he believes that the facts are such that his conduct is necessary and appropriate for any of the purposes which would establish a justification or excuse under this chapter, even though his belief is mistaken. However, if his belief is negligently or recklessly held, it is not an excuse in a prosecution for an offense for which negligence or recklessness, as the case may be, suffices to establish culpability. Excuse under this section is a defense or affirmative defense according to which type of defense would be established had the facts been as the person believed them to be.

§ 12.1-05-12—Definitions

In this chapter:

(1) "Deadly force" means force which a person uses with the intent of causing, or which he knows creates a substantial risk of causing, death or serious bodily injury. A threat to cause death or serious bodily injury, by the production of a weapon or otherwise, so long as the actor's intent is limited to creating an apprehension that he will use deadly force if necessary, does not constitute deadly force.

(2) "Dwelling" means any building or structure, though movable or temporary, or a portion thereof, which is for the time being a person's home or place of lodging.

(3) "Force" means physical action, threat, or menace against another, and includes confinement.

(4) "Premises" means all or any part of a building or real property, or any structure, vehicle, or watercraft used for overnight lodging of persons, or used by persons for carrying on business therein.

B. Current Law That Would Be Applied If the Case Were Prosecuted Today

North Dakota Century Code (1985 & Supp. 1998)
[The relevant statutes are unchanged, except for the following.]

§ 12.1-16-01—Murder
(1) A person is guilty of murder, a class AA felony, if *the person*:

(a) Intentionally or knowingly causes the death of another human being;

(b) Causes the death of another human being under circumstances manifesting extreme indifference to the value of human life; or

(c) Acting either alone or with one or more other persons, commits or attempts to commit treason, robbery, burglary, Kidnaping, felonious restraint, arson, gross sexual imposition, *a felony offense against a child under section 12.1-20-03, 12.1-27.2-02. 12.1-27.2-03, 12.1-27.2-04, or 14-09-22,* or escape and, in the course of and in furtherance of such a crime or of immediate flight therefrom, the person or [another] any other participant *in the crime* [if there be any] causes the death of any person. In any prosecution under this subsection in which the defendant was not the only participant in the underlying crime, it is an affirmative defense that the defendant:

(i) Did not commit the homicidal act or in any way solicit, command, induce, procure, counsel, or aid the commission thereof; and

(ii) Was not armed with a firearm, destructive device, dangerous weapon, or other weapon which under the circumstances indicated a readiness to inflict serious bodily injury; and

(iii) Reasonably believed that no other participant was armed with such a weapon; and

(iv) Reasonably believed that no other participant intended to engage in conduct likely to result in death or serious bodily injury. Subdivisions (a) and (b) are inapplicable in the circumstances covered by subsection (2).

(2) *A person is guilty of murder, a class A felony, if the person causes the death of another human being under circumstances which would be class AA felony murder, except that the person causes the death under the influence of extreme emotional disturbance for which there is reasonable excuse. The reasonableness of the excuse must be determined from the viewpoint of a person in that person's situation under the circumstances as that person believes them to be. An extreme emotional disturbance is excusable, within the meaning of this subsection only, if it is occasioned by substantial provocation, or a serious event, or situation for which the offender was not culpably responsible.*

§ 12.1-16-02—Manslaughter

A person is guilty of manslaughter, a class B felony, if he recklessly causes the death of another human being.

13. THE CASE OF BARRY KINGSTON (ENGLAND, 1991)

A. Existing Law Applied in the Case

Sexual Offenses Act, 1956, 4 & 5 Eliz.2, ch. 69

§ 15—Indecent Assault on a Man

(1) It is an offence for a person to make an indecent assault on a man.

(2) A boy under the age of sixteen cannot in law give any consent which would prevent an act being an assault for the purposes of this section.

(3) A man who is a defective cannot in law give any consent which would prevent an act being an assault for the purposes of this section, but a person is only to be treated as guilty of an indecent assault on a defective by reason of that incapacity to consent, if that person knew or had reason to suspect him to be a defective.

Regina v. Court, 1 A11 E.R. 120, 122 (1987) (the offense of indecent assault includes both a battery, or touching, and psychic assault without touching. If there was touching, it is not necessary to prove that the victim is aware of the assault or of the circumstances of indecency. If there is no touching, then to constitute an indecent assault the victim must be shown to have been aware of the assault and of the circumstances of indecency).

Regina v. Court, 2 A11 E.R. 221 (1988) (on a charge of indecent assault the prosecution must prove (1) that the accused intentionally assaulted the victim, (2) that the assault, or the circumstances accompanying it, are capable of being considered by right-minded persons as indecent, (3) that the accused intended to commit such an assault as is referred to in (2) above).

Cardle v. Mulrainey, SLT 1152 (1992) (where man drinks ale that has been secretly laced with amphetamine and subsequently attempts to steal a van, involuntary intoxication is a defense if, because of it, the man did not know the nature and quality of his acts or was suffering from a total alienation of reason). [This case was decided after the offense in *Kingston* but before the case came before the House of Lords.]

B. Current Law That Would Be Applied If the Case Were Prosecuted Today
[The relevant statutes are unchanged.]

14. THE CASE OF DAVID KENNY HAWKINS (NEVADA, 1986)

A. Existing Law Applied in the Case

Nevada Revised Statutes (1985)

§ 205.220—*Grand Larceny: Definition; Punishment*
[E]very person who feloniously steals, takes and carries away, leads or drives away the personal goods or property of another of the value of $100 or more, or the motor vehicle of another regardless of its value, is guilty of grand larceny, and shall be punished by imprisonment in the state prison for not less than 1 year nor more than 10 years and by a fine of not more than $10,000.

Shrader v. State, 101 Nev. 499, 504, 706 P. 2d 834, 837 (1985) (an entrapment defense has two elements: (1) an opportunity to commit a crime is presented by the state (2) to a person not predisposed to commit it).

B. Current Law That Would Be Applied If the Case Were Prosecuted Today

Nevada Revised Statutes (1997 & Supp. 1998)

§ 205.220—Grand Larceny: Definition
[A] person commits grand larceny if the person:
(1) Intentionally steals, takes and carries away, leads away or drives away:
(a) Personal goods or property, with a value of $250 or more, owned by another person; . . .

§ 205.240—Petit Larceny: Definition; Punishment
[A] person who:
(1) Steals, takes and carries, leads or drives away the personal goods or property of another, under the value of $250; . . .
. . . commits petit larceny and is guilty of a misdemeanor.

[*Shrader* remains the controlling case. See, e.g., *Roberts v. State,* 881 P.2d 1, 110 Nev. 1121 (1994).]

15. THE CASE OF RICHARD R. TENNESON (FEDERAL, 1954)

A. Existing Law at the Time of the Case

Uniform Code of Military Justice, 50 U.S.C.A. (1952)

§ 698 —Aiding the Enemy
Any person who—
(1) aids, or attempts to aid, the enemy with arms, ammunition, supplies, money, or other things; or
(2) without proper authority, knowingly harbors or protects or gives intelligence to, or communicates or corresponds with or holds any intercourse with the enemy, either directly or indirectly; shall suffer

death or such other punishment as a court-martial or military commission may direct.

§ 699 —*Misconduct as Prisoner*
Any person subject to this chapter who, while in the hands of the enemy in time of war—

(1) for the purpose of securing favorable treatment by his captors acts without proper authority in a manner contrary to law, custom, or regulation, to the detriment of others of whatever nationality held by the enemy as civilian or military prisoners; or

(2) while in a position of authority over such persons maltreats them without justifiable cause; shall be punished as a court-martial may direct.

§ 728—*General Article*
Though not specifically mentioned in this chapter, all disorders and neglects to the prejudice of good order and discipline in the armed forces, all conduct of a nature to bring discredit upon the armed forces, and crimes and offenses not capital, of which persons subject to this chapter may be guilty, shall be taken cognizance of by a general, special, or summary court-martial, according to the nature and degree of the offense, and shall be punished at the discretion of that court.

B. Current Law That Would Be Applied If the Case Were Prosecuted Today
[The relevant statutes are unchanged, but renumbered.]

16. THE CASE OF ALEX CABARGA (CALIFORNIA, 1982)

A. Existing Law at the Time of the Case

California Penal Code, 1972

§ 261—*Rape Defined*
Rape is an act of sexual intercourse accomplished with a person not the spouse of the perpetrator, under any of the following circumstances:

. . .

(2) Where it is accomplished against a person's will by means of force or fear of immediate and unlawful bodily injury on the person or another.

. . .

§ 261.5—Unlawful Sexual Intercourse with Female under Age Eighteen

Unlawful sexual intercourse is an act of sexual intercourse accomplished with a female not the wife of the perpetrator, where the female is under the age of 18 years.

§ 261.6.—Consent Defined

In prosecutions under Section 261, 286, 288a, or 289, in which consent is at issue, "consent" shall be defined to mean positive cooperation in act or attitude pursuant to an exercise of free will. The person must act freely and voluntarily and have knowledge of the nature of the act or transaction involved.

§ 264—Rape; . . . Unlawful Sexual Intercourse; Punishment

Rape, as defined in Section 261. . . , is punishable by imprisonment in the state prison for three, six, or eight years. . . . Unlawful sexual intercourse, as defined in section 261.5, is punishable either by imprisonment in the county jail for not more than one year or in the state prison.

§ 207—Abduction [Kidnaping]: Definition

Every person who forcibly steals, takes, or arrests any person in this state, and carries him into another country, state, or county, or into another part of the same county, or . . . who hires, persuades, entices, decoys, or seduces by false promises, misrepresentations, or the like, any person to go out of this state, or to be taken or removed therefrom, for the purpose and with the intent to sell such person into slavery or involuntary servitude, or otherwise to employ him for his own use, or to the use of another, without the free will and consent of such persuaded person . . . is guilty of Kidnapping.

§ 208—[Kidnapping] Punishment; Victims under Fourteen Years of Age at Time of Commission of Crime

Kidnapping is punishable by imprisonment in the state prison for three, five, or seven years.

§ 26—Persons Capable of Committing Crime; Exceptions

All persons are capable of committing crimes except those belonging to the following classes:

(1) Children under the age of 14, in the absence of clear proof that at the time of committing the act charged against them, they knew its wrongfulness;

(2) Idiots;

(3) Persons who committed the act or made the omission charged under an ignorance or mistake of fact, which disproves any criminal intent;

(4) Persons who committed the act charged without being conscious thereof;

(5) Persons who committed the act or made the omission charged through misfortune or by accident, when it appears that there was no evil design, intention, or culpable negligence;

(6) Persons (unless the crime be punishable with death) who committed the act or made the omission charged under threats or menaces sufficient to show that they had reasonable cause to and did believe their lives would be endangered if they refused.

B. Current Law That Would Be Applied If the Case Were Prosecuted Today

[There have been various alterations to the definition and grading of offenses, but none relevant to this case.]

17. THE CASE OF ROBERT "YUMMY" SANDIFER (ILLINOIS, 1994)

A. Existing Law at the Time of the Case

Illinois Compiled Statutes, Chapter 720 (1993)

§ 5/9-1—First Degree Murder; Death Penalties; Exceptions; Separate Hearings; Proof; Findings; Appellate Procedures; Reversals

(a) A person who kills an individual without lawful justification commits first degree murder if, in performing the acts which cause the death:

(1) he either intends to kill or do great bodily harm to that individual or another, or knows that such acts will cause death to that individual or another; or

(2) he knows that such acts create a strong probability of death or great bodily harm to that individual or another; or

(3) he is attempting or committing a forcible felony other than second degree murder.

(b) Aggravating Factors. A defendant who at the time of the commission of the offense has attained the age of 18 or more and who has been found guilty of first degree murder may be sentenced to death if:

. . .

(7) the murdered individual was under 12 years of age and the death resulted from exceptionally brutal or heinous behavior indicative of wanton cruelty; or

(8) the defendant committed the murder with intent to prevent the murdered individual from testifying in any criminal prosecution or giving material assistance to the State in any investigation or prosecution, either against the defendant or another; or the defendant committed the murder because the murdered individual was a witness in any prosecution or gave material assistance to the State in any investigation or prosecution, either against the defendant or another; or

. . .

(11) the murder was committed in a cold, calculated and premeditated manner pursuant to a preconceived plan, scheme or design to take a human life by unlawful means, and the conduct of the defendant created a reasonable expectation that the death of a human being would result therefrom; or

. . .

(c) Consideration of Factors in Aggravation and Mitigation. The court shall consider, or shall instruct the jury to consider any aggravating and any mitigating factors which are relevant to the imposition of the death penalty. Aggravating factors may include but need not be limited to those factors set forth in subsection (b). Mitigating factors may include but need not be limited to the following:

(1) the defendant has no significant history of prior criminal activity;

(2) the murder was committed while the defendant was under the influence of extreme mental or emotional disturbance, although not such as to constitute a defense to prosecution;

(3) the murdered individual was a participant in the defendant's homicidal conduct or consented to the homicidal act;

(4) the defendant acted under the compulsion of threat or menace of the imminent infliction of death or great bodily harm;

(5) the defendant was not personally present during commission of the act or acts causing death.

. . .

§ 5/9-2—*Second Degree Murder*

(a) A person commits the offense of second degree murder when
he commits the offense of first degree murder as defined in paragraphs
(1) or (2) of subsection (a) of Section 9-1 of this Code and either of the
following mitigating factors are present:

(1) At the time of the killing he is acting under a sudden and
intense passion resulting from serious provocation by the individual killed or another whom the offender endeavors to kill, but
he negligently or accidentally causes the death of the individual
killed; or

(2) At the time of the killing he believes the circumstances to be
such that, if they existed, would justify or exonerate the killing
under the principles stated in Article 7 of this Code [Justifiable Use
of Force; Exoneration], but his belief is unreasonable.

(b) Serious provocation is conduct sufficient to excite an intense
passion in a reasonable person.

(c) When a defendant is on trial for first degree murder and evidence of either of the mitigating factors defined in subsection (a) of
this Section has been presented, the burden of proof is on the defendant to prove either mitigating factor by a preponderance of the
evidence before the defendant can be found guilty of second degree
murder. However, the burden of proof remains on the State to prove
beyond a reasonable doubt each of the elements of first degree murder and, when appropriately raised, the absence of circumstances at
the time of the killing that would justify or exonerate the killing
under the principles stated in Article 7 of this Code. In a jury trial
for first degree murder in which evidence of either of the mitigating factors defined in subsection (a) of this Section has been presented and the defendant has requested that the jury be given the
option of finding the defendant guilty of second degree murder, the
jury must be instructed that it may not consider whether the defendant has met his burden of proof with regard to second degree
murder until and unless it has first determined that the State has

proven beyond a reasonable doubt each of the elements of first degree murder.

(d) Sentence. Second Degree Murder is a Class 1 felony.

§ 5/6-1—Infancy

No person shall be convicted of any offense unless he had attained his 13th birthday at the time the offense was committed.

§ 5/8-4—Attempt

(a) Elements of the offense. A person commits an attempt when, with intent to commit a specific offense, he does any act which constitutes a substantial step toward the commission of that offense.

(b) Impossibility. It shall not be a defense to a charge of attempt that because of a misapprehension of the circumstances it would have been impossible for the accused to commit the offense attempted.

(c) Sentence. A person convicted of an attempt may be fined or imprisoned or both not to exceed the maximum provided for the offense attempted, . . .

(1) the sentence for attempt to commit first degree murder is the sentence for a Class X felony, except that an attempt to commit first degree murder when at least one of the aggravating factors specified in paragraphs (1), (2) and (12) of subsection (b) of Section 9-1 is present is a Class X felony for which the sentence shall be a term of imprisonment of not less than 15 years and not more than 60 years;

(2) the sentence for attempt to commit a Class X felony is the sentence for a Class 1 felony;

(3) the sentence for attempt to commit a Class 1 felony is the sentence for a Class 2 felony;

(4) the sentence for attempt to commit a Class 2 felony is the sentence for a Class 3 felony; and

(5) the sentence for attempt to commit any felony other than those specified in Subsections (1), (2), (3) and (4) hereof is the sentence for a Class A misdemeanor.

§ 5/12-2—Aggravated Assault

(a) A person commits an aggravated assault, when, in committing an assault, he:

(1) Uses a deadly weapon or any device manufactured and designed to be substantially similar in appearance to a firearm, other

than by discharging a firearm in the direction of another person, a peace officer, a person summoned or directed by a peace officer, a correctional officer or a fireman. . . .

. . .

(13) Discharges a firearm.

(b) Sentence. Aggravated assault as defined in paragraphs (1) through (12) of Subsection (a) of this section is a Class A misdemeanor. Aggravated assault as defined in paragraph (13) of Subsection (a) of this section is a Class 4 felony.

B. Current Law That Would Be Applied If the Case Were Prosecuted Today

[The relevant statutes are unchanged, except for the following.]

Illinois Consolidated Statutes, Chapter 705 (1995 & Supp. 1998)

§405/5-36—Violent Juvenile Offender

(a) Definition. A minor having been previously adjudicated a delinquent minor for an offense which, had he or she been prosecuted as an adult, would have been a Class 2 or greater felony involving the use or threat of physical force or violence against an individual or a Class 2 or greater felony for which an element of the offense is possession or use of a firearm, and who is thereafter adjudicated a delinquent minor for a second time for any of those offenses shall be adjudicated a Violent Juvenile Offender if:

(1) The second adjudication is for an offense occurring after adjudication on the first; and

(2) The second offense occurred on or after January 1, 1995.

. . .

(d) Trial. Trial on the petition shall be by jury unless the minor demands, in open court and with advice of counsel, a trial by the court without a jury. . . .

. . .

(f) Disposition. If the court finds that the prerequisites established in subsection (a) of this Section have been proven, it shall adjudicate the minor a Violent Juvenile Offender and commit the minor to the Department of Corrections, Juvenile Division, until his or her 21st birthday, without possibility of parole, furlough, or non-emergency authorized absence. However, the minor shall be entitled to earn one day of good conduct credit for each day served as reductions against the period of his or her confinement. The good conduct credits shall be earned or revoked according to the procedures applicable to the allowance and revocation of good conduct credit for adult prisoners serving determinate sentences for felonies. . . .

Illinois Consolidated Statutes, Chapter 730 (1995 & Supp. 1998)

§ 5/3-10-11—Transfers from Department of Children and Family Services

(a) If (i) a minor 10 years of age or older is adjudicated a delinquent under the Juvenile Court Act or the Juvenile Court Act of 1987 and placed with the Department of Children and Family Services, (ii) it is determined by an interagency review committee that the Department of Children and Family Services lacks adequate facilities to care for and rehabilitate such minor and that placement of such minor with the Department of Corrections, subject to certification by the Department of Corrections, is appropriate, and (iii) the Department of Corrections certifies that it has suitable facilities and personnel available for the confinement of the minor, the Department of Children and Family Services may transfer custody of the minor to the Juvenile Division of the De, partment of Corrections provided that:

(1) the juvenile court that adjudicated the minor a delinquent orders the transfer after a hearing with opportunity to the minor to be heard and defend; and

(2) the Assistant Director of the Department of Corrections, Juvenile Division, is made a party to the action; and

(3) notice of such transfer is given to the minor's parent, guardian or nearest relative; and

(4) a term of incarceration is permitted by law for adults found guilty of the offense for which the minor was adjudicated delinquent. . . .

. . .

(e) In no event shall a minor transferred under this Section remain in the custody of the Department of Corrections for a period of time in excess of that period for which an adult could be committed for the same act.

Note on American Law Concerning Minimum Age for Criminal
(Adult Court) Prosecution

In twenty-seven states—Arizona, Arkansas, Delaware, Florida, Georgia, Indiana, Maine, Maryland, Massachusetts, Michigan, Mississippi, Montana, Nebraska, Nevada, New Hampshire, New York, Ohio, Oklahoma, Oregon, Pennsylvania, Rhode Island, South Carolina, South Dakota, Vermont, Washington, West Virginia, and Wyoming—Robert Sandifer could have been prosecuted for murder as an adult. See Department of Justice, *Juvenile Offenders and Victims: A National Report* 86-87 (1995).

Index

About the Author

Paul H. Robinson is the Edna & Ednyfed Williams Professor of Law at Northwestern University. He teaches courses in criminal law and advanced criminal law and a seminar in criminal law theory.

Professor Robinson earned a B.S. degree from Rensselaer Polytechnic Institute, a J.D. from the University of California at Los Angeles, where he was a comment editor of the *UCLA Law Review*, an LL.M. from Harvard University, and a Diploma in Legal Studies form the Cambridge University Law Faculty in Cambridge, England, where he served as a Harvard University Knox Traveling Fellow. From 1977 to 1992 he was a member of the faculty at Rutgers—The State University of New Jersey School of Law in Camden, New Jersey. In 1985 he was appointed Distinguished Professor and, in 1989 Outstanding Faculty Member of the Year for Rutgers. In 1989–90 he served as acting dean of the Law School. During 1998–99, he was a visiting professor at the University of Michigan Law School.

Professor Robinson's nonacademic work includes service as an attorney with the United States Department of Justice, Criminal Division, Legislation and Special Projects Section, then Special Assistant United States Attorney and federal prosecutor in Alexandria, Virginia. He served as counsel for the Subcommittee on Criminal Laws and Procedures of the United States Senate Judiciary Committee in 1977. In 1985 he was nominated by the President and confirmed by the Senate as one of the original Commissioners of the United States Sentencing Commission, where he served until 1988.

Professor Robinson is the author of several books, including *Structure and Function in Criminal Law* (Oxford 1997); *Criminal Law* (Little, Brown/Aspen 1997); *Justice, Liability, and Blame: Community Views and the Criminal Law* (with John Darley) (Westview 1995); *Fundamentals of Criminal Law* (Little, Brown, 2d ed. 1995); and *Criminal Law Defenses* (West Publishing Company 1984), a two-volume reference book for lawyers. He also has authored scholarly articles in the University of Chicago, Columbia, Northwestern, Texas, Stanford, UCLA, and Virginia law reviews, the *Yale Law Journal*, and the *Oxford Journal of Legal Studies*.

Professor Robinson is a member of the Advisory Committee of the criminal law journal *Zeitschrift für die Gesamte Strafrechtswissenschaft*, the American Psychological Association journal *Psychology, Public Policy, and Law*, and the *Buffalo Criminal Law Review*. He has lectured widely, nationally and internationally, including scholarly presentation in Moscow, Freiburg (Germany), London, Christchurch (New Zealand), Edinburgh, Vancouver, Helsinki, Uppsala (Sweden), Siracusa, Tel Aviv, Minsk, and Cambridge. He has served as a visiting professor at the University of Canterbury in Christchurch, New Zealand, and at the United Nations Asia Far East Institute for the Prevention of Crime and the Treatment of Offenders (UNAFEI) in Tokyo, Japan.